D1222896

ALL GOOD BOOKS ARE
CATHOLIC BOOKS

VOLUMES IN THIS SERIES

CUSHWA CENTER STUDIES OF CATHOLICISM IN
TWENTIETH-CENTURY AMERICA
edited by R. Scott Appleby, University of Notre Dame

Catholics in the American Century: Recasting Narratives of U.S. History
edited by R. Scott Appleby and Kathleen Sprows Cummings

On the Irish Waterfront: The Crusader, the Movie, and the Soul of the Port of New York
by James T. Fisher

Horizons of the Sacred: Mexican Traditions in U.S. Catholicism
edited by Timothy Matovina and Gary Riebe-Estrella, SVD

Habits of Devotion: Catholic Religious Practice in Twentieth-Century America
edited by James M. O'Toole

Ballots and Bibles: Ethnic Politics and the Catholic Church in Providence
by Evelyn Savidge Sterne

Catholics and Contraception: An American History
by Leslie Woodcock Tentler

Claiming the City: Politics, Faith, and the Power of Place in St. Paul
by Mary Lethert Wingerd

ALL GOOD BOOKS ARE CATHOLIC BOOKS

PRINT CULTURE, CENSORSHIP, AND MODERNITY IN TWENTIETH-CENTURY AMERICA

UNA M. CADEGAN

CORNELL UNIVERSITY PRESS

Ithaca and London

First published 2013 by Cornell University Press

Printed in the United States of America

Library of Congress Cataloging-in-Publication Data

Cadegan, Una M., 1960– author.
   All good books are Catholic books : print culture,
censorship, and modernity in twentieth-century
America / Una M. Cadegan.
         page cm. — (Cushwa Center studies of
Catholicism in twentieth-century America)
   Includes bibliographical references and index.
   ISBN 978-0-8014-5112-6 (cloth : alk. paper)
   1. Catholic literature—History and criti-
cism.   2. Catholic literature—Publishing—United
States—History—20th century.   3. Catholics—United
States—Intellectual life—20th century.   4. Censorship—
Religious aspects—Catholic Church.   5. Modernism
(Christian theology)—Catholic Church.   6. Catholic
Church—United States—History—20th cen-
tury.   I. Title.

   PN485.C324 2013
   810.9'921282—dc23
                                                    2013004903

Cornell University Press strives to use environmentally
responsible suppliers and materials to the fullest extent
possible in the publishing of its books. Such materials
include vegetable-based, low-VOC inks and acid-free
papers that are recycled, totally chlorine-free, or partly
composed of nonwood fibers. For further information,
visit our website at www.cornellpress.cornell.edu.

Cloth printing   10 9 8 7 6 5 4 3 2 1

For my parents

I write the way I do because (not though) I am a
Catholic. This is a fact and nothing covers it like the
bald statement. However, I am a Catholic peculiarly
possessed of the modern consciousness, that thing
Jung describes as unhistorical, solitary and guilty.
To possess this *within* the Church is to bear a burden,
the necessary burden for the conscious Catholic. It's
to feel the contemporary situation at the ultimate
level. I think that the Church is the only thing that is
going to make the terrible world we are coming to
endurable; the only thing that makes the Church
endurable is that it is somehow the body of Christ
and that on this we are fed. It seems to be a fact that
you have to suffer as much from the Church as for it
but if you believe in the divinity of Christ, you have
to cherish the world at the same time that you
struggle to endure it.

—Flannery O'Connor, letter to A., 20 July 1955

Contents

Acknowledgments   ix

Introduction: The Cultural Work of
Catholic Literature   1

1. U.S. Catholic Literary Aesthetics   20

2. Modernisms Literary and Theological   47

3. Declining Oppositions   64

4. The History and Function of Catholic
   Censorship, as Told to the Twentieth
   Century   85

5. Censorship in the Land of
   "Thinking on One's Own"   104

6. Art and Freedom in the Era of
   "The Church of Your Choice"   123

7. Reclaiming the Modernists,
   Reclaiming the Modern   153

8. Peculiarly Possessed of the Modern
   Consciousness   171

   Epilogue: The Abrogation of
   the Index   192

Notes   197

Index   221

ACKNOWLEDGMENTS

If you work on a project long enough, you find yourself swimming in a great ocean of gratitude.

Thanks first, as is always most appropriate for historians, to the generous and knowledgeable archivists and librarians at so many places: especially Charlotte Ames, Kevin Cawley, and Wendy Clauson Schlereth at the University of Notre Dame; and many others at Boston College, the Archdiocese of Chicago, Georgetown University, the Midwest Jesuit Archives in St. Louis, the University of Pennsylvania, Stanford University, and the University of Dayton's U.S. Catholic Collection and Marian Library.

Thanks especially to colleagues and friends at the Cushwa Center for the Study of American Catholicism at the University of Notre Dame, who have supported my work from its earliest days to the present: Jay Dolan, Scott Appleby, Barbara Lockwood, Kathleen Sprows Cummings, Timothy Matovina, and Paula Brach. A Research Travel Grant from the Cushwa Center was the first external funding I ever received.

Thanks to those skilled and patient editors at Cornell University Press and Westchester Publishing Services who made the manuscript into a book: Michael McGandy, Sarah Grossman, Susan Specter, and Melody Negron, along with the book's indexer, Linda Webster.

Thanks to the great scholars and generous human beings who shaped my thinking on literature, history, and culture—Anthony N. B. Garvan, Henry H. Glassie, Francis J. Henninger, Murray G. Murphey, Janice A. Radway, Barbara Herrnstein Smith, and Don Yoder. Thanks also to the supportive administrator-scholars, my colleagues and friends at the University of Dayton, without whom few of us could do what we do, especially Frank Lazarus, Paul Morman, Mary Morton, Paul Benson, and Julius Amin.

Thanks to the colleagues and friends who read and discussed and responded to endless versions of the project—Mike Barnes, Dennis Doyle, Jim Heft, Therese Lysaught, Jack McGrath, Maureen Tilley, Terry Tilley, Sandra Yocum (all former stalwarts of the DGDG), and several lively and useful colloquia with my History Department colleagues.

Thanks to other gracious colleagues and friends in Catholic Studies, at the University of Dayton and elsewhere—Phil Gleason, David O'Brien, Jim Fisher, Nicoletta Hary, John McGreevy, Maggie McGuinness, Bill Portier, Ellen Skerrett, and Tony Smith.

Thanks for general solidarity and sustenance of all kinds to dear friends Liesl Allingham, John Benvenuto, Ellen Fleischmann, Larry Flockerzie, Mary Harvan Gorgette, Barbara Heath, Carol Engelhardt Herringer, Kelly Johnson, Caroline Merithew, and Bill and Sue Trollinger.

Three colleagues and friends read the manuscript at a crucial point, and their (independent) responses convinced me that it was a book: Steve Dandaneau, Carol Herringer, and Jim Heft.

My deepest thanks to all of these people, because it is thanks to them that I was able to bring this project to completion. Its strengths are largely theirs; its weaknesses are all mine.

This is, first and foremost, for my parents, William and Sarah Cadegan, because if we are, as I believe, nothing other than the culmination of all the ways in which we have been loved, then most of the good of any kind of which I am capable is due to them.

Introduction
The Cultural Work of Catholic Literature

At the close and climax of James Joyce's 1916 novel, *A Portrait of the Artist as a Young Man*, the protagonist Stephen Dedalus announces to himself and to the ages his newly embraced mission: "Welcome, O life! I go to encounter for the millionth time the reality of experience and to forge in the smithy of my soul the uncreated conscience of my race."[1] In its emphasis on the primacy and immediacy of individual consciousness, and on the artist's making something that had no previous history, Stephen's pronouncement is perhaps the most famous epigraph of literary modernism. *Portrait of the Artist*'s stylistic innovations and its story of a young man's severing of every tie that had defined him—family, church, nation—exemplify modernism's break with the past, its rejection of artistic and social convention, its restless attempt to see the world afresh.

On the other side of the Atlantic, *Catholic World*, a literary magazine that had by 1917 been published for nearly fifty years by the Paulist Fathers, included a review of *Portrait of the Artist* in its June "New Books" section. The review took a less exalted view of Stephen Dedalus's ambition, describing Joyce's work as a "story of a young Irishman's loss of faith" and "the picture of the inside of one abnormally self-centred mind." The reviewer conceded that the novel's distinctive stylistic features—"cutting of transitions, the deliberate lack of reserve which forces upon the reader an appalling intimacy, the

1

formlessness which concentrates attention upon the central personality"—
were "successful," "creating an irresistible effect of sharp, first-hand reality."
In the end, though, "by the irony that avenges broken laws," the protagonist's (and, by not-so-subtle implication, the author's) self-absorption "leads
this apostle of self to speak of finding freedom when he has left truth at
home, and to desire self-expression so ardently that, to compass it, he aban-
dons God."[2]

Time would seem to have vindicated Stephen Dedalus. Joyce reigns as
one of the towering literary talents of the century. His early champions appear prescient and discerning, his opponents—most notoriously those in
Ireland, England, and the United States who sought to prevent publication
of his 1922 masterwork, *Ulysses,* on grounds of obscenity—repressed and
repressive, deserving of the mockery and rejection to which Joyce and his
contemporaries subjected them.

Joyce's opponents might be forgiven for failing to perceive the signs of a
sea change in modern sensibilities. Writing in 1924, Virginia Woolf devised
one of the most useful hyperboles in twentieth-century literary criticism:
"On or about December 1910 human character changed."[3] The phrase captures both the rupture triggered by the emergence of literary modernism
and the impossibility of dating it precisely. It captures as well Woolf's conviction that modernists were expressing—must express—a transformation
that had occurred in the world outside the novel. Those capable of recognizing and expressing the change belonged to the future; those incapable, to
the past.

Was the *Catholic World* review therefore simply predictable evidence of a
reflexive antimodernism, of the inability of a Catholic publication to recognize contemporary genius and to sympathize with contemporary dilemmas? A yes-or-no answer to such a question obscures what is most interesting
about the issues and people involved. In reviews like this one, in dozens of
magazines and hundreds of books—in fact, within an entire alternative
literary culture—U.S. Catholics worked out a distinctive literary vision,
shaped not solely by opposition to the century's secular literary trends but
more deeply by their own categories and criteria for defining and evaluating
literature. In so doing, they simultaneously addressed theological, philosophical, and historiographical questions crucial to the relationship between
Roman Catholicism and modernity. The responses they formulated to these
questions make U.S. Catholic literary culture—its literary vision, the people
who articulated it, and the institutions within which it was fostered—a
valuable and overlooked source for understanding the intellectual history of
U.S. Catholicism in the twentieth century.

U.S. Catholic Literary Culture

At the century's beginning, and particularly in the moment immediately following the Great War, the distance between Catholicism and modernity could seem very wide. The rift had been apparent, and deepening, for centuries. By 1917 Roman Catholicism was into its fifth century of opposition to many elements constitutive of political and cultural modernity in the West, including the individualist orientation and antihierarchical critique advanced by Reformation Protestantism; the secular and anti-aristocratic, anti-monarchical bent of the modern nation-state; Enlightenment rationalism *and* Romantic self-expression. This philosophical distance was intensified by the increasing nineteenth-century influence of political and economic liberalism, which were to many Catholics unacceptable because of the insistence on secularism and the consequent overthrow of authorities historically loyal to the Church.[4] Pope Pius IX's physical separation from the transformations Italy underwent in the decades of his pontificate resonated as a symbol of Catholicism's political distance from modernity. Economic liberalism was also, as the nineteenth century progressed, more and more deeply implicated in worsening industrial poverty, about which church authorities became increasingly concerned both out of a newly clarified sense of social justice and out of fear that workers' discontent would make them susceptible to the century's other great threat, socialism.

In defining both socialism and liberalism as enemies of Catholicism, the Vatican had backed itself into a political and philosophical corner. Despite the early signs of what would emerge as a century-long body of papal teaching on social justice, Vatican sympathy and support in the decades before the Great War were mostly with those suspicious of the corrosive effect of modernity on the faith. The Bolshevik Revolution and the apparently permanent threat of socialism served only to intensify this reaction.

And yet, for U.S. Catholics the immediate postwar moment seemed to pose new possibilities for their involvement in American culture. During the war the U.S. bishops had formed the National Catholic War Council, an instrument of national self-consciousness, organization, and centralization that intensified the sense of being a national church. Participating in the war effort, both in the military and on the home front, gave many Catholics a newly tangible sense of citizenship. Even the promulgation of a revised Code of Canon Law, begun years earlier but issued in 1917, was seen as the timely provision of an ancient resource newly honed to cope with rapid change and unforeseen questions.

U.S. Catholics' enthusiasm for the postwar moment was complicated by the large percentage among them who were recent immigrants or the children of immigrants. The immense wave of Catholic immigration before the war ceased almost instantaneously with the restrictive immigration acts of 1921 and 1924. The closing of immigration meant that assimilation was a widely shared cohort phenomenon to an extent never before experienced. Jay Dolan notes that by 1920, six groups—Irish, German, Italian, Polish, French Canadians, and Mexican Americans—made up at least 75 percent of the Catholic population, but that the remaining 25 percent included twenty-two additional ethnic groups (four—Slovaks, Lithuanians, Ukrainians, and Czechs—the largest among these).[5] The divisions within the U.S. Catholic community produced by this wide variety of ethnic difference, while sometimes bitter and lasting, were tempered by the unity enforced by common membership in a suspect minority. The wave of immigration that swelled the percentage of Catholics in the U.S. population to nearly 30 percent by 1930 also swelled the nativism of those who saw a threat to autonomous American selfhood in the assimilation of large numbers of Catholics, especially because their birth rate was higher than that of the rest of the American population.[6] Immigration restriction stabilized the Catholic population and allowed for several decades' focus on assimilation, on the particularities of the second- and third-generation immigrant experience, rather than on the more urgent issues that faced new immigrants.[7] It also, however, highlighted the reality of anti-Catholicism and the extent to which some components of American cultural and intellectual identity depended on Catholicism as a foil, even an outright opponent.

Catholics were painfully aware in the 1920s of the renewed strain of anti-Catholicism in American life; they were also aware that American Catholics were lagging behind their compatriots in many areas of educational and political achievement. But at the same time, Catholics were energetically engaging some of the liveliest institutions in American society, such as popular culture and entertainment, and municipal and national politics. If in the 1920s and 1930s Catholics were absent from the loftiest heights of American achievement, they were inarguably making a rapid ascent on which they had started much later than many of their compatriots.

Literary work was one of the fields U.S. Catholics engaged most extensively in the years immediately before and after the Great War. In these decades Catholics created a wide network of literary production and evaluation that included authors, readers, publishers, booksellers, editors, reviewers, critics, teachers, censors, librarians, and journalists. There were Catholic publishing houses and bookstores, Catholic newspapers and periodicals, catechisms and textbooks for children in Catholic schools, Catholic novels and etiquette books and calendars and encyclopedias and comic books. Measured both in real terms and in degree of self-consciousness, Catholic literary and print culture grew, strengthened, diversified, and professionalized in the first half of the twentieth century.[8] Newspapers alone were declining in importance; by 1920 most Catholic newspapers were diocesan and thus organs of official opinion and instruction. Enormous entrepreneurial, professional, and apostolic energy characterized nearly every other phase of print culture. Magazines and periodicals proliferated and grew in circulation. The growth of Catholic colleges and universities led to more self-conscious reading and criticism of "Catholic literature" as well as the creation of professional programs in journalism. Professional associations for Catholic journalists, critics, editors, and librarians were created—and in their turn founded journals that contributed to the vast output of Catholic print culture.

Catholic publishers were primarily firms that had been founded by European immigrants in the nineteenth century, then handed on to the next, more assimilated generation, or in some cases sold to other owners by the early decades of the twentieth century. Most Catholic publishers were also dealers in religious goods—the conventional wisdom was that selling rosaries, vestments, and communion wafers was necessary to subsidize the usually unprofitable books. Most so-called "Catholic" literature, however, was put out by secular publishers, some of which, especially by the 1930s and 1940s, developed Catholic imprints as they became aware of the growth and increasing education levels of the Catholic population.

At the same time that Catholic material was popular and profitable for secular publishers, U.S. Catholics nonetheless created separate institutional contexts for virtually every aspect of literary production. They established reading groups and professional associations, held conferences, published trade papers and scholarly periodicals, built buildings, founded businesses. In short, an entire infrastructure, human and material, grew up around Catholic literary work in the United States. This infrastructure was more than an ad hoc accumulation of attempts to quiet fears about the relationship between Catholicism and contemporary U.S. culture. Instead, it shared enough of a common sense of meaning and purpose that it is best understood as a culture. "Culture" is notoriously difficult to define, but we can begin with Clifford Geertz's definition as a "shared framework of meaning" ("Man is suspended in webs of significance he himself has spun"), tempered with Murray Murphey's acknowledgment that a somewhat more discursive explanation is necessary. Culture consists of what is learned, not genetic, including the material products of that knowledge. As such, it consists also of norms, standards for perceiving, believing, and doing, including the relationships among these norms. It is shared, but pinning down the contours of the sharing is difficult.[9] It is not solely conscious, but sketching the outlines of its conscious content still leads the observer a long way down the path of understanding: Folklorist Henry Glassie writes, "Culture is a mental construct built by individuals in shifting experience. Moving together in communication, people become alert to problems requiring action. Their thought becomes oriented to key paradoxes around which interpretations coalesce. Agreeing on the importance of certain issues, people come into social association and link their destinies through compatible understandings, at once making a culture among themselves and cutting a collective track through time."[10]

In the years between the end of the Great War and the immediate aftermath of the Second Vatican Council, what U.S. Catholics thought, wrote, and taught about literature cut a collective track through time, one that has subsequently remained largely unexplored. Although not univocal, their views, language, and categories were notably consistent and pervasive. These "mental constructs," informed by both religious belief and national identity, reflected and interpreted the "shifting experience" of this turbulent half-century. They performed "cultural work," in Jane P. Tompkins's phrase, "providing society with a means of thinking about itself, defining certain aspects of a social reality which the authors and their readers shared, dramatizing its conflicts, and recommending solutions."[11]

Catholics who wrote and thought about what literature was and should be played a key role in dramatizing the conflict between Catholicism and modernity, broadly considered. They had within this larger context a particular mission, which was to respond to the distinctively literary manifestation of modernity known as modernism. This was a delicate task, because something called "Modernism" had been solidly condemned by the Vatican in 1907. Theological modernism was distinct from literary and other forms of artistic modernism, but there was enough overlap in themes and attitudes that Catholics who thought and wrote about the latter were inescapably also somehow thinking and writing about the former. The path, the collective track, these works cut through time reveals the creation of a set of intellectual resources by means of which Catholics could not simply reject or acquiesce to modernity but accommodate it on their own terms. That this had happened in key ways by the time of the Second Vatican Council is a commonplace of twentieth-century Catholic intellectual history; that literature and literary culture played a key role is not.

These grand purposes often had mundane facades, but their participants were well aware of the grandeur. Catholic literary and print culture consciously took up a number of tasks its participants believed necessary to the right relationship between Catholicism and American life. First, it claimed the possibility of being thoroughly Catholic, inarguably American, and identifiably modern. Second, it made this case both internally (to Catholics anxious about the corrosive effect of American culture on the faith) and externally (to compatriots worried about the effect of Catholicism on American life). Third, these goals required guarding both the Church and American society against the greatest dangers of the age, particularly socialism. Fourth, taken together these emphases reflect the broad underlying imperative within Catholic literary culture to transform society toward the vision of unity in Christ articulated by the popes and embraced by a wide variety of U.S. Catholic clergy and laity.

Catholic, American, and Modern

A number of the most prominent and influential Catholic literary enterprises were explicit that their main purpose was to claim a distinctive Catholic ground that was also unambiguously American. This claim is apparent in the inaugural editorial—and the name—of the Jesuit periodical *America*, founded in 1909 as a weekly review of politics, art, and culture from "the" Catholic perspective. "The object of this Review," the editors wrote, "is . . . to supply in one central publication a record of Catholic achievement and a defense of Catholic doctrine, built up by skilful [*sic*] hands in every region of the globe." Its mission was not solely internal; non-Catholic Americans, the editors asserted, "are not only . . . ready to hear our views, but they are also eager to have us exert our proper influence in the national and social life." To that end the editors pledged "strict avoidance of proselytism and of all unnecessary controversy."[12] The editors presume not just the need to shore up the U.S. Catholic community, but also that outsiders are watching and listening and can be edified or scandalized. The more populist *Our Sunday Visitor*, founded in 1912 by Bishop John F. Noll of Fort Wayne, Indiana, though with a less urbane veneer, exhibited much the same confidence that Catholicism could and should speak from the center of American society in unapologetically Catholic terms. The first issue included the headline "The Church Law of Annual Confession and Communion Strongest Basis of Society."[13]

The desire to have Catholicism included and accurately portrayed in the grand drama of American life was pervasive. The desire to do so with a certain contemporary efficiency and flair was also apparent in, to take a perhaps unlikely example, the *Catholic Encyclopedia*. Its fifteen volumes and more than twelve thousand entries were born of dissatisfaction with the way Catholic subjects were treated in secular encyclopedias.[14] Published over seven years (1907–14), the *Catholic Encyclopedia* attempted to encompass all aspects of life within its covers. Though its main purpose was to set the record straight on Catholic doctrine and history, it also presented Catholic views on contemporary topics such as socialism and psychotherapy. Its editors stated that they were "fully aware that there is no specifically Catholic science, that mathematics, chemistry, physiology and other branches of human knowledge are neither Catholic, Jewish, nor Protestant; but, when it is commonly asserted that Catholic principles are an obstacle to scientific research, it seems not only proper but needful to register what and how much Catholics have contributed to every department of knowledge."[15] Nearly every account of the *Encyclopedia*'s genesis highlights its publication by an independently established corporation, its financing by a combination of subscriptions and lay investors, and the profit they reaped from their investment. This group of Catholics claimed a place on the American landscape that was both intellectual and commercial, defined equally by scholarly expertise and business savvy.

The modernity of Catholic literary and print culture lay not just in its adoption of new technologies but also in its assimilation of contemporary notions of the self and its relation to society. The Catholic reading circles that formed in increasing numbers after 1886 drew on the same rhetoric of "self-culture" and "self-improvement" in describing their purposes as had the largely Protestant Chautauqua movement after which they modeled themselves. They also saw the circles as filling the same need for women to continue their education despite being excluded from university degree courses. The Catholic reading circles adopted reading lists that combined titles recommended for the Chautauqua groups and for other religiously unaffiliated groups (such as William Henry Goodyear's *Roman and Medieval Art*), but also added titles by Catholic authors, especially on particularly contested subjects such as the Reformation (Martin John Spalding's *History of the Protestant Reformation*) or socialism (Victor Cathrein's *Socialism Exposed and Refuted*).[16] From one angle these efforts look purely defensive, an attempt to wall off Catholics (and especially educated young Catholic women) from engagement with contemporary ideas. However, in their literary travels these readers and writers invoked Matthew Arnold and John Ruskin with as much ease as they did Catholic writers, sometimes critically but also as influential authorities. Indeed, sometimes the commentators embodied the coming together of the two worlds. Proposing in 1893 the establishment of an "Institute for Women's Professions," F. M. Edselas—Episcopalian convert, cloistered nun, and contributor to the Columbian Exposition's World Parliament of Religions—counseled how to judge whether a course of study had prepared a student well: "[Is she] fully equipped and ready to respond to calls from any quarter? Is she in touch, body, mind, and soul, with the needs of humanity? Has she that culture which, as Matthew Arnold says, is 'the knowledge of the best that has been thought and said in the world'—and we may add with the power of a well-trained mind to make it of constant service?"[17] In their embrace of so much of middle-class reading culture, American Catholics assumed they had a place at the table and that they were benefiting American life and culture by adding their voice to the conversation.

The 1920s underscored the foreignness of Catholic immigrants and of Catholicism in ways that literary culture could and did address. For example, the 1916 *Ideal Catholic Reader* (fourth in the series), by "A Sister of St. Joseph," included a frontispiece of Murillo's *Immaculate Conception* along with reproductions of works by Michelangelo, Raphael, and Doré.[18] It was a simple lesson in art history, but it was also an attempt both to elevate the taste of the children of immigrants who populated Catholic school classrooms and to recall and celebrate for those same children the role Catholicism played in the history of art and culture. Some of the urgency in the desire to elevate the taste of the Catholic reader came from this sense that there was an imperative to live up to a grand heritage, often derided in contemporary life, that needed adherents worthy of it.

Internal and External Focus

The interwar self-consciousness of American Catholics, and the presence among them of large numbers of recent immigrants, meant that a primary purpose of Catholic literary culture was to define and support that community and to mediate its interactions with the world around it. American Catholics' idea of community, however, not only defined the community's boundaries but propelled its members beyond them. The intended audience of Catholic literary culture was seldom solely internal. The editors of the *Catholic Encyclopedia* aimed explicitly to shape the views not only of Catholics but also of the readers of *Appleton's Cyclopedia*, the work to which they saw their opus as an important corrective. Whether readers who were not Catholic consulted the *Catholic Encyclopedia* in large numbers is difficult to say, but some 80 percent of the libraries listed in the WorldCat database as holding copies of the original *Catholic Encyclopedia* are not Catholic libraries. Even if some of these libraries had a significant proportion of Catholics among their patrons, the fact that such a high percentage of the holders of the *Catholic Encyclopedia* were public libraries, research universities, and Protestant seminaries suggests that the *Encyclopedia*'s editors may have achieved their goal.

In context, even materials that seem the most internally oriented have an explicitly external dimension. It is true that much of Catholic print culture existed primarily to produce the print materials necessary for Catholic practice and formation: Bibles, prayer books, official liturgical texts, devotional guides (for private rather than public worship), missals, spiritual reading, catechisms, and textbooks for Catholic schools. Producing such a wide array of materials, and closely monitoring them for conformity to official doctrine, was necessary because of the threat that intellectual and cultural modernity posed to the fidelity of the U.S. Catholic community. Because the secular, materialistic U.S. context was so different from that of Catholic Europe, extra vigilance was required to provide American Catholics with easy access to accurate, attractive versions of the truth. For example, the *Baltimore Catechism*, central to the folklore of and nostalgia for pre–Vatican II Catholicism, surely reflected a real concern for accurate doctrine. But it also resulted from an extensive process of consultation that drew on contemporary pedagogical research and cognitive psychology and was in turn a business opportunity with a potential market of every Catholic seven-year-old, so that the many versions published before its standardization in 1941 competed with each other via cosmetic changes, such as cover color and illustrations, and innovations motivated by pedagogy (glossaries for each chapter, divisions into separate texts for different grade levels, simpler language for younger children) and by theology (arrangement of topics according to their place in the liturgical year or the addition of scriptural support and justification for the catechism's doctrinal content).[19]

Catholic literary culture was inevitably inflected by the hierarchical polity of Roman Catholicism. But it was equally characterized by the collaboration and interdependence of hierarchy and laity. Ventures initiated by clergy usually depended on laypeople for labor and professional expertise and often for capital. Lay publishers, including secular publishers, sought ecclesiastical permission for works such as catechisms and textbooks that they intended to market to a Catholic public. Lay Catholics sought less legalistic affirmation from bishops and other clergy, as well, asking for unofficial endorsement of periodicals, for example, even if not strictly required to do so under canon law. Some collaborations were primarily financial, some deeply personal. The overall picture is a blend of legal requirement, political expediency, earnest acknowledgment of legitimate authority, and genuine personal connection.[20]

Guarding against the Socialist Threat

In their confidence that they could demonstrate to audiences both internal and external the compatibility between Catholicism and American life with all its modern sheen, some of the enterprises of U.S. Catholic literary culture had a boosterish veneer (and a few a boosterish soul). But they also had a sense of profound urgency, because the people involved in them believed that the contemporary world needed what American Catholicism had to offer, not just as one useful element in the melting pot but as the key ingredient that could save the whole thing from disaster. At the center of this sense of urgency was the apparent threat posed by socialism.

This concern long predated the 1917 Bolshevik Revolution. Pope Leo XIII's 1891 encyclical *Rerum Novarum*, which acknowledged the Church's responsibility to address workers' needs, was greeted with relief and energetic action by U.S. Catholics who wanted a Catholic alternative to both socialism and laissez-faire political economics. Nearly universally before 1917 and afterward in some quarters for nearly two decades, Catholic critics of socialism and communism were clear that one of the major causes of both was capitalism. The injustices of the industrial social order fell so heavily on workers that the promises of socialism were compelling. Opposing socialism, therefore, required ameliorating the most destructive aspects of capitalism, which in turn required imagining an appropriate role for the material prosperity of American life.

Catholic print culture, occasionally in surprising ways, was a key vehicle for the opposition to socialism. Sometimes the assault was a frontal attack. *Our Sunday Visitor* enthusiastically condemned socialism (and later the Soviet Union), emphasizing the obligation of U.S. Catholics to resist any Bolshevik incursion. "Socialism's Foundation Shattered" read a headline in the first issue in 1912.[21] Others, though, constructed a vision of industrial society in which workers would not be drawn to socialism because they would share sufficiently in the wealth produced by their efforts. Moral theologian and social justice advocate John A. Ryan published a series of articles in *Catholic World* arguing for a living wage that would provide families with both security and leisure. He specified not only the minimum a family would need to achieve these things but also a maximum beyond which it was probably not moral to strive.

Less overt but probably equally intentional is the argument implicit in the plot of *The Rich Mrs. Burgoyne* (1912) by Kathleen Thompson Norris (1880–1966), surely one of the most popular novelists of the twentieth century. She published ninety-six books, primarily novels aimed at an audience of women readers, in the course of a writing career that lasted from 1911 until the late 1950s. *The Rich Mrs. Burgoyne* was Norris's first novel; her first published full-length work, *Mother*, had been an autobiographical reminiscence that originally appeared in 1911 after its popularity as a piece in *Ladies Home Journal* led *Journal* editor Edward Bok to issue it separately. As late as the early 1940s it was still a popular Mother's Day present.[22] Norris's focus on romance and family and her reliance on formula and sentiment have led to her almost complete eradication from literary memory. But *The Rich Mrs. Burgoyne* is an intriguing example of a work that "defines certain aspects of a social reality which the authors and their readers shared, dramatizes its conflicts, and recommends solutions."[23]

The novel's title character is rumored to possess a fortune of $8 million when she moves to an up-and-coming California town and startles the striving inhabitants with the economy and generosity of her household. Mrs. Burgoyne's entertaining combines simplicity, elegance, and grace—a perfectly prepared steak and salad, for example, instead of numerous elaborate courses. Her style refreshes those burdened (the wives with preparation, the husbands with too many heavy foods) by the complex conventions of Victorian dining. At the end of the novel the townspeople find out that Mrs. Burgoyne's fortune does not exist, and that her economies were not the new fashion but simple necessity. Not a radical story, but in suggesting that there could be an "enough" in the burgeoning of American consumption Norris creates a literary landscape in which the elements of John A. Ryan's vision of the social order come to life. Fiction and nonfiction both imaginatively reconfigure American economic life.

The distinctive place on the American landscape that Catholic print and literary culture had to map needed to be a middle ground that made room for notions of the common good (but resisting the "collective") while rejecting the atheism, the state ownership of the economy, and the eradication of the individual that Catholics believed to characterize socialism and communism. The complexity of the emerging constellation can be seen in a comment made by Brother Leo (Francis Meehan, 1854–1943). As professor of English and chancellor of St. Mary's College in Moraga, California, Brother Leo influenced Catholic literary culture through not only extensive writings but also compelling lectures for students, the general public, and occasionally a national radio audience. His vision of St. Mary's as "a translation of high European Catholic consciousness to California" suggests the scope of the ambition he and a number of his contemporaries shared.[24] In a 1928 letter to Francis Talbot, then literary editor of *America*, regarding the need for a Catholic book club to complement or counter the recently established Book-of-the-Month Club, he wrote, "I share your surprise that so standardized a fashion of spreading literature should appeal to intelligent men and women, even in America where we have more standardization than is good for us; but since the idea seems to have won favor, it will be at least an interesting experiment to try on a Catholic following. I detest the goose step; but obviously reading in goose step is better than not reading at all."[25] In this two-front battle, Catholicism needed to stand against both the commercial depersonalization of industrial-consumer society and the martial depersonalization of totalitarianism.

"Mighty Futures"

More than simply resisting the encroachment of socialism, American Catholics who were engaged in literary work saw a role for literary art in transforming culture on a cosmic scale. Poet Thomas Walsh (1875–1928), for example, noted that Les Jeunes, as he referred to the most recent generation of Catholic poets in the 1920s, "are carrying on their shoulders a golden ark of Christian beauty, and they seem to be quite conscious of their responsibility. . . . The multiple voices clamoring around them, the modern doubts and dubious invitations of the 'isms,' seem to have made them slightly cautious in tone; it is evident the ages of Faith are no more and the building of the City of God must have strengthened foundations and modern embellishments, more than mere retouching of old ornament, to fit them for the mighty futures that are preparing."[26]

This task of bridging past, present, and future took on an increasingly heroic cast as the storm clouds gathered in the 1920s and 1930s. William Halsey argued influentially in 1980 that U.S. Catholics between the wars represented a "survival of American innocence"—a lingering confidence in progress and order that had been shattered for other, more highly attuned Americans by the Great War. "Innocence," though, seems too passive a metaphor for the task Catholics saw themselves shouldering, and the late nineteenth century too limited a time horizon.[27] Daniel A. Lord, SJ, although atypical among his contemporaries in energy and sheer output, shared with very many of them a sense of urgent and unique crisis. "It was left for this generation," Lord wrote in 1930, ". . . to discover the astounding fact that books have no effect on life or conduct. Every other age in history was sure that books were one of the really powerful forces that drive ideas into the very soul of mankind, foment revolutions, fire national conflagrations, start new religions, corrupt human hearts, sweep kings off their thrones, and set men on the way to heaven or to hell."[28] Born in 1888, Lord found his life's work early and nearly by accident, when a bout of typhoid prevented him from moving on to his third year of full-time college study (the "philosophate," when Jesuits began serious study of philosophy) with his Jesuit classmates. Instead he spent a year working in St. Louis with The Queen's Work Press. "A magazine and a movement," The Queen's Work (the Queen being Mary) sought to provide the print materials necessary to bolster its "sodalities," groups organized around using the resources of Catholic tradition to address the issues facing the contemporary world.[29]

Over the course of the next four decades Lord became a one-man culture industry, working out his version of the church's relationship to modernity in books, magazine articles, pamphlets, novels, sheet music, children's books, large-scale historical pageants, radio broadcasts, and musical comedies based on the Church's social teachings and other papal encyclicals. "The Matrimonial Follies of 1939," a 1939 St. Anthony Messenger profile noted, "had as its theme the marriage encyclicals of the late Pope Pius XI."[30] Although Lord's output "defies accurate listing,"[31] The Queen's Work put the official tally (in their commemoration of him on what would have been his seventy-fifth birthday) at 30 books, 12 booklets, 224 pamphlets, 48 children's books, 25 plays, 12 pageants, 3 musicals, and 5 published songs.

Lord's prolific output and charismatic persona kept him at center stage in the drama of redeeming modernity, but he was part of a cast of thousands. He and his contemporaries in the 1930s understood their work as writers and fosterers of Catholic print and literary culture to be a key component of the larger enterprise known as Catholic Action—the diffuse constellation of activities and initiatives, christened by Pope Pius XI (r. 1922–39) and echoed in multiple Catholic venues in the middle decades of the twentieth century, aimed at drawing on the expertise and energies of lay Catholics to bring about the transformation of society. Responding to Pius's exhortation to "bring all things to Christ," advocates of Catholic Action took on the obligation to diagnose the problems of contemporary society, make judgments about the best way to address the problems, and act in an attempt to improve the situation. Literature was an essential tool in the Catholic Action kit.

This tool could be and was wielded in multiple venues by a wide variety of actors. The National Catholic Welfare Conference, for example, sponsored a publication entitled *Catholic Action*. Its "study topic" for January 1936, headlined on the cover of that month's issue, was "Youth and Today's Literature." The guide exhorted young Catholic Action participants: "By reading Catholic books, periodicals and newspapers steep yourself in the literature, culture, and the spirit of the Church. In this way, you will obtain an increasingly luminous understanding of the magnificent vision of Catholic life and its power to transform society."[32] A 1931 headline in *Catholic Library World* read "Suggesting Catholic Books as Xmas Gifts a Practical Form of Catholic Action."[33]

Catholic Action mobilized in many areas of U.S. Catholic life and culture, exhorting laity to use their secular vocations "to restore all things in Christ." The role laity were expected to play in this enterprise helps to explain what can seem like a contradiction—at the same time that a strong critique of modernity was being articulated, Catholic editors and publishers were marshaling all the technological and professional innovations they could muster to produce, teach, and evaluate literature of all kinds. Peter Wynhoven, vice president of the Catholic Press Association in 1939, wrote (in a piece entitled variously "We May Well Learn from the Enemy," and "Sacerdotal Salesmanship"), "Although the Catholic Church is the biggest business in America, she alone is not yet convinced [of] the great need of publicity, the strength of the printed word. . . . Some of our Catholic literature may not have a striking reader appeal. Our able editors are handicapped by lack of sufficient finances to publish something up-to-date that will catch the fancy of our present-day public."[34] This sense of the urgent need to enlist the most innovative contemporary methods in the service of ancient traditional goals is a hallmark of much activity that went by the name of Catholic Action.

Additionally, proponents of Catholic Action in the United States saw as one of its great hopes the revival or renaissance in Catholic literature that had begun in Europe in the final decades of the nineteenth century and was continuing, in American eyes, to deepen and flourish there while being frustratingly slow to take root in U.S. soil. The writers named as constituting the revival almost always included, among others, John Henry Newman, G. K. Chesterton, Hilaire Belloc, Gerard Manley Hopkins, and Francis Thompson, in England; Georges Bernanos, Leon Bloy, Paul Claudel, Jacques Maritain, and Francois Mauriac, in France; and Sigrid Undset, in Norway.[35] Undset's Nobel Prize in 1929 for the massive medieval epic *Kristin Lavransdatter* in particular seemed to reinforce the achievement, to confirm that Catholic subject matter and commitments could yet carry real artistic weight in the twentieth century.

In the United States, Catholic literary culture and Catholic Action drew on and contributed to each other. Burton Confrey published *The Moral Mission of Literature and Other Essays* two years after the anthology *Readings for Catholic Action*.[36] The Catholic Library Association said of the task it described as "peculiarly ours—promoting Catholic literature": "Apathetic concern in this matter on the part of any Catholic librarian is a shameful monstrosity. We are crusaders in the cause of Catholic Action."[37] Layman Thomas McDermott, in his chapter on the United States in his and Stephen Brown's *Survey of Catholic Literature*, voiced a lament typical by the late 1940s concerning the absence of laity among U.S. Catholic writers. He was very clear about the remedy: "The failure of our laity to contribute to American Catholic literature is their own and can be corrected only by themselves. Catholic Action is the simple and complete corrective."[38] Literature needed Catholic Action, Catholic Action needed literature, and the world needed both.

Plan of This Book

In his 1933 *Introduction to Catholic Booklore,* Stephen Brown (described in 1947 as the "dean of Catholic librarians"[39]) explained why Catholic bibliography included books on subjects besides religion, such as history, science, politics, and art: "It is but an application of the principle that one's religion is not the church one goes to, but the world one lives in."[40] This distinctively polymathic view of literary and print culture as encompassing all of life was what gave rise to the sprawling network of Catholic literary enterprises, and to the shared framework of meaning that animated them beyond their differences. It also over time produced an incisive and thoroughgoing cultural commentary on the relationship between Catholicism and modernity that facilitated their reconciliation.

As philosopher Charles Taylor has argued, one of the distinguishing features of modernity is the shift from "higher time," the time of premodern societies in which the here and now connects to eternal time, to "secular time," the linear, ordinary time of the modern era.[41] As twentieth-century intellectuals, Catholics had to live in both. They needed, and developed, an intellectually credible rationale within which this coexistence could be coherent. Historian Thomas J. Shahan, writing on the study of church history in 1922 in the *Catholic Historical Review,* articulates a view of where Catholicism stands in the history of the world that seems to set it outside the very historical time he is examining:

The most sublime event of the world's history is the foundation of that Church, by which a new and supernatural factor entered into the world's life, and new principles of thought and conduct supplanted forever the old *Weltanschauung*. It was as another flood, after which the individual, the family, the state, human society found themselves in absolutely new conditions. In the place of error came truth, in the place of idolatry adoration in spirit and truth, in the place of heathen folly and corruption with its pollution of human worth and degradation of the family and extinction of personal liberty, there came Christianity proclaiming the freedom of the children of God, the supernatural dignity and end of man, the equal dignity of woman and children and slaves; in place of darkness there came the reign of light and life and grace and truth.[42]

Such a view seems incompatible with the professional study of history, but in the same article Shahan also explicitly embraced a wide array of ideas and methods for the contemporary study of Catholicism: scientific method, honesty about the study of church corruption, the historical-critical study of scripture, examination of the role played by climate and topography, and the evolution of dogma. He was clearly confident that all these things were compatible.

This confidence stems from one of the most pervasive beliefs about preconciliar Catholicism: that it was timeless and unchanging. That belief could be and was the source of some of the unfortunate stasis in Catholic intellectual life in the twentieth century. But it was simultaneously a strategic choice. Affirmation of the Church's unchanging essence was not simply reflexive antimodernist rejection, but also a way of defining the playing field. Shahan and his fellow Catholics in history, literary work, and other disciplines used these apparently self-contradictory analyses to lay out the conditions under which Catholics would participate in the debate over the nature of modernity. To the extent that self-consciously and explicitly Catholic intellectual perspectives were unwelcome in the secular academy, the institutions of Catholic literary and print culture provided a physical space for this debate to play out; to the extent that considerations of the compatibility between modernity and Catholicism were unwelcome in Catholic intellectual culture, the assertions of timelessness provided a temporal space for the same debate.

Literary work posed a similar task, and Catholics involved in literary work responded analogously. In "The Catholic Theory of Arts and Letters," her contribution to the 1923 *Catholic Builders of the Nation: A Symposium on the Catholic Contribution to the Civilization of the United States*, Blanche Mary

Kelly asserts, "[The] Catholic Church has always steered a characteristically sane middle course between the pagan cult of the lust of the eye and the Puritan rejection of material beauty as an inherently evil thing. With God she has looked upon the work of His hands and seen it to be good." Although she is unable to assess "the modern theories of art and literature such as Futurism, Imagism, Da-daism, *Vers libre*, etc.," as anything other than "expressions of revolt and anarchy," she nonetheless includes them as part of her survey.[43] Literary modernism was one of the most influential genres of the day and required a response. To be both intellectually credible and defensibly Catholic, this response needed an aesthetic grounding that was both substantive and versatile. Much of the effort of Catholics involved in literary work in the interwar years was directed toward honing just such a set of aesthetic tools, which helped them transform the debates in which they were participants.

This book looks at roughly two generations of participants in Catholic literary work. The members of the first, born long enough before the Great War to have reached intellectual maturity before it began, shaped the literary and print culture that was already flourishing by the end of that war and often continued to be active participants, influencing the discussion through works that continued to be read and cited. The members of the second generation were born mostly in the first decade or two of the twentieth century and came to intellectual maturity after the Great War. For them, modernism of one sort or another was part of the air they breathed—officially to be avoided theologically and philosophically, but de facto something within their literary job description.

Chapter 1 describes the content of the literary aesthetic developed by U.S. Catholics in the early decades of the twentieth century, which helped to create the space within which questions that were largely off-limits to other areas of Catholic intellectual culture could be addressed. Chapter 2 looks in detail at the question of "modernism"—as the subject of theological debate and ecclesiastical condemnation and, simultaneously, in a different but related form, one of the main features of contemporary literary life. Chapter 3 discusses the daunting obstacles to Catholic literary analysis that were raised by literary modernism.

An even deeper rift between Catholic literary culture and intellectual modernity seemed apparent in the most anomalous feature of Catholic print culture: censorship. Chapter 4 examines the history of Catholic regulation of books and reading and describes the censorship system in the twentieth century. Chapter 5 looks at the ways the system was "translated"—explained and rationalized—to the Catholic reading public and also to and by Catholic scholars, writers, and intellectuals in a century and a nation that prided themselves on intellectual autonomy and artistic freedom. These explanations and rationalizations create a conceptual bridge to the topic of Chapter 6: efforts by Catholics to influence the content of American popular culture, especially motion pictures. Debates over Catholic control of print and of popular media drew on and reconfigured the basic elements and ideas of Catholic literary culture.

Chapters 7 and 8 return to the literary per se in the 1950s and 1960s to examine the changing ideas and institutions that reflected and made available the results of the previous decades' criticism and debate. By the mid-1960s, Catholics involved in literary work had reimagined their place on the cultural and intellectual landscape. This was no naive or escapist reimagining, but one forged by the century's cataclysms and the ongoing fear of nuclear annihilation. The chastening of hopes seemed in turn to contribute to a reimagining of Catholics in secular literary circles, whereby once-benighted medievals were now uniquely attuned to the century's experience. The period of this study opened in 1917 with the promulgation of the revised code of canon law that prescribed the censorship legislation governing Catholic literary work for the rest of the century, and it closes in 1966 with the "abrogation" of the authority of the Index of Forbidden Books. The Epilogue reflects on this symbol of the changed relationship between Catholicism and intellectual modernity to offer some conclusions about the importance and limits of literary culture as a resource for understanding twentieth-century U.S. Catholic intellectual history.

CHAPTER 1

U.S. Catholic Literary Aesthetics

In 1921, Condé B. Pallen published an article in *America* entitled "Free Verse." Pallen by this time had been prominent in Catholic literary culture for decades. As editor of *Church Progress and Catholic World* of St. Louis, poet, literary scholar and critic, popular lecturer on literary topics, and managing editor of the *Catholic Encyclopedia*, Pallen in his career linked literary and nonliterary work, institution building with scholarly and creative productivity. In "Free Verse," he wrote, " 'Shredded prose' is an apt description, if not an exact definition of what its advocates call free verse. That it is free, as free as madcap caprice, may be granted; that it is verse, which is built on metrical units, is to be denied. People may speak of a square circle, but there is no such thing; contradictions in terms are only a way of registering the impossible." So far, a formal argument from a disgruntled conservator of ossified stylistic convention. But as Pallen continues, an alternative cosmology becomes apparent. "The free-verse movement, like many other radical movements of the day, is a reaction from law and order. . . . Like free verse, cubism and futurism have flared up, the dawn of new things, only to be consumed in the lurid flame of their own incandescent folly. Free verse is only another *ignis fatuus* blown from the miasmic jungles of disorder. You cannot escape the law. God made the world in measure, weight and number, and in measure, weight and number it will endure."[1] This is an argument not just about literary style, but about the nature of the world. Its alternative cosmology is theocentric, and the order and purpose of the universe are discernible to humanity.[2]

Pallen was not alone in his conviction that the literary was connected to every other aspect of reality. Indeed, he shares with his co-religionists this and other beliefs that put them at odds with many of their contemporaries—not just religiously, but also philosophically, politically, historically, and literarily. For this generation, the "root source of modern disorder," as Philip Gleason puts it, lay in society's rejection of Catholicism's perennial truth and legitimate authority. Equally important, Catholics also believed they knew how—and were obligated—to address modernity's deepest discontents.[3] Catholics who took up this obligation via literary work needed not just institutions and publications, not just organizations and printing presses; they needed an aesthetic—a conscious, explicit philosophical framework for defining and evaluating literature. Such a framework had already been shaping U.S. Catholic literary work for some time, as Condé Pallen's critique suggests. Its role in the cultural work of Catholic literature can be more clearly demonstrated by sketching its contours, describing some of its major elements, and examining its role in appraising one of the major literary movements of the generation before the era of the Great War, realism.

Interwar Catholic Literary Culture

Catholics involved in literary work were shaping and employing their literary aesthetic in an era when changes in the secular literary academy significantly affected the nature of their task. Two of these changes are especially important here. Beginning in the early 1920s, American literary culture was becoming simultaneously professionalized and nationalized. In the generation of the "genteel tradition," late Victorians writing between the U.S. Civil War and World War I, literature had been more avocation than profession, the province of "men of letters" who wrote and read primarily in mainstream middle-class periodicals.[4] As university study and research became more specialized in the first decades of the twentieth century, departments of "English" began appearing, and literature increasingly became the province of the universities, requiring professional study and credentialing, especially to undertake the work of the critic. A cause and consequence of this change was the growing legitimacy of American literature as an object of serious study. Earlier generations had considered reading post-Renaissance English-language literature to be leisure, not scholarship—and if this was true of authors such as George Eliot and Thomas Hardy, how much more true must it be of Washington Irving and James Fennimore Cooper?[5] As literary scholars began to discern an "American Renaissance" in the writings of a number of mid-nineteenth-century Anglo male Protestant New Englanders, however, they expanded the body of work deemed suitable for professional literary consideration. The result was a prolonged burst in the study, teaching, and celebration of American literature per se for the first time.

Accompanying this shift was a call for critics to write a "national" literary history—to construct a history of American writing that would embody a national consciousness in a list of masterworks created by great American artists. The writers of the "American Renaissance"—Ralph Waldo Emerson, Henry David Thoreau, Walt Whitman, Nathaniel Hawthorne, Herman Melville, and a handful of others—were increasingly believed by interwar literary critics to represent an authentically American literary tradition. The culmination of this retrieval of a native tradition was the publication in 1941 of F. O. Matthiessen's *American Renaissance*, which identified Emerson, Thoreau, Whitman, Hawthorne, and Melville as central. In reaching back beyond the previous generation's celebration of the genteel tradition as represented by poets Henry Wadsworth Longfellow, John Greenleaf Whittier, Oliver Wendell Holmes, and James Russell Lowell, Matthiessen and other interwar critics saw themselves as "liberating America's cultural past from the deadly grip of WASP Victorianism." It is equally plausible to note that they thereby "helped place this past within the confines of WASP modernism."[6] The literary culture that came to dominate the U.S. academy through the 1950s, therefore, espoused a nationalism that implicitly figured American identity as Protestant.[7] As interwar Catholics participated in the professionalization of literary study in their own universities and other institutions, accommodating this second change within their views of literature was a key conceptual task.

Three aspects of Catholic literary culture set it at odds with these emerging characteristics of the literary mainstream. First, at a time when literature was supposed to express the freedom of the individual liberated from the stifling past, Catholic literary culture set itself the task of shoring up a unified communal identity. It was hierarchical and also collaborative, oriented internally and also externally. It was fractious and variegated, but thoroughly permeated by the sense of obligation to seek unity. "Seeking unity" did not necessarily imply harmony—it could mean excoriating errant brethren in decidedly inharmonious terms. Divisions existed between ethnic groups; between midwesterners and east coasters; between clergy and laity; between men and women; between conservatives and liberals; between anticommunists and union organizers and supporters; between low, middle, and high brows; between a largely blue-collar and rural emphasis on pastoral and devotional concerns and a more upper-class elite emphasis on high culture and cosmopolitan engagement with the contemporary. Catholic literary culture was one site within which these conflicts could be addressed and where they were sometimes fought out with damaging and lasting recrimination. Despite the depth and reality of the divisions, both theology and polity required that ultimate (even if only eschatological) unity be asserted.

Literary texts of all kinds were implicated in a dense web of mutual cooperation and obligation, writers linked to readers in an enterprise with great—indeed, cosmic—social implications. In *Religion and the Study of Literature*, Brother Leo wrote: "Literature springs from the heart of a man who knows much about life and who sympathizes deeply with life; and its educational, its cultural value springs from the fact that the reading of literature produces a corresponding growth of human knowledge and human sympathy in the heart of the student."[8] Names and descriptions for this growth varied: to Daniel O'Neill, literature "excites the noblest of emotions"; Stephen Brown said that "ordinary people find in the reading of fiction . . . at lowest a distraction, a thread of interest that catches the imagination and holds the attention for the time, at best a widening of experience, an enlargement of interest, a setting free of the more generous emotions, a certain humanizing influence"; Burton Confrey stated flatly that "the moral mission of literature is . . . to make us live better lives" and to "help [our fellowmen (*sic*)] achieve the goal which God has set as our final end."[9] All these descriptions have in common a sense that literature is an encounter between human beings, with effects for which the participants in the encounter are responsible.

Second, not only was Catholic literary culture relentlessly communal at a time when art's exaltation of individual freedom was nearly unparalleled. In addition, at a time when putting art at the service of ends other than itself was suspect as a symptom of incipient totalitarianism, Catholic literary culture set itself the task of changing the world. The literary aesthetic of Catholic Americans had a clear activist dimension. Literary work (in addition to theological and pastoral writing) had to *do* as well as *be*, had to serve as a means by which ends beyond and above the printed word were achieved. An activist aesthetic may seem like a contradiction in terms, but it animated Catholic literary efforts at many levels. Some efforts were in-house, such as the attempt by *America* editor Francis X. Talbot and Daniel Lord to compile a "Gallery of Living Catholic Authors," a showcase of the progress being made by Catholic Action. But even the thoroughly mainstream critical endeavors of poet Allen Tate, much better known as a southern writer and a New Critic than as a Catholic writer, were increasingly informed by a desire to save modernity from the perils created by its gnosticism and abstraction.[10] Catholic revivalists from Tate to Chesterton to Eliot were convinced that literature had a role to play in transforming society and an obligation to play that role. The end for the individual was always, ultimately, salvation, and art had to at least not interfere with that goal. The best art moved the reader directly toward that goal—helped, in fact, to achieve it. As Catholic Action began more and more to permeate Catholic literary culture, however, this individual focus continued to widen to include not just protection of individual salvation but the active initiative of redeeming modernity—of dramatizing the life and power of Catholicism in such a way that it could help people reimagine the world.

Adopting a literary aesthetic that was both communal and activist meant holding works and the people who produced them accountable for their effects, for how they facilitated the soul's journey toward heaven and the transformation of the world. This accountability was sometimes voluntary, sometimes involuntary. Some Catholic authors took up literary work as an apostolate, as a calling by which they attempted to further the work of the apostles in the contemporary world. But this accountability was also applied to authors who had no intention of holding themselves to these standards— non-Catholics and those in the category of so many twentieth-century U.S. authors who left the Church in order to pursue success in the literary world. So Catholic book reviewers and literary critics, for example, regularly assessed works by standards their authors were never attempting to meet, as in Theodore Maynard's somewhat sheepish but determined explication of "The Catholicism of Dickens."[11] Thus also Brother Leo's analysis of H. G. Wells's novel *When the Sleeper Wakes*. Wells was notorious within Catholic literary culture on account of his *Outline of History*, in which the Church appears as the opponent of progress and freedom. In the novel the protagonist wakes in the future, finds that poverty and suffering still exist, and despairs. Leo calls this an "indictment of the theory of human perfectibility through merely human means, that grotesque faith in the ability of man to lift himself by pulling at his own bootstraps."[12]

Their belief in the theocentric order of the universe and the obligation to bring it to bear on the travails of modernity led Catholic critics to develop a view of literature as being always at the service of extraliterary ends. They had the misfortune of embracing and articulating this view at precisely the moment when it was most intensely out of favor in mainstream artistic thought. Both for late Victorian belles-lettres gentry and for their modernist supplanters, art existed only for itself, only to be, and to suggest that it should "do" anything was to disqualify it as art.

An aesthetic in the service of nonaesthetic ends negated itself and resulted not in art but in propaganda. This term's entry into English (and a number of other languages, including French, Spanish, Dutch, and German) has a distinct anti-Catholic cast. "Propaganda" derived from the Latin name of the Congregation for the Propagation of the Faith (*Propaganda Fide*), also known as the Holy Office of the Inquisition. Once the term entered into aesthetic discussion, it served to delineate one of the most rigorously policed dichotomies in twentieth-century art, between art and propaganda. In refusing to accept that these were their only options, Catholics involved in literary work set themselves a difficult intellectual and institutional task. They needed to construct and apply a literary aesthetic that could span the very gap against which it defined itself.

A key tool in spanning this gap, the third aspect of this communal, activist literary culture, was its reliance on the trope of "timelessness." The belief that Catholic truth was timeless, and in particular that the post-Tridentine Church represented the persistence of timeless truth in a world of widespread error and chaos, was not solely an instrument of separatism. It was also a means of engaging intellectual questions central to the definition of modernity. When that engagement became increasingly difficult for Catholic theology in the first half of the twentieth century, it continued in Catholic literary culture.

The conceptual framework within which Catholics involved in literary work carried out their task was an evaluative system of some considerable scope and ingenuity. To be properly called "Catholic" (as opposed to "middle-class" or "clerical" or "conservative"), this aesthetic had to speak to church and culture, to modernist poetry and comic book, to New York literary critics and midwestern radio listeners. How, it seems fair to ask, could any given philosophical stance fit such a varied bill? Even further, could anything that had to bear this much cultural and theological weight properly be *called* an aesthetic? A set of literary practices, yes; certainly "cultural work" in Jane Tompkins's sense. But is it "aesthetic" or "literary" in any sense other than, perhaps, ethnographic?

The contexts within which Catholics defined and evaluated literature reveal the contours of a variegated but clear, surprisingly flexible aesthetic philosophy. Some of these evaluations do not hold up very well, as in *America*'s 1925 dismissal of *The Great Gatsby* as "an inferior novel, considered from any angle whatsoever . . . feeble in theme, in portraiture and even in expression."[13] Other analyses are highly elaborated, conscious, and reflective. In

The Well of English, Blanche Mary Kelly acknowledges that she places herself outside the critical mainstream in attempting to demonstrate "that Catholic Christianity infused into English literature a quality which accounts for most of what it had of greatness," but Kelly uses nuanced aesthetic distinctions that take into account the intentions and frames of reference of the authors she analyzes as she fits them into her own, theologically inflected scheme.[14] Whether deftly or clumsily wielded, the critical tools of Catholics involved in literary work shared a great deal in common.

The Contours of a Catholic Literary Aesthetic

The primary framework for Catholic aesthetic analysis was scriptural and Thomistic. Early and mid-twentieth-century U.S. Catholic literary culture conceptualized these elements distinctively and in terms that would shift dramatically by the century's end. Understood in context, these are the historical and intellectual linchpins around which Catholic literary analysis turns.

To say that Catholic aesthetic analysis was scriptural means that the Bible formed the primary point of reference for most works that addressed themselves to the definition and evaluation of literature from a Catholic standpoint. Those who are well informed about twentieth-century U.S. Catholic theological history may find this counterintuitive: Catholic theological culture was notorious for its retrograde approach to biblical study. The historical-critical study of scripture was too much associated with the liberalizing tendencies of Protestant theology and was for the most part proscribed for Catholics and Catholic scholars. In addition, Catholics were discouraged from individual study of the Bible, on account of the danger of misinterpretation resulting from the lack of guidance. But to say this is not to say that the scriptures were unfamiliar to most Catholics, whether scholars, critics, or ordinary readers. The ideas and stories and people of the biblical account throng the writings of Catholics concerned with the nature and evaluation of literature. They provide a narrative and doctrinal reference point within which these writers attempt to work out in their contemporary context the age-old relationship between art and religion.

The starting point, in more ways than one, was the idea of creation. Because the primary relationships that structured human identity and experience included the relationship to God as creator, all artistic creation was in some ultimate sense an echo of that original role. On the one hand, the relationship necessitated humility, because the artist was dealing with a world

and an order that were given, which put necessary limits on the artistic enterprise: "In his theme the imaginative writer must pledge unswerving fidelity to human nature. In observing this standard he is merely obeying reason,
for a new theme could mean only an attempt to improve upon the work of
the Creator Himself."[15] On the other hand, the comparison to God as creator uniquely exalted the literary enterprise. Boston College English professor John L. Bonn, SJ, argued that because "literature is the only art chosen
by God as the medium of revelation," it is "the most divine of the arts."[16]

The unique importance of literature was solidified by the metaphor for
the unity of divinity and humanity in Jesus that opens the gospel of John:
"In the beginning was the Word, and the Word was with God, and the Word
was God." Flannery O'Connor made perhaps the most widely quoted connection between her work and the doctrine of the Incarnation, but it was
far from the first or only one.[17] In 1897 in his opening chapter on "The
Catholicity of Literature," Condé Pallen had called the Incarnation the
"pivot of the world's history." Another of Bonn's arguments for literature as
the most divine of the arts was that "the Son of God is not by metaphor,
but by actuality, the Verbum." Harold Gardiner in 1941 made the same connection: "Our Catholic creed is a culture, a way, or rather *the* way of life. . . .
It is a fact that actually happened in the course of history, and it will always
remain a fact, whether we ever think of it or even realize it, that human
nature has been caught up into the Divinity, that it has been consecrated in
the person of the Word made Flesh, the God Man. All that is good, positive
in human nature, then, is potentially Christian and Catholic"[18]—this in the
introduction to a book of recommended reading for children.

Scripture not only provided the bedrock images on which Catholic
understandings of literature were founded. It was also an inexhaustible
source of references, comparisons, and titles, such as Valentine Long's 1935
Not on Bread Alone. Thomas Walsh begins his 1923 essay "Our Catholic
Poetry": "From the earliest days of exploration and missionary voyage the
passing of the Cross was to the accompaniment of echoes of the Psalmist's
Lyre."[19] Brother Leo entitled one chapter of *Religion and the Study of Literature* "The Perfect Short Story"—that is, the story of the Prodigal Son. From
the standpoint of much biblical criticism of the era, many of the examples
these writers used appear naive or ahistorical. But it is impossible to deny
the centrality of the biblical narrative and cast of characters to ideas about
literature in early twentieth-century Catholic literary culture.

The Bible was crucial not just as a repository for metaphors and examples. It was, as a historically situated document central to the cultural history of the West, a key element in the literary history Catholic writers

constructed and within which they located themselves and their ideas. When Joseph Pernicone tells the history of ecclesiastical censorship, he begins with the burning of books at Ephesus recounted in Acts 19:19.[20] A Catholic writer or critic who thus asserted credentials stretching vicariously back to biblical times, part of a tradition that claimed credit for shaping much of what Western culture regarded as literary, was also asserting the authority to speak to literary issues of the day despite the sea changes that had drastically altered the contemporary scene.

As it moved through the centuries, this justifying narrative lingered longest in the thirteenth, to pick up the two figures who most towered over early twentieth-century Catholic literary analysis—Dante Alighieri and Thomas Aquinas. Dante was important as an example of two things. First, he was a symbol of the greatness of the Middle Ages; the loss of that era's synthesis of religion and culture was frequently lamented as U.S. Catholics grappled with the fragmented reality of industrial consumer culture. Second, Dante's *Divine Comedy* was also for early twentieth-century Catholic literary commentators definitive refutation of the idea that religious belief somehow inhibited the creation of great art. As these writers and editors and teachers struggled to figure out what an American Catholic art might look like, they could point to Dante as the most inspiring example of what Catholic artists should be able to attain.

Aquinas's role was less as example and more as animating philosophical spirit.[21] His thought—or, more accurately, the version of his thought that went by the name of neoscholasticism—provided the most influential philosophical framework for thinking through literary issues. As with most twentieth-century uses of Aquinas's thought, writers and critics less often returned to his original text and more often invoked a set of principles rooted in Aquinas's work. A 1937 essay on the "philosophy of classification" (of library books) opens with this reflection: "The function of the wise man, according to the definition which Saint Thomas takes from Aristotle, is to discern the true nature of things, that he may with certainty discriminate among them and dispose of them each to its proper end. If this be true, the classifier of books, who achieves even a measure of the potentialities of his task, may well be honored as sage among the servants of those who read."[22]

Some teachers and critics used neoscholastic categories to argue for Catholicism's more holistic view of literature and the human person. In lecture notes titled "The Problem of Reality," John Bonn distinguishes among three views: "1. Only the material is real: materialists; 2. Only the spiritual is real: idealists; 3. Both are real: Scholastics."[23] Thomistic categories were useful for defining aspects of language other than the literary, as well: as Notre Dame English professor Richard Sullivan, in notes titled "Punctuation," dated January 8, 1940, put it:

> Grammar like civil law
>   based on natural law
> Punctuation rules a little
>   more like social customs—
>   etiquette.[24]

Thomistic categories helped situate and structure the literary at the same time as they reinscribed Catholic conceptual patterns back into the understanding of contemporary society.

Central to Catholic definition and evaluation of works of art was the necessary unity and harmony among the three criteria of goodness, truth, and beauty. Among early- and mid-twentieth-century Catholic critics, these became and remained distinct, interrelated criteria for judgment. At first glance this triad may seem unremarkable. It characterized a great deal of Victorian literary analysis, drawing on Aristotle via Matthew Arnold. Many American Catholics were comfortably part of the Anglo-American culture of belles lettres and guardians of the genteel tradition. This comfort, however, reflects not so much a vestigial Victorianism as the conviction that the Victorian categories had been unmoored from their actual scholastic origins. Catholic literary analysis reconnected goodness, truth, and beauty to medieval theological and philosophical ideas. Philip Vitale, of DePaul's English department, wrote as late as 1958, "For the Catholic critic, there is no good or truth opposed to God; neither is there beauty opposed to God. For God is the Good as he is the Truth; he is Beauty itself and confers beauty upon all creation 'because he is the cause of all harmony and brightness.' Thus every consonance or harmony, every beauty in creatures, is nothing but a similitude of, or participation in, Divine Beauty."[25] As a critical framework, what it lacked in neologistic flair it made up for in flexibility. Applied in a remarkable variety of ways—deftly, clumsily, pedantically, ingeniously—to a remarkable variety of texts, it was a key tool in the task of fashioning unity out of disagreement and disarray. Furthermore, it was a conscious response to what Catholics saw as modernism's (and modernity's) truncated vision of humanity, society, and creation.

"Goodness" translated into the moral content of a literary work. "If literary history teaches one thing more insistently than any other," Brother Leo maintained in *Religion and the Study of Literature*, "it is that in the judgment of the ages—which is the court of last appeal in literary matters—the book that is ignoble from the viewpoint of morals cannot be a masterpiece from the viewpoint of art."[26] Evaluation according to the moral criterion had at least two expressions, one producing the repressive condemnation of works of art largely on grounds of sexual morality, the other an understanding of the nature of morality that propelled Catholics beyond the boundaries of Catholic literary culture and into collaboration with a variety of fellow citizens. The first expression has gotten much more attention than the second. The image of the religious prude attempting to censor either great works of art (Joyce's *Ulysses*) or essentially harmless items of popular culture (dime novels and pulp magazines) would seem to personify the moral criterion in action. Heavy-handed application of the moral criterion produced most of the howlers in Catholic evaluation of literature—the critical judgments that seem most narrow, least literary, and most deliberately obtuse about where the seriousness and greatness of twentieth-century literature lay. It is difficult, for example, to defend the judgment that the final scene of *The Grapes of Wrath*, in which Rose-o'-Sharon nurses a man dying of hunger, is obscene.[27] It would, however, be a mistake to think that only critics who made such judgments were taking Catholic understandings of the moral law into account when making literary judgments.

The rapidity of the shift in cultural mores in the years after the Great War caused anxiety not just among Catholics. Public support was growing for legalizing divorce and contraception. The passage of the constitutional amendment granting woman suffrage was accompanied by a dramatic loosening of prewar strictures regarding women's dress and public presence. Short skirts, short hair, smoking in public, driving around in automobiles with men to whom they were not married or even engaged—all these symbols of changed cultural expectations had their supporters and their detractors, provoked anxiety as well as enthusiasm, among Catholics and their fellow citizens. As these changing standards made their way into literary depiction, both popular and high, they provoked a new level of literary debate in which the moral criterion was central. Most Catholic critics agreed on the general principle that literature should depict human experience honestly; where they diverged was over what that depiction looked like in practice. Much of the discussion centered on issues of sexual morality. At every brow level there was cause for concern—frankness about sexuality and rejection of nineteenth-century social mores were defining features of serious fiction. "There is a widespread notion," Irish writer John Desmond Sheridan wrote in 1935, "that good writing, if it tends toward realism, must be a trifle indecent, and some Catholics are even inclined to think that good writing excuses indecency."[28] Even popular fiction, while more conventional and reticent in some ways, seemed to Catholic critics to rely increasingly on divorce, for example, for dramatic effect and plot resolution.

Prudery is insufficient as an explanation of the functioning of the moral criterion in Catholics' evaluation of literature and other art in the 1920s and 1930s, as they adjusted to the rapid shifts in society. As Sheridan also observed, "The decadence of today is a new departure and must not be confounded with the decadence of the day before yesterday. It stands apart, because it is a philosophy rather than a fashion."[29] Not everyone would share his definition of what constituted "decadence," but he pinpoints an emerging and explicit philosophical understanding of morality that both was distinctively Catholic and at the same time propelled Catholic writers beyond the boundaries of Catholic literary culture. Understanding of the good, for Catholics, was grounded in the belief in the existence of a moral law built into the nature of the universe by God but discernible through human reason. This more philosophically rigorous notion did not, admittedly, operate in every campaign against indecency in comic books, but it featured more prominently than one might suspect. Because it presumed the existence of natural law, it presumed also that moral truths were available to "all people of good will" and that Catholics therefore had an obligation to collaborate with their fellow citizens in protecting the moral good.

Besides fostering collaboration, this philosophical aspect of the moral criterion led Catholic critics to identify, celebrate, and lay claim to a shared moral vision in writings produced in a wide variety of contexts. Oscar Wilde, for example, was suspect for both his notorious lifestyle and for his apparently decadent artistic philosophy. At the same time, his deathbed conversion to Roman Catholicism, along with the earnest moral tone of some of his work, led some Catholic critics to include him in the fold, albeit with qualifications. Thus Brother Leo assessed Wilde's *De Profundis*, written while the author was imprisoned in Reading Gaol, as "a bit of glowing, soul-stirring, matchless prose even though the man who fashioned it in the furnace of a grief-scorched heart was a sinner of nameless sins."[30]

The Catholic literary aesthetic was grounded in the neo-Thomistic unity of goodness, truth, and beauty. Indeed, the three criteria display a coherent continuity along a cumulative spectrum. The cumulative aspect seemed to function this way: A critic needed to deal preliminarily with the moral criterion in order to focus primarily on issues of truth or doctrine, and, successively, needed to deal with any challenges to both moral and doctrinal criteria in order to focus primarily on the aesthetic. Conformity to the moral law, for example, was necessary, but for Burton Confrey it was far less than sufficient to qualify as work as good: "If a novelist . . . who attends a Catholic church offers a sentimental potpourri of kissing affairs in which the heroine thinks one of her numerous partners married, but Kind Providence later reveals that he is not, we would not approve the claptrap nor would we, by our silence, recommend it."[31] Boston College's John Bonn, SJ, makes the same distinction and qualification in notes entitled "Lecture on Literature (Philosophical)": "In all forms of literature the moral effect is secondary; even in rhetoric the moral purpose must be subordinate to the aesthetic purpose if it is to be classified as art. But legitimate to judge it on these grounds: the end of art is a proximate end; but a proximate end is subservient to an ultimate end; and the ultimate end is a moral end; therefore art is subordinate to morality; But it is not good art because moral."[32] The awareness of this relationship could be deeply grudging; James J. Daly, SJ, concedes, "I am aware that literature is the expression of human nature, good and bad, and the bad must be noticed if literature is to be properly taught," before he goes on to say, "I am also certain that the bad is not so to be noticed in a classroom as to become a menace to a youth's spiritual growth." "If genius *mal logé* is waiting to be discovered anywhere," he observes, "the discoverers need not be Catholic critics, least of all, Catholic schoolrooms."[33] The result of this distinction, in practice, was a sometimes paradoxical situation in which the critics whose discourse seems the least sectarian, because it was so much engaged with the language of the contemporary academy, was the most densely embedded in Catholic literary culture, because the writer had had to come to terms with all three criteria in order to concentrate most fully on the aesthetic dimension.

The "truth" component of goodness, truth, and beauty can be thought of as the doctrinal criterion. Most simply, it meant fidelity to truth as Catholics understood it, including the role of the Church as custodian and teacher of that truth. It, too, had its literal and sectarian applications, some of them built into the particular roles people played within Catholic literary culture: as book reviewers for Catholic publications, for example, or as those in charge of accession for Catholic libraries. In a generally positive review of a textbook on American literature, the reviewer concludes, "The real objection to the book as a pupil's text is the philosophic undercurrent which . . . characterizes as good-humored and matter-of-fact the 'twentieth-century way' of ignoring the fundamental principles of religion."[34] However, while Catholics writing about literature were pervasively concerned that the beauty of Catholic truth be widely known among Catholic readers, none suggests that Catholic readers read only, even primarily, about Catholics or Catholicism.

This is perhaps because of the other important aspect of the doctrinal criterion, which, like the belief in natural law, propelled Catholics beyond parochial boundaries even while helping to define them. Belief in creation and incarnation meant that all created reality and all human experience potentially revealed the presence of God. Fidelity to truth in literature, then, was not solely replication of or even adherence to Catholic doctrine, but the artist's responsibility to depict human life in its fullness and the recognition that this depiction would include things distinct from Catholic doctrine and practice. The capaciousness of certain definitions of truth as they applied to evaluating literature depended, once again, on art's analogical connection to creation. Novelist Richard Sullivan argued in characteristically diffident fashion in a lecture entitled "The Intention of the Novel" that "any novel, if it is a re-creation of *real* human experience, honestly made, without distortion or falsification, with no contradiction of truth, is worthy of our most profound respect and gratitude. I believe this because I believe there is no human experience which is without meaning. I think that to re-create human beings in action, through words, is important and good. It may even, if one considers the sacramental character of creation, be holy. . . . Nothing that can be honestly said of man is unworthy of our attention."[35]

The two aspects of the doctrinal criterion could conflict with each other, and the resolutions could be creative. Recall Brother Leo's gloss on H. G. Wells's determinedly pessimistic and atheistic vision of the future, in *When the Sleeper Wakes*, which becomes instead a reaffirmation of human dependence on God.[36] Also exemplary is the 1945 *Catholic World* review of Richard Wright's *Black Boy*, which was willing to cede ground on issues of morality and on manifest respect for the church. The reviewer excused both a certain "irreverence" in Wright's depiction of Christianity as well as "a few really objectionable passages in the book . . . for though the author never excuses immorality, he does describe sordid scenes without delicacy or reticence," enough to "ban the book for immature readers." The reviewer, Rev. Michael McLaughlin, "critic and sociologist," suggested an expurgated edition: "It would serve a great need, for the safety of democracy and intellectual honesty demand that Americans know the horrible story of racial injustice."[37] Expurgation is too clearly a mode of censorship to seem a reasonable solution today, but in context what predominates is an earnest desire to find some means both to protect those who legitimately require protection and to maintain fidelity to the truth of American life, a truth that can be served, occasionally, even at the expense of due deference to religion. When necessary the doctrinal criterion could be applied as deftly as the moral criterion, in order to accommodate continually renewed understandings of the truth.

The concern with "beauty" became a distinct aesthetic criterion. Catholics writing about literature frequently invoked Aquinas on beauty's three elements: integrity or perfection, proportion or harmony, and *claritas* (translated both as "clarity" and "brightness").[38] This trio derives from a section of the *Summa Theologiae* (part 1, question 39, article 8) concerned with whether it is appropriate to attribute characteristics to the three persons of the Trinity (since such attribution could be seen as somehow limiting the limitlessness of God). Aquinas replies yes; he argues further that "species or beauty" can be applied appropriately to the Son, using the language of analogy: "Our intellect, which is led to the knowledge of God from creatures, must consider God according to the mode derived from creatures. . . . Species or beauty has a likeness to the property of [*similitudinem habet cum proprio*] the Son."

"For beauty includes three conditions," he continues, "'integrity' or 'perfection,' since those things which are impaired are by the very fact ugly; due 'proportion' or 'harmony'; and lastly, 'brightness' or 'clarity,' whence things are called beautiful which have a bright color."[39] Thus the language of Catholic aesthetics was even more deeply woven into the biblical and Thomistic fabric: the definition of "beauty" relies on the properties belonging to the second, incarnate, person of the Trinity; and human reason is capable of discerning in that beauty something analogically true about the nature of God.

This nexus helps to explain why Catholic writers so firmly rejected the notion of "art for art's sake," which gained in prominence in the early years of the century but persisted as a common trope for decades. From one angle, Catholics saw the idea as idolatrous, because it separated art from— and to some extent substituted it for—religion. They saw it also as decadent, due largely to its association with aestheticism as a movement. Anthony Yorke commented in *Catholic World* in 1897 on Walter Pater: "Such is the culture which comes down to us from the Greeks. It is pagan to the end of the chapter. . . . 'L'art pour l'art!' To live for the sake of, and merely for the sake of, the ecstasy which devotion to art produces. What a little thing to feed an immortal soul on!"[40] Brother Leo describes an aesthetic that retains the connection between art and religion as "sane" and "wholesome," in contrast to that of "certain nineteenth century apostles of art for art's sake," whose views and the art they produced were "morbid," "précieuse," "barren," "ship-wrecked," and "stillborn."[41] Similarly, a decade later, Daniel J. O'Neill: "Literature, one of the fine arts, expresses the beautiful. Those who preach *Ars gratia Artis* would alienate the beautiful from the good and the true. They would propose: Here is virtue; it is beautiful. Here is vice; it is beautiful. Or again: Here is a novel the theme of which is soul-inspiring; it is literature. Here is a novel, the theme of which is loathsomely degenerate; it is literature. No art is autonomous; it exists for the inspiration to higher ideals of living. Literature is not autonomous; its mission is legitimately to enrich intellectual and social experience, nobly to exalt moral experience."[42]

At the same time Catholic critics vigorously defended beauty per se against utilitarian critiques of its uselessness or inefficiency as well as against their own co-religionists who worried about its distracting or seductive powers. Beauty, like all other aspects of created reality, had its origins in God and was therefore inherently good. Again, this position predates the bounds of this study, but is consistently articulated well into the twentieth century. "Uncreate [*sic*] beauty," Condé Pallen wrote in 1897, "which is absolute and infinite, condescending to our state, and sacrificing its immensities and its intimate glories, enters into the boundaries of time and space, that their softening shadows and our finite faculties may find power to gaze upon its reflected beauty without being consumed by its splendors."[43] In 1911 Agnes Repplier wrote, "No creed that has ever held and swayed the soul of man has ignored the avenues of approach . . . that can make a just appeal to his senses, and turn his innate love of loveliness to love of God." She then goes on to use as an example "the muezzin who from the fretted balcony of a minaret sends out his voice in that appealing cry which penetrates the soul of all good Moslems. . . . At dawn, at noon, at sunset, at nightfall, he calls upon the faithful to adore the Power which set the sun in the firmament, and which casts a mantle of darkness over the weary earth."[44] The point has a remarkable staying power in the Catholic analytic tool kit. Still in 1935 writers were arguing that because "the thirsty craving after beauty, implanted in human nature, yet unsatisfied or disappointed this side of the grave" was part of the nature of the human person as created by God, seeking to satisfy it was evidence of the longing for God.[45] The impulse could be distorted or misdirected, but was in itself good and evidence of goodness.

Explicitly Catholic literary criticism did, then, take the aesthetic into account, but in a way that grounded even the most purely formal appreciation in categories that were as theological as they were literary. Beauty in the aesthetic sense was not an independent variable or an autonomous source of meaning; it depended on the theological idea of God's beauty, and on an idea that followed from it—that a faithful rendering of the created, and fallen, world was beautiful in this sense. In this critics were once more in harmony with Aquinas, who noted in the same *Summa* article that "an image is said to be beautiful, if it perfectly represents even an ugly thing."[46] This concept of beauty was complex: formal properties counted, but they were insufficient as criteria by which to judge a work's success. Rather than being inherently satisfying, beauty instead necessarily evoked an unfulfilled longing directed beyond it, whether or not the reader or listener or viewer knew this.

Aesthetics, Modernity, and Realism

Within this Catholic literary aesthetic, the mutual interdependence of goodness, truth, and beauty was not solely a critical tool for the evaluation and interpretation of literature. It was in addition explicitly and sometimes militantly a reinterpretation of the preceding half millennium of Western intellectual and cultural history. The entire modern English literary tradition, according to Valentine Long, gave voice to "the struggling sadness of a child crying for its mother." "The truer instincts of English poetry . . . are sad, unspeakably so, . . . because a sixteenth-century misfortune of a Queen has robbed them of hope, of their birthright, has orphaned them of a Mother."[47] The same intertwining of the literary and historical, with the addition of political and economic threads, can be found in the "discussion outline" (a typical teaching tool of Catholic Action, especially for young people) written by Jesuit Herbert O'Halloran Walker and published by The Queen's Work Press in 1938. Discussion 5 of *The Power and Apostolate of Catholic Literature*, entitled "Books Make Nations and Culture," retells the history of the West from the Incarnation to the present day.[48] By the nineteenth century, the villain of the piece was, not surprisingly, liberalism. ("This liberalism killed Christianity in so far as it was able to do so. Churchgoing on Sunday was still considered good form, but religion was something reserved only for Sundays.") Perhaps more surprisingly, the rise of liberalism had literary implications:

> With liberalism came the "success literature."
>   "From the spring seat of the grocery wagon to the big house behind the golf course." Horatio Alger, etc.
>   With liberalism too came big profits and small wages—and Karl Marx and Engels—and communism and the *end of individuals*.
>   Dictators rule two thirds of the world. (27)

This constellation of causation would be easy enough to mock, or to dismiss, were it as idiosyncratic as it may appear. But although it is perhaps more cryptic than most such analyses, its linkage of literary quality to economic inequality to the threat of socialism to the radical diminution of the human person that enables totalitarianism to flourish is more typical than not.

A less baroque variant of the same analysis can be found in the ur-text of the Catholic literary revival, Calvert Alexander's *The Catholic Literary Revival: Three Phases in Its Development from 1845 to the Present.*[49] Born in 1900, Alexander worked as a reporter in St. Louis to help support his family until he entered the Jesuits in 1924. Written during his scholasticate, *The Catholic Literary Revival* focused primarily on the world of serious, high-culture literature to describe a movement, worldwide and a century long, of writers bringing the resources of Catholicism to bear on the great artistic and cultural questions of the age.

The volume's introduction re-reads the history of the preceding century, asserting "the necessity of understanding the relation between the Catholic Revival and the secular history with which it is everywhere in contact. This relation," Alexander maintains, "is primarily one of revolt" (3–4). In Alexander's dramatization of the era's grand conflict, the modern world is losing; the mindful members of the generations preceding him have come to understand the limitations of the secular worldview and the poverty of all proposed alternatives. Alexander describes the situation in stark terms: "Complete loss of faith in the old secular world would mean a renewed faith in the new supernatural world. It would either mean that or abysmal despair. So true was this that a wise nineteenth-century man could have predicted with accuracy that when the consciousness of the old world's death became widespread, equally widespread would be the turning of men to Catholicism." Personal and cultural history merge in the conversion of apparently increasing numbers of writers and intellectuals to Catholicism: "All those vital differences that once gave a semblance of life have disappeared," he says, referring to the debates over classicism and romanticism, conservatism and radicalism, that had characterized the literary world of the preceding century, "leaving only monotonous uniformity from which little notable vitality results. Catholic literature is written by those who intellectually have stepped clear of this 'waste land' into a world full of an abundant and varied life" (15).

In this and other works, we see a decades-long attempt by Catholics engaged in literary work to disentangle themselves from the grasp of Anglo-American cultural hegemony and reconstruct a cultural history of the modern era in which they are not the obstacles and hindrances to intellectual and artistic achievement but its preservers and insurers. One arena in which this struggle was still being waged in the 1930s was the issue of realism in art and literature. By the final years of the nineteenth century, American Catholic writers and critics had a clear and unambiguous position on realism—they either entirely rejected or thoroughly embraced it, depending on how it was defined and who was doing the defining. What was at issue, most fundamentally, was what the word "reality" encompassed.

Realism in literature was not a new category in the 1890s—it had been around for nearly half a century. It meant different things in Europe than it did in the United States, which affected Catholic commentary more than that of their compatriots, since Catholics saw themselves as implicated in European, especially French, realism in a way that other Americans were not. In Europe, "realism" was more likely to graphically portray poverty and sexuality and to suggest that suffering and embodied experience were the most real, or the only real, aspects of human existence. U.S. Catholic critics objected to this sort of realism on grounds of sensibility and of philosophy. "The glib phrase, 'Honi soit qui mal y pense,'" wrote Thomas J. Hagerty in 1899, "will not answer when we set ourselves against a realism which gloats over woman's shame and man's dishonor; for virtue cannot be abashed by the charge of squeamishness nor deafened by the blare of publishers' trumpets."[50] Condé Pallen's contemporaneous analysis was more philosophically grounded (and characteristically apocalyptic). To him, the story was of a literary and philosophical fall in which literary realism was a direct result of philosophical skepticism: "In art, [skepticism] denies beauty and exalts the ugly to her high place. In literature, it begets—if a negative can be said to beget—Realism, and this much it does, not that it seeks to affirm anything, but by way of so many steps in the descent to the abyss."[51] Such objections were bolstered by the fact that all works (*opera omnia*) by the preeminent practitioner of this sort of realism, Émile Zola, had been listed on the Index of Forbidden Books.

In the United States, "realism" as a movement came to be distinguished from "naturalism"; by the 1920s these were seen as the constitutive strands of American literary tradition in the years after the Civil War and before the heyday of modernism. Realism's U.S. progenitor was William Dean Howells, perhaps the most influential literary person in the post–Civil War United States. Howells earned both fame and criticism for his meticulous portraits of the emerging American middle class in all their bourgeois glory and complacency. At the time they were published, novels such as *The Rise of Silas Lapham* (1884) seemed like bold assertions of ordinary American life as a suitable subject for literature; within a decade or two, however, they were overshadowed by the much bleaker work of Howells's protégés Stephen Crane, Theodore Dreiser, and Frank Norris. These younger writers more consciously asserted that "realism" required accepting the materialist nature of reality, and their naturalism depicted a brutal social and economic order that reflected the reality of a godless cosmos.

Catholic critics saw this emerging U.S. school in the wider context of European realism and judged in those terms. One of the most prominent Catholic critics in the nineteenth-century United States, Maurice Francis Egan, writing in *Catholic World* in 1887 upon the publication of Howells's *The Minister's Charge*, stated flatly that Howells was "not a realist." "He impresses us as a sincere and pure-minded gentleman who arranges his groups, carefully chosen, each member with his working-clothes on, and then photographs them. But this is not realism. Turgueneff, and Tolstoi, and De Goncourt, and, above all, Zola, would repudiate this method and manner. When Mr. Howells aims to be most realistic he generally succeeds in being commonplace."[52] Coming from Egan, no admirer of Zola, this was not a compliment. It does, however, make clear that Catholic literary culture featured substantive discussions about realism decades before the Great War.

Indeed, realism was the key issue in Virginia Woolf's choice of 1910 as the pivot point on which "everything changed"—the reaction, positive and negative, to the first large public exhibition of post-impressionist painting in London in 1910 was one of the factors that led her to select that year.[53] Further, her analysis overlapped with Catholic discussion of precisely the issues to which she was responding. When in her 1924 essay "Mr. Bennett and Mrs. Brown" Virginia Woolf coined the famous aphorism, she was defending modernism—including her own work—and criticizing the Edwardian realism of English novelist Arnold Bennett and his fellow writers H. G. Wells and John Galsworthy. Her essay was one volley in an ongoing match. Bennett's work had earned Woolf's dismissal by minutely depicting the material surroundings of a character and neglecting to convey her interior depths. Bennett had recently deepened his offense by criticizing a novel of Woolf's on the grounds that "the characters in it were not alive."[54] Woolf argued that the realists were so trapped in the stifling conventions of contemporary life that new writers had to struggle toward an entirely new mode in which to write. James Joyce's *Ulysses* resorted to indecency, according to Woolf, but it was "the conscious and calculated indecency of a desperate man who feels that in order to breathe he must break the windows."[55] As Woolf influentially formulated the issue, there were only two sides, representing the past and the future. We might expect, then, that Catholics engaged in literary work would line up with Arnold Bennett in defense of realism and of the past. Not so, in two ways.

First, Catholics also had their problems with Bennett. The feeling was mutual and had been for some while. Bennett was a participant in a high-profile 1907–8 exchange in *New Age* magazine among Bennett, Hilaire Belloc, G. K. Chesterton, George Bernard Shaw, and H. G. Wells over the nature of modern society and modern belief, touched off by Bennett's essay "Why I Am a Socialist." In 1917 Bennett published an edited collection of his weekly columns from *New Age*, in which he included his review of Chesterton's 1909 essay collection, *Tremendous Trifles*.[56] His comments, and Chesterton's response, were highlighted as the last item in the September 1917 issue of *Catholic World*. "In my opinion," Bennett wrote, "at this time of day, it is absolutely impossible for a young man with a first-class intellectual apparatus to accept any form of dogma, and I am therefore forced to the conclusion that Mr. Chesterton has not got a first-class intellectual apparatus."

Chesterton's response was an exemplary move in the game of using assertions of timelessness to make very timely arguments: Bennett's temporal metaphor, according to Chesterton, "exposes and explodes his whole philosophy." Chesterton highlights the absurdity, which he presumes Bennett would acknowledge, of believing in reincarnation "at 12:30 a.m., but not at 3:30 p.m." and goes on to assert that "it is every bit as irrational to deal thus with mere centuries as to deal thus with mere hours. . . . He does not worship an eight-day clock . . . and I will not worship an eight-century clock either."[57] Bennett's realism, though fusty and conventional to Virginia Woolf, was to Catholics such as Chesterton (and the approving *Catholic World* editors who printed his riposte) more like than unlike Virginia Woolf's work in its rejection of reality's sacred basis and the reasoned interpretation thereof that, for Catholics, gave rise to dogma. Therefore, because both evaded so much of what was "real" about the world and human experience, both equally forfeited any claim to the term "realism."

Catholic analysis of realism in art had three key components. First, realism, to be accurately so termed, had to reflect the reality that the world was not solely material but included a spiritual dimension within which humanity had an ultimate destiny. If a work did not somehow (even by absence or negation) point to the fullness of the creation and redemption of the world by an incarnate and still-present God, it could not claim realism. Second, artists had not just the right but the obligation to depict all aspects of human experience, including evil and sin. Novelist Compton Mackenzie confidently asserted the Catholic novelist's obligation "to drag his trawl as fearlessly in the depths as to cast his fly upon the sparkling shallows."[58] Third, these two points were integrated and mutually sustaining—the depiction of the realities of human experience had to be oriented in some discernible way toward helping readers achieve their ultimate destiny. Elizabeth Monroe wrote that the novel "may represent lust, adultery, violence, or filth, but it represents these things as defections from reason or morality, not as the norms of human experience." Monroe even argued that such treatment was not so much a moral principle as an aesthetic one: a "novel loses aesthetic distance by appeals that are too immediate"—that is, by "making passion or sin an end in itself or representing it with undue vividness."[59] Richard Sullivan qualified his remarks quoted earlier by noting that although "the spread of the novel is coextensive with reality; novels deal with people; nothing, *nothing*, that involves human beings is out of range as a subject," still "the mind and art of the novelist must be up to what he treats: altitude is essential."[60] These principles could be crisply articulated, but there was perennial disagreement over their application. One person's searingly honest portrayal was another's sordid obscenity.

The work of Norwegian author Sigrid Undset elicited precisely this divided response. Undset's three-volume novel of medieval Scandinavia, *Kristin Lavransdatter*, was simultaneously hailed as a Catholic classic and assailed for depicting passion, adultery, and too many of the specifics of daily life. *America* editor Francis X. Talbot, SJ, defended Undset in 1929 shortly after she won the Nobel Prize for Literature. "What can be done," Talbot asked, "about our modern Catholic writers who are trying to express contemporary life in the modern idiom? . . . What care must they exercise in deleting every sentence that might prove suggestive to an immature or an oversensitive imagination?"[61] The equation of an appreciation for realism with maturity and adulthood reflects anxiety over changing gender roles and shifting loci of cultural authority that appeared in many assessments of literature in the 1920s and 1930s. Those such as Talbot who criticized the oversensitivity of some Catholic readers were not suggesting that the moral law was not relevant to the evaluation of literature; far from it. They were instead suggesting that if the moral vision integral to a work was consistent with Catholic teaching, then some undesirable elements could be ignored in appreciating the whole.

Undset's work even today wields emotional force in its stark depiction of the hardship and violence of medieval life. Especially in the 1920s, objections to her work might be explained as evidence of the difference between American and European sensibilities. What is truly striking about Talbot's article, to the point of reshaping the debate over realism, is that in it he also felt the need to defend Kathleen Thompson Norris.

In 1929 Norris had been famous for almost twenty years as the author of wholesome stories of romance and family life that were among the most popular works of the century. Over the five decades following the bestselling *Mother* in 1911, Norris published ninety-six books, mostly novels. The few mentions of her in twentieth-century literary history or criticism assess her works as though they were interchangeable, but a look at the scope of her career through the lens of Catholic literary culture reveals a great deal. Norris was highly praised by none other than William Dean Howells, particularly for her realism. In a 1914 article in the *North American Review* he put her in the company of Dickens and "the great Russians." "Her art is always art for truth's sake and goodness's sake, and mostly for hope's sake."[62] Norris's pedigree as a realist was yet more distinguished, however, as she was married to Charles Norris, novelist brother of American naturalist Frank Norris.

Early in her career Norris was advised to "soften the Catholic atmosphere" in her work so as not to limit her audience to Catholics.[63] By the mid-1920s she was successful and confident enough to depict Catholic families openly in her novels—confident enough to set the opening of her 1925 novel *Little Ships* during exposition of the Blessed Sacrament. Her role as a Catholic writer was not without controversy, however, which she addressed in an essay in *Fiction by Its Makers*, writing of the "one hundred and fourteen letters of protest, most of them scornful, some of them angry," which she received after "putting flowers on the altar on Holy Thursday." Her response to what seems to have been vocal and persistent criticism, from which even her extremely positive portrayal of American Catholic family life did not shield her, appeals with some asperity to the artist's freedom and duty to depict reality as it is: "When the day comes when we can point to all the bad persons in the world, and say truthfully, 'Those are not Catholics,' and to all the good ones, and say, 'Those are,' then Catholic fiction may be both truthful and palatable."[64] Francis Talbot noted in his 1929 article that Catholic critics "with a keen eye for righteousness" saw in Norris's novel *Red Silence* "suggestive passages." These presumably had to do with the novel's primary plot thread, in which the ne'er-do-well friend of an ex-lover blackmails heroine Dory Penfield to keep the knowledge of her affair from her husband, Jerd. The truth, once revealed, prompts Jerd not to condemnation but forgiveness, and on perhaps surprisingly egalitarian terms: "Why should a man do a thing, casually and simply, and forget it, and a woman be dragged through agonies of shame, sometimes as far as a scaffold, for the identical thing—for the same response to a natural feeling." But Norris is also careful to have her heroine note, resisting her husband's forgiveness, "But there *are* wrong things in the world, Jerd." To which Jerd replies, "'Ah, yes, of course there are! But it's the clinging to them, the feeling that one can't forgive them, that they leave permanent stains, that's the stupid part.'"[65] Not classical moral theology, but a rather carefully thought-out moral framework nonetheless.

Talbot's exasperation with such critics still had cause as late as 1941. In that year *Sign* columnist Katherine Burton criticized Norris's novel *The Venables* in emotional terms: "It comes close to being something that Margaret Sanger could use as an example and a defense." Burton's evidence was the reaction of a "young friend," who told her that "had she read these chapters before her baby was born she would have been wild with fear about having him born, so terrible were the descriptions of childbirth. . . ." The scenes Burton seems to be referring to, of the birth of a wanted child into a devout and loving Catholic family, do make clear, indirectly and allusively, that even normal childbirth at home involved considerable suffering, along with worry over whether mother and child would live. To see it as birth control propaganda is striking evidence of the almost impossibly wide variations in sensibility that Catholic literary culture had to bridge. Nonetheless, for Burton, "This book is realism trimmed with very green grapes of wrath."[66]

Criticism of Norris is especially instructive because, despite William Dean Howells's commendation of her realism, she was more often criticized—indeed, was something like shorthand—for excessive sentimentality. A 1937 Gluyas Williams cartoon depicts a young woman waving as she rides away from the house of the justice of the peace in a posh car with a handsome man while her fiancé watches forlornly from the front porch; the cartoon bears the caption: "The Kathleen Norris heroine who didn't wait for Mr. Right." Richard Sullivan urged the editor of his 1946 novel *The World of Idella May* to avoid the "Kathleen Norris approach" in approving the book's dust jacket.[67] She was also a key point of reference two years later in Sullivan's cautious approval of his friend Harry Sylvester's *Atlantic Monthly* article on "Problems of the Catholic Writer." The article, Sullivan wrote to his (and formerly Sylvester's) agent, "will do, I'm sure, a lot of energetic stirring among persons who think that Kathleen Norris is the world's greatest writer: persons who feel that the virtue of a novel lies in its making one feel either holy (this is preferable) or just plain peachy (which is next best)."[68]

As Hawthorne with the "d——d mob of scribbling women," Sullivan (twenty years Norris's junior) was probably protesting a bit too much. And in fact he was subject to similar criticism the next year in response to the publication of his first novel, *Summer after Summer*. A *Books on Trial* reviewer scathingly dismissed the novel as "peep-holing" in its depiction of a young couple awaiting the birth of their second child. Sullivan's colleague at Notre Dame (and head of the philosophy department), Philip C. Moore, CSC, wrote to John C. Tully, editor of *Books on Trial*, taking him to task in strong terms for printing the review. In defending the book against these charges, Moore made a typical distinction: "In *Summer after Summer* we are at last getting true American Catholic fiction, shot through with Catholic realism. This is in happy contrast to American Catholic fiction of the past which was either sticky with piety or juvenile. Mr. Sullivan's book is not milk for babes, but good solid food for those who have attained to full intellectual Catholic manhood."[69]

Debates over realism revealed fissures in American Catholic literary culture—between what we might call, in Rochelle Gurstein's terms, the "party of reticence" and the "party of exposure," between popular and "serious" literature, between women and men.[70] The gendered terms of Philip Moore's defense of Richard Sullivan were not incidental, as the sentimentality of the fiction preferred by many Catholic reviewers was regularly attributed to the novel's being primarily written for and read by women.[71] Such divisions were real, but what Catholic commentary about realism reveals most clearly over time is how flexibly Catholic critics (amateur and professional) could apply shared aesthetic categories. Catholics attempting to safeguard the most delicate prewar reticence could appeal to the same critical terminology as those attempting to encompass the bleakest terrain of postwar despair.

The framework was capacious enough to accommodate a text such as Pietro di Donato's 1939 *Christ in Concrete*, which appeared somewhere at the intersection of naturalism and Catholicism. Di Donato's story of Paul, a brickworker's son who has to take on the trade as a boy when his father dies in an accident, could quite easily have been rejected by a Catholic reviewer: the Church in the form of a selfishly oblivious priest fails the family badly, Paul at the novel's end rejects the Church and adopts socialism, and throughout the work the naturalistic detail is straightforward. *America*'s reviewer, however, Joseph R. N. Maxwell, attributed to the work "all the pathos of a Greek tragedy." He noted its "uncompromising frankness and plain-spoken realism," that not everyone would agree with the theme of the novel, and that it was at times too graphic, but he ended with praise for "his delineation of the character of [Paul's mother] Annunziata, who with her dying breath prays for Paul and closes her story with a note of hope."[72] Maxwell's judgment reflects a shift that gradually broadens the category of realism while the debate over it remains self-consciously Catholic. The shift is not strictly linear (the Norris and Sullivan examples above come two and three years after *Christ in Concrete* was published), but over the course of the interwar decades the category comes to encompass more instead of less, to prove indefinitely expandable.

These categories and the strategies for applying them existed not to circumscribe an autonomous arena called "art," and within that arena to delineate a yet-smaller circle called "great," but conversely to incorporate within the category of the literary as much and as many as it could possibly hold. Contemplating an aesthetic with such a range—popular and high; past, present, future; material and supernatural; things seen and unseen; local and global; immediate and ultimate—might tempt one to say (sing) with Gilbert and Sullivan, "When every one is somebodee, / Then no one's anybody!" If the usual purpose of an aesthetic, as of any conceptual system, is to help make distinctions and judgments, it is a marker of how distinctive Catholic approaches to literature were in the twentieth century that, as a system, it insisted on bringing all of reality within its scope and judging it in the light of eternity and yet functioned across a wide variety of contexts in the pragmatic day-to-day decisions people made about what to write and read.

The framework for literary analysis used by Catholics writing self-consciously and explicitly as Catholics remained remarkably stable over the decades from just before the Great War to just before the next war, but this stability is misleading if it is taken as evidence of disengagement. Encompassed by a supposedly timeless entity, Catholics could delve deeply into their particular times as though the times were—indeed, *because* they were—of ultimate significance. Catholics writing about literature were deeply conscious of the ways in which Roman Catholicism had stood and was standing—institutionally, philosophically, culturally—against much of what constituted the modern world. But by continually insisting that all aspects of human experience were appropriate, even necessary, subjects for literature, they turned their minds again and again to the preceding two centuries and eventually helped to reknit the conceptual fabric of modernity.

Catholic literary culture provided the space and time within which Catholics could work out this accommodation with modernity on their own terms. The accommodation was in part concrete and pragmatic, as in the establishment of new institutions like the Catholic Book Club, which poet and critic Katherine Bregy endorsed this way: "For the 'general reader' must always, I suppose, be more or less directly directed—and it seems fairly obvious by this time that neither the Literary Guild nor the secular Book-of-the-Month Club can do the work for Catholics quite satisfactorily."[73] In the years after the Great War, Catholics adapted the standardizing and professionalizing trends of secular print culture to address the situation of their own assimilating immigrant population.

Participants in Catholic literary culture also accommodated with modernity by elaborating and honing a set of ideas. This conceptual component was less concrete but not therefore any less pragmatic, nor less addressed to the needs of the immediate moment. Interwar Catholic writers and critics confronted the ideas reverberating through U.S. intellectual culture, confident that their distinctive resources were up to the challenge. The preceding generation had developed a response to realism in literature that both delineated a Catholic ground on which to define reality and at the same time enlarged the borders of that ground to encompass ever-larger swaths of the real. The postwar generation continued to use these ideas about the real to address and inflect—for both church and culture—one of the most pervasive, compelling, maddening, and fluid ideas of the twentieth century: modernism.

CHAPTER 2

Modernisms Literary and Theological

A defining aspect of Catholic intellectual life in the 1920s was the 1907 Vatican condemnation of something termed "Modernism," a set of theological positions the Vatican considered incompatible with Catholic belief. Although this condemnation did not deal quite the death blow to Catholic intellectual life that historians long maintained, virtually no American Catholic intellectual of the interwar years would have defended modernism per se.[1] What then could Baptist minister John Roach Straton possibly have meant when he warned in 1928 of the danger ahead should Al Smith be elected president, because Smith "represented 'card playing, cocktail drinking, poodle dogs, divorces, novels, stuffy rooms, dancing, evolution, Clarence Darrow, overeating, nude art, prize fighting, actors, greyhound racing, and modernism'"?[2] At the very least, "modernism" could appear in a wide variety of guises in the 1920s, in unexpected corners of cultural discourse. Evident almost everywhere, it was (and remains) notoriously difficult to pin down neatly.

The cultural work of Catholic literature in the middle years of the twentieth century was to tend the boundaries of Catholic culture at the same time that it facilitated contact and influence across those boundaries. Straton's rollicking Al Smith constellation suggests that Catholic culture bordered on a number of different territories, all of them part of the landscape with which Catholic literary culture engaged, reinforcing the ideology of essential unity among Catholics of all classes at the same time that it revealed fissures and distinctions. To do so it established and drew on an extensive network of alternative literary institutions animated by a simple and flexible literary aesthetic that was able to address literary issues at all levels. Because within this aesthetic literary issues were always also theological and philosophical, discussion of topics such as realism, as we have seen, concerned not solely or even primarily formal aesthetic criteria but debates about the nature of the cosmos, history, and humanity.

If thinking about "realism" plunged Catholics engaged in literary work into active discussion of the relationship of U.S. Catholicism to its time and place, how much more is this true of the even more influential and pervasive literary modernism? As it happens, in December 1910 (the very month when "human character changed") *Catholic World* in its "Foreign Periodicals" section took note of a Vatican pronouncement recently recorded in the Italian Jesuit review *Civiltà Cattolica*. "'Literary modernism,'" the short notice read, "is not a new kind or a new form of Modernism, distinct from the forms of Modernism condemned in the Encyclical *Pascendi*; but is the use of various kinds of literature to spread abroad Modernist doctrines."[3] Did such pronouncements close off engagement with literary modernism as they did the theological variety? Not if we judge by the fact that when *Portrait of the Artist as a Young Man* was published in 1916, *Catholic World* reviewed it—that is, engaged its ideas and evaluated it in light of the American journal's own views of literature *and* of modernity. It did so, perhaps notably, without using the word "modernist" to describe the novel or its author, and without reference to the Vatican's decrees.

Like James Joyce, a number of the people who undertook key elements of the (literary) modernist project—literarily and institutionally—were somehow identifiable as Catholic. As a result, U.S. Catholic critical energies and attention (both favorable and unfavorable) were directed toward modernism that might otherwise not have been. Because Catholic literary critics had to keep talking about "modernism" during the very same time that Catholic theologians were prevented from talk about "modernism," we find in literary discussions considerable overlooked evidence of the means by which the philosophical reconciliation between Catholicism and the modern world came about. In this way, literary history is perhaps more central to the intellectual history of twentieth-century U.S. Catholicism than has yet been appreciated.

Literary modernism, like its counterparts in the visual and musical arts, foregrounded ideas about aesthetics and society, history and human nature, that often collided with the philosophy that grounded Catholic literary aesthetics. Because both modernism and Catholicism were complex entities with their own occasional internal contradictions, their interaction defies simple characterization.[4] But for U.S. Catholics involved in literary work in the years after the Great War, the collision could and did result in stark oppositions that seemed to pit Catholics against modernity in an unresolvable battle. As we will see here and in Chapter 3, however, Catholic literary critics, by continually questioning the oppositions apparently imposed on Catholicism by modernism, developed a set of intellectual resources that not only eventually reclaimed modernism in literature as part of the century's spiritual heritage but also helped bring about the reengagement with modernity that characterized the Church by the time of the Second Vatican Council in the 1960s.

Theological Modernism and U.S. Catholic Intellectual Life

In the history of Catholic theology in the twentieth-century United States, "modernism" refers primarily to the heresy condemned (and, some would say, created) in Pope Pius X's 1907 encyclical *Pascendi dominici gregis*. The condemnation grew out of a long and deepening rift between Catholicism and "modern" thought that stretched back in some sense at least to the sixteenth century. The condemnation is also inseparable from papal and ecclesiastical politics of the nineteenth century, and the conflation by a number of major participants in the controversy of the political liberalism that in their view had led to a century of destructive revolution with the philosophical liberalism that seemed to reduce humanity to the material and empirical and the created world to a mechanism.

Virtually every account of theological modernism, from 1907 to the present, pleads severe difficulty in defining the term. The difficulty stems in large part from the diffuse nature of the phenomenon. A number of different thinkers in France, England, Germany, Italy, and elsewhere were attempting to assimilate the findings of historical biblical criticism, the significance of the rise of science, and the philosophical implications of democracy into Christian understandings of the human person and the nature of tradition and authority. These scholars and thinkers were often, though not always, acquainted with each other and each other's work, but they were not in any meaningful sense an organized movement. They were, almost without exception until the 1907 condemnation, deeply committed to the Roman Catholic Church and, while interested in church reform and reconciliation with modernity, were not attempting or intending subversion or revolution. Most were taken aback and deeply hurt by the intensity of the papal condemnation. As Scott Appleby documents, a number of the most prominent figures in the group left the Church or were excommunicated but nonetheless maintained a personal commitment to Catholicism and Catholic tradition.[5]

Pascendi famously condemned modernism as the "synthesis of all heresies." So sweeping was its characterization of the position, and so intense its rejection, that it left virtually no intellectual elbow room for response or debate. One would not be wrong, the encyclical states, "in regarding them as the most pernicious of all the adversaries of the Church. For, as We have said, they put into operation their designs for her undoing, not from without but from within. Hence, the danger is present almost in the very veins and heart of the Church, whose injury is the more certain from the very fact that their knowledge of her is more intimate. Moreover, they lay the ax not to the branches and shoots, but to the very root, that is, to the faith and its deepest fibers. And once having struck at this root of immortality, they proceed to diffuse poison through the whole tree. So that there is no part of Catholic truth which they leave untouched, none that they do not strive to corrupt."[6] The principle means of modernist corruption, according to *Pascendi*, was the conviction that religion along with all other aspects of human experience needed constantly to change and evolve in order to remain alive and vital. A central aspect of this change was religion's need to reform itself by incorporating new scientific understandings so as to abandon anything demonstrated by science to be untrue. In nearly a century's hindsight, *Pascendi* pretty clearly overstated both the changelessness of even post-Tridentine Catholicism and the infatuation with innovation of the people it condemned as modernist. But it makes quite clear how deep the rift was within a tradition committed to reason when reason came to be defined in such a way that it contradicted or rendered irrelevant supernatural truth.

Because, in the manner of most papal communication, *Pascendi* named no names and targeted no individual thinkers directly, the encyclical encouraged the suspicious to see modernists everywhere. Historians of the reaction to the encyclical have documented the speed with which American Catholic intellectuals, some of whom for years had eagerly pursued the implications of ideas potentially characterized as modernist, repudiated them in the encyclical's wake.[7]

The condemnation of modernism occurred in a U.S. climate already chilled less than a decade earlier by *Testem benevolentiae*, an 1899 Vatican condemnation of an even more amorphous set of positions termed

"Americanism." Directed toward a group of American bishops who had for more than a decade advocated enthusiastically the study of the American situation as a type case for how the Church should exist in the modern world, *Testem*, like *Pascendi*, conflated a number of differing positions into one heresy. Its most basic criticism was of the "false principle that the church's adaptation to modern civilization requires not only changes in church discipline but also in doctrine. Americanism minimizes doctrine to make the church more acceptable to non-Catholics."[8] It is unclear, and has been unclear since 1899, that anyone actually advocated in their entirety the positions *Testem* condemned, and historians of Americanism have located the origins of the condemnation in a specific series of controversies in the United States and, most proximately, France in the 1880s and 1890s.[9] To the extent that it existed at all as a coherent entity, modernism was a European rather than an American phenomenon. But it occurred so soon on the heels of the condemnation of Americanism that the two were largely conflated in U.S. Catholic intellectual history and reverberated together through U.S. Catholic intellectual life for generations.

Historians and theologians continue to debate the legacy of theological modernism for U.S. Catholic intellectual life, and the debate tends, unsurprisingly, to reflect current divisions within U.S. Catholicism. Contemporary liberals tend to see the condemnation as having had a disastrous effect on the vitality of theology in the United States, discouraging original work for at least fifty years, if not longer. Conservatives, while sometimes acknowledging the severity of the condemnation, tend to adopt a version of its basic premise—that uncritical acceptance of the positions that characterize modern philosophy undermines church authority and tradition. Some even go so far as to reject the authority of the Second Vatican Council (1962–65), claiming it was influenced too much by modernist principles. The diversity of these reactions indicates that a neutral assessment of theological modernism and its condemnation can be only limited and tentative, but the controversy nonetheless reveals clearly the contours of the conflict between Catholic tradition and intellectual-philosophical modernity.

The key to interpreting the effects of theological modernism, whether from the left or from the right, lies in judgments about just what should accommodate to what in the reconciliation between church and modernity. So-called modernists and their predecessors a generation earlier saw a pragmatic and moral imperative in the adaptation of church structures and teachings to modernity. Antimodernists, both before and after the formal condemnation of the heresy, affirmed the universality and timelessness of Catholic truth, tying that affirmation to specific doctrinal formulations and institutional structures—and if we now see these formulations as undeniably contingent and mutable, we do so with an additional century's experience of and confidence in the possibility of their persistence in the face of modernity's challenges.

The conflict, then, was real; given the totality of political, social, intellectual, and cultural circumstances, the new ideas being posed did require change, did have an internal logic that could and did propel some of their proponents beyond the institutional church, did threaten the existence of the Church as it was understood.[10] At the same time, engagement with these ideas was unavoidable; any Vatican hope that they could be extinguished or evaded was culpably naive. That both of these statements can be true seems unlikely; such is the nature of the impasse created by the collision of Catholicism and modernity at the turn of the last century.

This collision and the resulting impasse established Catholicism in an intellectually adversarial relationship with philosophical modernity for much of the twentieth century. In theological study especially, historians and other scholars agree that much of the work necessary to bring Catholic theology into meaningful dialogue with modern philosophy was delayed for decades. What Catholic seminarians and other students of theology studied instead was, as *Pascendi* prescribed, neoscholasticism—the thought of Thomas Aquinas as it had been distilled and refined over the preceding centuries ("that which the Angelic Doctor has bequeathed to us").[11] Although the static and uncreative nature of neo-Thomist philosophy has been overstated, even at its most nimble it could not adequately address the questions posed by post-Kantian philosophy.

These questions were not, however, the only ones animating the American intellectual scene in the years after the condemnation of modernism. U.S. Catholic scholars and writers in a number of fields other than theology and philosophy applied and extended Catholic categories of analysis in addressing themselves to some of the most lively intellectual questions of the day. Catholic sociologists drew on natural law tradition and Catholic understandings of the human person to argue against what they saw as the deadening materialism characterizing academic sociology. Economists and political theorists developed influential models of the relationship between the state and the economy that they used to criticize both socialism and unrestrained capitalism. Legal theorists crafted and attempted to defend an alternative tradition of legal reasoning that opposed the increasingly influential "legal realism" championed by Oliver Wendell Holmes and his successors.[12]

As we have seen, Catholics thinking and writing about literature were at least as active and energetic in this period as those working in other fields.

Unlike the work of Catholic sociologists, political scientists, and legal theorists, however, literary work has not for the most part been studied as part of the period's intellectual history. This neglect stems in part from the disciplinary history of "English" in the twentieth century, which helped to define the arts as a realm distinct from the "intellectual," a place where intuition and creativity could reign without the limits imposed by rationality.[13] This trend intensified through the middle decades of the century, so that by the 1950s mainstream academic literary criticism was about as far as it ever was to be from gauging literary value in anything other than formal aesthetic terms. But as we have seen, literary work was for Catholics more so than perhaps for any other group of American intellectuals in this period a matter of conscious theological and philosophical reflection (with clearly political and cultural ramifications) as well as a creative exploration of what lay beyond reason. Literature and literary analysis are essential to the story of American Catholic intellectual life in the aftermath of the condemnation of modernism, because literary critics had to keep talking about something called "modernism," perhaps the single most influential aesthetic movement of the century.

On the one hand, such was the intensity of *Pascendi*'s effect that self-conscious Catholic writers generally distinguished their treatment of the issue of "modernism" in nontheological contexts from anything having to do with the condemned heresy. In addition, modernism from its late nineteenth-century beginnings was evidently at odds with Catholic literary aesthetics in any number of ways. Formally, modernist artists and authors drew on developments in the science of perception and cognition to argue that realism was not "realistic," and that formal experimentation (abstraction in painting and sculpture, free verse in poetry, stream-of-consciousness in prose) could more effectively convey the flux and contingency of these new understandings. Modernism's themes and subjects reflected its contention that confidence in a coherent worldview grounded in metaphysical certainty belonged to the childhood of humanity, and needed to be abandoned—especially after the carnage of the Great War—and the reality of fragmentation and dissociation accepted. Even the personal mores of many modernist artists evinced the belief that rejecting convention in form and content was consistent with rejecting social conventions such as marriage, sexual fidelity, heterosexuality, and nationalist allegiance that were rooted in the same bourgeois history.

On the other hand, despite the way in which modernist aesthetics differed from Catholic, the inhabitants of Catholic literary culture regularly engaged with key modernist texts. To what extent were they, inevitably but obliquely, also engaging with the ideas condemned in *Pascendi*? ("Far, far

from the clergy be the love of novelty!" [par. 49] would not serve a reviewer well as a critical tenet.) The ambiguity inherent in the situation
helped to define a space for a particularly delicate job of cultural work.

Recall the Vatican's unequivocal 1915 announcement that "literary modernism is not a new kind or a new form of Modernism, distinct from the
forms of Modernism condemned in the Encyclical *Pascendi*; but is the use
of various kinds of literature to spread abroad Modernist doctrines."[14] By
1947 an article for *Catholic Digest* about the Index of Forbidden Books
noted precisely the opposite: "Books written in our time in any language
which find their way to the Index are almost exclusively works of theology,
written by priests, containing errors of Modernism, a technical term for
certain theological errors, having nothing to do with 'modernism' in the
current sense."[15] Theological modernism was still a terminal error, but one
with no connection to artistic modernism. How was this separation effected?
What conceptual tools helped to rationalize—literally, create a rationale to
make sense of—literary modernism as something distinct from the century's major theological land mines?

Within the field of literary criticism and even literary work more broadly
defined, Catholics were not propelled as abruptly along the trajectory noted
by Scott Appleby; that is, their work seldom generated sufficient controversy
that they were forced to the point of having to repudiate either their own
ideas or the authority that was condemning them. Instead, within the literary
realm a *sotto voce* Catholic-modernist conversation could continue. Because in
any given literary discussion there was on the surface less at stake than in an
analogous discussion of theology or philosophy, Catholic literary workers
had a little more intellectual and artistic latitude. But because the literary discussion for Catholics was based on an explicit and explicitly theological philosophy, it became one means by which to work through philosophical issues
without directly addressing them. As literary discussions sought an appropriate
stance toward potentially dangerous or heretical ideas, they became an important site of Catholic engagement with philosophical modernity.

Literary Modernism and Catholic Antimodernism

The Roman Catholic conflict with modernity was genuine and pervasive,
but it was not univocal. There was no single vision of what the best, most
"Catholic" alternative to modernity—and eventually to modernism—might
be. Instead there was a sustained conversation within which voices of different regions, classes, "states of life" (Catholic-speak for clergy, religious, and

laity), and brow levels brought their interpretation of Catholic truth to bear on what they believed to be the most pressing issues of the day.

In a number of important ways, Catholic antimodernism preceded Catholic modernism.[16] At least since 1789, Roman Catholicism had been opposed to many of the philosophical and political changes that constituted the major developments of the nineteenth century. At least since 1848 and certainly since the definition of papal infallibility at the First Vatican Council in 1869–70, U.S. Catholic apologists had had a difficult job of understanding and justifying to their compatriots Roman consolidation of authority and rejection of philosophical modernity.[17]

Ultramontanism (an increased emphasis on the centralization of teaching authority in the pope) was probably the clearest trend of Roman Catholic history in the twentieth century, but U.S. responses to the idea were multivalent. Some U.S. observers defended the Vatican uncritically and were as Romanly antimodern as it was possible to be. Others, in contrast, were deeply disturbed by Vatican actions and pronouncements and sought to find in U.S. society models for the relationship between church and modern culture that could replace rearguard Roman reaction. Because so much intellectual energy was devoted to faithfully countering the extremity of Roman reaction, antimodernism can ironically be seen as a catalyst to both Americanism and theological modernism. The differences of opinion represented by these different U.S. reactions to Roman centralization produced serious divisions and conflicts within the U.S. hierarchy, which were part of the cause of the Americanist crisis of the late 1890s. The variety of intellectual rationales reflected a multiplicity of conceptual schemes for the relationship between Catholicism and modernity as embodied in the U.S. experience. The 1907 condemnation of modernism per se entered into political and theological conversations already in progress.

In fact, by the years after the Great War, U.S. Catholic responses to modernity were sufficiently multivariate that "antimodernism" does not quite capture their characteristic stance. Catholics still articulated a critique of various aspects of modernity, both material and philosophical, but the intent was increasingly to figure out how to enter into and redeem modernity, not simply how to safeguard against it, still less to repeal it or reverse its tide. "Countermodernism" conveys this attempt to formulate feasible alternatives but still suggests reaction rather than invention or creativity. Without intrusive neologizing it is difficult to find a single word or phrase that captures American Catholic responses to modernity, especially in the 1920s and 1930s. Perhaps it would be most accurate to think of them as attempting to renarrate or reanimate modernity. That is, by the time of World War I and increasingly thereafter, U.S. Catholics accepted as (at least potentially) active goods the constitutive structures of modernity over which earlier generations had contended—in particular, democracy, capitalism, and science—but understood them as needing the spirit that only Catholicism offered to keep them from descending into materialism. In a variety of voices and venues, Catholics retold the story of modernity to make clear their special expertise in protecting the goods of modernity from the inherent dangers. These retellings sought to restore continuity with a past that increasingly seemed not so much severed as misplaced or misdirected.

In the realm of philosophy, some key elements of Catholic response to the Enlightenment project were genuinely antimodernist, in that they consisted of outright rejection. As scientific naturalism came to predominate in intellectual work generally and in the U.S. academy in particular, the divide between it and the epistemology presumed by neo-Thomistic philosophy became deeply entrenched. That is, a significant and sustained conflict between naturalism, which presumes that the necessary starting point for truth is the absence of assumptions, and neoscholasticism, which assumes as the basis of truth a revealed, a priori system of knowledge external to the knower, shaped much of the encounter between Catholicism and the twentieth-century academy.[18] However, the very existence of the conflict reveals that Catholics did not ignore emerging scientific ideas. On the contrary, because one of the basic tenets of neoscholasticism was that nothing true about the universe could conflict with Catholic truth, an extensive cottage industry evaluated and attempted to reconcile (or in some cases discredit) ideas that had come to have widespread scientific and cultural currency. The best-known example is evolution, but there was also an ongoing debate, full of confidence and caution in apparently equal measure, about the growing pervasiveness of Freudian categories in discussions of psychology.[19] For example, *America* published a series of articles on psychoanalysis in 1924 and 1925 by E. Boyd Barrett, SJ, that raised some questions about their orthodoxy and produced a call from one of Barrett's Jesuit superiors to have future articles submitted for censorship. The first articles contain virtually nothing that would indicate they were being published in a Catholic periodical except for the "SJ" after the author's name. The ensuing controversy, however, which will be described in Chapter 5, indicates the institutional and intellectual complexity of Catholic efforts to engage intellectual modernity in all its forms.

Catholics rejected not only the notion that philosophical principles could change but also de facto shifts in social mores. As attitudes toward moral-social issues such as marriage and divorce, birth control, and premarital sex changed at an accelerating pace in the first three decades of the century, Catholics maintained an alternate viewpoint that derived not only (or even primarily) from residual Victorianism but rather from a self-consciously articulated alternate view of the nature and purpose of the human person. "Modernity" in many early twentieth-century discussions was inseparable from this alarm over increasingly lax morality (in this, of course, Catholic commentators were far from unique).[20]

Politically and economically, Catholic antimodernism can look conservative or liberal, depending on the angle of vision. Politically, nineteenth-century European Catholicism had been largely reactionary, as revolutionary movements were often also at least anticlerical and more often openly antireligious. The rise of the secular state, the single most dominant political trend in the West of the eighteenth and nineteenth centuries, seemed to Rome not only not an unqualified good but a clear and present danger.[21] The Vatican refused well into the twentieth century to endorse the separation of church and state as a positive good. This stance posed a considerable problem for Catholic Americans, who began developing a line of thought and a set of arguments that led eventually to the work of Jesuit John Courtney Murray, whose views on religious liberty were regarded as suspect in the 1950s but who served as a *peritus*, or expert advisor, to the U.S. bishops at the Second Vatican Council only a decade later and was the primary author of the Council's Declaration on Religious Freedom. In the intervening years, Catholic political thinkers developed a rationale under which the separation of church and state appeared at least as beneficial to religion as the close relationship that had characterized "Christendom" real and idealized. This rationale was "antimodern" to the extent that it refused to embrace or was prevented from embracing the democratic celebration of individual autonomy as an unqualified moral advance for humanity; but it did not so much reject political modernity as reimagine it, not only as compatible with Catholicism but as requiring Catholicism to make it fully humane.

Economically, as Catholicism in both Europe and the United States came to grips with industrialization, antimodernism took a variety of forms. There was, all things considered, relatively little attempt to turn back the clock to the feudal era economically, though there was considerable medieval nostalgia, some of it only self-indulgent, some of it giving rise to well-thought-out alternative social programs that resulted in real social change.[22] Officially, and more pervasively, Catholicism's response to the social upheaval resulting from industrialization was to make economic matters secondary to other, more central, concerns. If, as reformers and eventually the pope argued, industrialization made living dignified, moral lives more difficult for large numbers of people, then the economic conditions would have to be altered. As Paul Misner points out, Leo XIII's landmark social encyclical *Rerum Novarum* was no liberal manifesto; it was as much about clearing the way for the reassertion of rightful authority, and minimizing the ravages of capitalism to take the steam out of socialism, as it was about supporting the rights of workers to organize.[23] The same could not be said, however, of John A. Ryan's arguments for the living wage and the program of social reform adopted by the U.S. bishops in 1919, both of which actively embraced capitalism's beneficial aspects and sought primarily to temper its negative effects so as to make the benefits as widely available as possible.[24]

Similarly, Catholic literary studies also engaged with contemporary trends in order to winnow the wheat from the chaff—celebrating what could be drawn into the mission of redeeming modernity, while identifying along the way what was harmful and tending toward despair. In a 1925 analysis of the work of H. G. Wells, Paulist and *Catholic World* editor James M. Gillis wondered, "That an evolutionist can despair of the world is a mystery. . . . We who do not consider evolution a key to all mysteries, and a solution of the Riddle of the Universe, are not despondent. We believe in God—not an impotent God who is only doing the best He can, but a God Who has ten thousand times set the world right again when everything seemed wrong, a God Who can and will bring the race out of the morass into which it has so willfully strayed."[25] As Catholics in a variety of different fields engaged the ideas and institutions that constituted the modern world and found there a complex mix of familiarity and distance, so those involved in literary criticism approached literary modernism.

Historians of literary modernism plead the same difficulty of definition as do their theological counterparts. While historians of the phenomenon locate its origins as early as the work of Rimbaud in the 1870s, modernism became part of public consciousness and public discussion in the United States during the second decade of the twentieth century, with the advent of, among other works and events, T. S. Eliot's "The Love Song of J. Alfred Prufrock," Ezra Pound's *Cantos*, James Joyce's *Portrait of the Artist as a Young Man*, and the 1913 New York Armory Show.[26] In the next decade literary modernism saw in world events—in the war, especially—a radical break from history, tradition, and convention. This break produced divergent impulses within modernism that add to the complexity of defining it. From one angle the bankruptcy of Western bourgeois culture and imperialism made apparent by the ferocity and nihilism of World War I led some modernists to something like despair. The other path, though, saw and sought in the disintegration of the idea of the West opportunities for the liberation of humanity from political and social constraints. For both strains, however, the radical break with history resulted formally in the need for a new language and style to express a new way of perceiving the world, to express the alienation and dissociation and fragmentation believed to be newly unique to Western society after the Great War.

And on this common ground literary modernism and Catholicism met. For both groups, the horrors of the war, its seemingly complete destruction of any belief in human perfectibility, seemed to confirm much of their pre-war critiques.[27] Both sought to revive a vivid sense of life that they thought was in some sense being snuffed out by modernity. Their paths diverged dramatically at that point, but the urgent moment of response to the trauma of the Great War became a turning point in how they interpreted each other. Modernism went on to become the dominant artistic and critical language of the century. Literary and artistic modernists defined themselves in opposition to what came before, seeing (even exaggerating) a radical break with history and with earlier modes and understandings of perception and experience. But in many, if not most, of its defining elements, literary modernism seemed tailor-made to alienate Catholics. Philosophically it at least toyed with and at most entirely rejected all the propositions neoscholasticism depended on to exist. Socially it mocked and flouted, in the name of self-expression and human freedom, conventions that for many Catholic observers were grounded in timeless moral law.

Some Catholics recognized early on, though, that modernism was not solely rejectionist. It was at least as much concerned with taking things apart to understand how they worked and to increase a reader's (or listener's or viewer's) self-consciousness about the distance between sensation and awareness. Modernists took melody apart, they took narrative and rhyme and meter apart, they took perception apart, they took social convention apart, they took history apart. The truncated lines in the penultimate stanza of Eliot's "The Hollow Men" (1925), which immediately precede the famous "*This is the way the world ends,*" convey more effectively than meticulous meter could the inadequacy, even the impossibility, of traditional prayer as a stay against despair:

For Thine is
Life is
For Thine is the

Similarly, the confusing and colliding points of view in William Faulkner's 1929 *The Sound and the Fury* illustrate the instability of the white supremacist narrative of southern history, its vulnerability to the voices it put so much force into suppressing (including those of its most privileged white sons). As Ann Douglas has observed, "Conventional literary strategies of plotting were apparently among the casualties of the Great War."[28]

Even at the points on which modernists and Catholics could find little common cause, however, they performed unlikely services for each other. In dismantling many of the received certainties of the prewar world, even the modernists who most scandalized Catholic critics helped clear a space on which Catholics could rebuild to their own liking. For Catholic critics, the human chaos that resulted, in their view, from the materialism and self-indulgence of certain modernist writers underlined the need for the "sanity" that the Christian worldview provided. In return, what Catholics did for the artistic modernists was to pay them the compliment of continuing to find them dangerous. Modernism by the 1920s had begun to find itself embraced by the cognoscenti and occupying the very center of Anglo-American literary life. In subsequent generations that indignity deepened into modernism's becoming the established conventional wisdom against which others defined themselves, or with which they allied themselves.[29] Catholic critics, however, continued to take the modernist critiques seriously long after secular and academic critics had defanged, tamed, and enthroned them.

The task of the Catholic critic, as we have seen, was a delicate one. How to discuss issues of "modernism" when something by that name had been anathematized by the Vatican? How to review writers of seriousness and weight whose approach to the great human questions clashed so severely with Catholic tradition and practice? How to account for the apparent necessity that artists leave the Church in order to be taken seriously by the artistic establishment? Answering these questions, accomplishing these tasks, was the job description of Catholics in positions of literary influence in the middle decades of the century. It was a variant, a subspecialty, of what John Murray Cuddihy calls the "task of the modernizing intellectual"—the responsibility of members of a believing community to attempt to reconcile the tenets of the tradition with "the sheer irreversible actuality of that modern religiously pluralistic situation that confronted them in America," while maintaining personal integrity both as practitioner of the tradition and as a scholar within the academy.[30] Without their ever claiming the task in these terms, these writers were their own sort of "modernists," in that they sustained the engagement between Catholicism and modernism.

The task was made difficult not only by Vatican anathemas, but by an academic and cultural context that used Catholicism as one of its defining "others." As John McGreevy put it, "discussion of Catholicism . . . helped define the terms of mid-twentieth-century American liberalism. Those terms included the insistence that religion, as an entirely private matter, must be separated from the state, that religious loyalties must not threaten national unity, and that only an emphasis on individual autonomy, thinking on one's own, would sustain American democracy."[31] The stance of opposition was to some extent not chosen by Catholics but imposed on them by the culture and politics of their time. As the "other" against which American artists and intellectuals defined themselves, Catholics occupied an ideological niche that constrained the reception of their views. What McGreevy has characterized as "thinking on one's own" is invaluable conceptually as a framework for describing the ground of difference between Catholic and secular intellectuals.

Politically, American intellectuals such as John Dewey and Walter Lippmann saw Catholicism through a lens that highlighted the apparent obstacles it posed to a robust defense of democracy and the formation of democratic citizens and a culture of democracy. Analogously, literary and cultural critics celebrating modernism effectively conflated Catholicism with the "tradition" against which modernism largely defined itself, "tradition" in this instance being synonymous with the constraint of the individual and of art, the repression of passion and expression, the suffocation by history and institution. Ezra Pound announced that the Christian era ended when Joyce finished writing *Ulysses* near the end of 1921.[32] Within such a configuration, in the early years of the prominence of literary modernism the only response available to Catholic critics seemed to be opposition. This circumscription was both external and internal; that is, while Catholic theology and polity made antimodernism the default mode for Catholic criticism of all sorts, literary modernism equally effectively posed what appeared to be a stark choice: between present and past, innovation and reaction, relevance and inconsequence.

By somewhere around 1955 these choices no longer appeared as stark. The shift was incremental, impossible to separate into discrete steps or even clear periods, but it is discernible nonetheless. What happened? In some accounts of the shift, Catholicism simply came to its senses and accepted the reality of the modern world after years of "hear-no-evil, see-no-evil" innocence. Undoubtedly the positions taken by Catholic critics in the 1950s were different from those taken by their co-religionists in the 1910s and 1920s. However, they represent something other than acquiescence or simple loss of innocence. They represent the reshaping of the terms of the debate, a reshaping that reveals the extent to which Catholics participated in the debate rather than simply reacting to it.

Catholics who were engaged in the writing, publishing, reading, and evaluating of literature evaded the oppositions imposed on them by the various modernisms with which they were entangled. They took on the "task of the modernizing literary critic" by refusing to stay put on the conceptual map within which they were inscribed. Catholic literary work, over time, *declined* oppositions imposed both internally and externally—"declined" in the sense of polite and indirect rejection, combining things that were not supposed to be combined, and gradually reincorporating excluded elements; "declined" also in the sense of grammatical inflection—they took the terms and structures available and inflected them according to their own critical system, eventually producing a synthesis, a dialect that included both terms of the oppositions. They did not thereby solve every problem or heal every division, but they did develop a reservoir of intellectual resources that assisted in the eventual accommodation of American Catholic culture to intellectual modernity.

Catholics saw themselves as opposing literary modernism to the extent that it seemed to embrace meaninglessness, fragmentation, or nihilism, and to embody those stances formally. In defining and evaluating literature, Catholic writers and critics navigated between the poles that structured the specific terms of the general debate over the relationship between Catholicism and modernity. That is, while we can describe a broad context within which they worked out this general conflict, what shaped the broad context was a series of debates over its component ideas. In the debate over literary modernism and its relationship to Catholic literary aesthetics, four pairs of opposed terms and the constellation of ideas they represented were crucial: individual/community, iconoclasm/orthodoxy, innovation/repetition, and openness/closure.

These sets of ideas were central to the definition of modernism and to the debates over excellence and modernity in literature. In each case, in the early years of the flourishing of literary modernism, Catholicism was strongly associated with one term of the opposition and seemed poised to define itself at least in part by rejecting the other term. In each case, however, by the 1950s what had appeared four decades earlier to be an irreconcilable opposition was instead a complexly understood interrelation. Despite the apparent starkness of the early twentieth-century choice, Catholic critics over time declined to choose one term over the other, to privilege one and reject the other, and instead elaborated a rationale that included both terms of the opposition, newly defined in some cases, within the scope of a Catholic literary aesthetic.

Various kinds of Catholic critical discourse and even certain kinds of Catholic fiction worked throughout the century to reconcile the oppositions to include the "Catholic" term, and to define the Catholic term as legitimately or remedially modern—that is, as being at least as much of the age as the "mainstream" or "secular" term of the opposition, or as being an emphasis abandoned to the detriment of the modern world (and thus within the Catholic writer's responsibility to recover). Conversely, the "secular" or "modernist" term was simultaneously brought within the Catholic critical orbit or universe. The result was not so much Hegelian synthesis as an uneasily sustained balance.

Whether the resulting system was or is useful as a tool of literary criticism—that is, whether it was effective in distinguishing good work from bad work, or whether its judgments could carry any critical weight today—is not the primary question here. A cultural historian is instead concerned with how certain groups used the conceptual tools available to them to structure meaning. The terms and complexities of Catholic aesthetics functioned not only in the high-style realm of literary modernism and judgments about literary value, but also in the realm of popular and mass culture. In both realms, self-conscious and explicitly Catholic participants in cultural production navigated the landscape by remarkably similar coordinates.

CHAPTER 3

Declining Oppositions

It is probably not an accident that in George Shuster's *The Catholic Spirit in Modern English Literature* the word "modernism" does not occur, despite the work's appearing in modernism's *annus mirabilis*, 1922, the year of publication for both *Ulysses* and *The Waste Land*. The only time the word "modernist" appears is in an approving description of Hilaire Belloc's attempt to "uncover the medieval walls upon which modern Europe rests" in *The Path to Rome*: "He laughs with the Catholic peasant at the expense of the modernist; he joins eagerly in the dozen democratic things which people who are free in practice think it natural to perform" (257). Shuster, who would soon move on to *Commonweal* magazine and eventually to the presidency of Hunter College and to a variety of positions within the U.S. government, including seventeen years with UNESCO, almost certainly was aware both of the work of those who embraced the term and of the condemnation by the Vatican of a set of theological positions collected under the same name. The absence of the term while Shuster explores "modern" English literature is most usefully seen not as evasion but as engagement, but engagement on territory on which many combatants had been warned not to tread and had therefore to proceed delicately, alert and wary.

The boundaries they were attempting to circumvent were not solely literary, and they were policed not solely by Catholics. In a 1929 review in the

American Journal of Sociology, Chicago Theological Seminary's Arthur E. Holt reviewed Shuster's 1927 *The Catholic Spirit in America* along with Winfred Garrison's *Catholicism and the American Mind*. In the review, Holt approvingly quotes Garrison's zero-sum formulation of the predicament facing Catholics such as Shuster: "The men who defend the principle of toleration for all varieties of religious opinion, assume either that all religions are equally true or that the true cannot be distinguished from the false. On no other ground is it logically possible to accept the theory of indiscriminate and universal toleration." Holt assesses this as "a rather hard nut for a man of Mr. Shuster's liberal tendency to crack."[1]

This sense, perceived and articulated on both sides of the divide, of the incompatibility of Catholic stances with the foundations of modernity generally and with modernism in literature in particular, could take on epochal dimensions, as in Ezra Pound's announcement of the end of the Christian era when James Joyce wrote the last words of *Ulysses*, an end he saw as so definitive that he proposed that 1922 become "year 1 of a new era."[2] But as we know, Catholic writers both of and about literature refused to stay put on their side of this divide. How did they navigate in order to eventually remap the divide, claiming the entire territory as their homeland? Four dimensions of the problem distinctive to the literary will be central, two of which—individual and community, iconoclasm and orthodoxy—have to do with literature's content, and the two others—openness and closure, innovation and repetition—with literature's form.

Individual and Community

The modernist project exalted the creative individual, the person who was able to shed the strictures of history and society and see and render the world afresh. In its European forms, the history and society against which modernism defined itself were inescapably Catholic. As American critics began articulating an indigenous modernism, they made the development of American literature into a variant of this story writ large. That is, American history itself was the story of the independent and autonomous, democratic spirit of Protestantism finding fertile soil in the New World to cultivate a society free from the conventions and hierarchies of the old. The most "American" literature, increasingly by the 1920s, was that which told this story. By the 1940s, "American literature" (the canon of valued texts) was deeply inflected by Protestant-romantic notions of the authentic self, free of the constraints of society, history, and community. Huck Finn "lighting out for the territory," Ahab desiring to "strike the sun if it insulted me," Jay Gatsby's believing in the green light, "the orgiastic future that year by year receded before us"—these protagonists stood contentiously against their soft, compromised compatriots and boldly faced the world without the support of convention or community. Narratives and other forms that emphasized the elements of classical comedy, for example, the restoring of social order and traditional symbols of authority, seemed to critics increasingly less interesting, even less literary. They might function as a kind of therapeutic medication for audiences unable to bear up under the loneliness of modernity, but they could not be said to speak for the age the way real literature must.

Paul Giles's *American Catholic Arts and Fictions: Culture, Ideology, Aesthetics* recognized and described an alternative Catholic trajectory within American literature, one that imagined the modern individual still embedded in and created by community, and aware—if often ironically—of the claims of history and tradition.[3] This awareness might be manifested as much by rejection as by participation, as in the case of Theodore Dreiser and James T. Farrell. Nonetheless, the thread that Giles traces from Orestes Brownson in the nineteenth century through the novelistic and cinematic crime sagas of the 1960s and 1970s spins a different American story. The fact that he can discern this distinct and distinctively Catholic thread demonstrates the extent to which the trajectory of "American" literature had been determined by the Protestant narrative that defined itself against a medieval Catholic past.

Catholic publications about literature in the early years of the twentieth century highlighted views that saw and criticized modernist exaltation of the self, including those written by non-Catholics such as the Oberlin-educated writer and teacher Catherine Beach Ely. "Mean minds in modern drama, fiction and verse can see nothing beyond their own inflated ego," Ely wrote in *America* in 1922.[4] In fact, a significant component of what Catholics and sympathetic compatriots saw as the pathology of modernity had to do with the individual's having thrown off not only all legitimate authority but all traditional self-control as well, allowing the most elemental urges to dominate. A certain amount of Catholic criticism of literary modernism exhibited a deep revulsion at the passions and impulses modernism not only indulged but celebrated.

This particular dichotomy was perhaps the least polarized of the four we are examining here. To modernists, the opposition was defining; they needed society, history, and tradition as foils against which to celebrate the author creating something new and the protagonist reinventing himself and the world. Catholic critics, however, refused from the beginning to accept this as a dichotomy and to stay put in their place on the spectrum. They insisted, not that individuals did not exist or should not express themselves, but that they achieved fullest expression as individuals in the context of history and community. In addition, two different emerging threats gave Catholics a greater sense of common cause with their fellow citizens—with "all people of goodwill"—in the defense of the individual. The impersonality of consumer culture, the homogenizing effect of increasing emphasis on material wealth and accumulation, threatened individuality as much from the standpoint of Catholic theology as from that of liberal humanism. "Here are five novels by Americans," Maurice Francis Egan wrote in 1921, "but if they are American novels, God help America! . . . It seems the business of the American novelist writing today to assume that man lives by bread alone, and that after he has eaten his bread, with all the jam he can get, there is nothing left for him."[5] In addition, even before 1917 and with increasing fervor for decades after, Catholics saw themselves allied with their compatriots as defenders of the sacred individual against the dehumanizing collectivity of socialism and then of Soviet communism. They took up this challenge zealously and brought overtly Catholic resources to bear on it. "On another question particularly urgent today," English convert and writer E. I. Watkin wrote in 1939, "Catholicism as expressed by the liturgy keeps the *via media* and occupies the centre. It is the relation between the individual and society, between individualism and 'sociality,' or if to avoid this barbarism I may be allowed so to style it, 'socialism.' "[6]

The prominence of English and other non-U.S. voices in such discussions (Watkin's book was published by Sheed and Ward, itself an English publishing house that made the works of many European Catholic writers available to a U.S. audience for the first time) underscores one of the most important ways in which Catholic literary culture diverged from the mainstream between the wars. In the years after the *annus mirabilis* of 1922, in which *The Waste Land* and Joyce's *Ulysses* were both published, literary modernism in the United States increasingly took on the cast of American literary culture as it was being defined by the growing and centralizing professions of critic and professor. In the years after World War I it became increasingly nationalist and formalist in character—it simultaneously sought to retrieve and foster a distinctively American tradition of great literature and to define literary value in ways that increasingly permitted only formal considerations.[7] The resulting literary consensus drastically narrowed the range of works that could be included within the definition of "great American literature." Just as Catholic literary self-consciousness was deepening, "American literature" was being defined in such a way as to more effectively exclude Catholic definitions from the category of the literary, most particularly its inherently international reach and scope, and its insistence that content mattered in considerations of literary value.

As Barbara Herrnstein Smith has argued, maintaining a consensus about literary value requires some mechanism by which to discount the opinions of groups who do not share the consensus, "for example, those not yet adequately acculturated." In exercising its "normative authority," the group whose norms and tastes currently prevail must privilege their own authority absolutely and "pathologiz[e] all other contingencies."[8] Scholars of women's literature have demonstrated the extent to which the prevailing norms that defined literary excellence for much of the twentieth century served to exclude virtually all writing done by women. For example, Kathleen Thompson Norris's husband, Charles, brother of naturalist writer Frank Norris, was by all accounts unfailingly supportive of her writing, but it is still one of the exigencies of the history of popular writing by women that copies of his half dozen (serious, ambitious) novels with virile one-word titles like *Seed* and *Flint* are much easier to come by in the used-book world than are copies of any of the eight dozen ("ephemeral," "sentimental") books by his wife (including *Passion Flower, Maiden Voyage,* and *Rose of the World*). Catholic conceptions of literature shared with much literature by women an emphasis on continuity over time, on an individual's place within a larger pattern, and on the intricate working-out of that place. These emphases contrasted dramatically with the intense assertions by twentieth-century canon builders that American literature was about freedom from history, about starting over, about the creation of new norms and institutions.[9]

In one example, strikingly, these similar emphases coincide. Willa Cather biographer Sharon O'Brien has traced the process by which Cather went from being considered a major American writer to a minor one. Critics had praised Cather's accounts of U.S. pioneer life in novels such as *O! Pioneers* and *My Antonia* and had seen her as on track to be a major American novelist. According to O'Brien, the shift in critical opinion came about as a result of Cather's decision to turn for subjects to the past and to the world of women. For example, Lionel Trilling in *After the Genteel Tradition* "linked Cather's decision to write historical fiction [*Shadows on the Rock*] with a 'defiant' rejection of her own time, which he in turn associated with her fondness for limited female interests." O'Brien goes on to explore how "softness," "smallness," and "female interests" became linked in critical discourse with inferiority as a writer.[10] The two novels arguably most crucial in Cather's turn to the past, however—*Death Comes for the Archbishop* (1927), a fictionalized life of the first bishop of Santa Fe, and *Shadows on the Rock*

(1931), set in seventeenth-century Quebec—had explicitly Catholic subject matter. The disappointment that critics such as Trilling, Granville Hicks, and Newton Arvin expressed at what they perceived as Cather's rejection of her own time is also attributable to the sense that she had turned away from the main currents of American narrative to the backwaters of southwestern and Canadian Catholicism.

Not surprisingly, Catholic critics seized on and celebrated Cather's shift in subject matter, believing her artistry to be deepening, not softening. The reviewer for *Catholic World* said of *Shadows on the Rock*: "No one should miss reading this book. And Catholics, especially, should be reminded of the wealth of tradition which is our heritage."[11] Catholic critics saw in Cather's novels a gradual and admirable progress "from one level of meaning and value to another; from the level of nature to the level of mind, and from the level of mind to the level of spirit." By 1941, when Cather published *Sapphira and the Slave Girl*, Catholic critics agreed that she "demonstrates herself steeped in Christianity: *anima naturaliter christiana*."[12] Catholic critics implicitly rejected the evolving dichotomy—between the present and the past, between individual initiative and historical insight—that Sharon O'Brien describes. They celebrated Cather's inscription of Catholicism onto the landscape of American history and claimed Cather as one of their own. At the same time, they brooded over why a non-Catholic American should have produced "Catholic" novels so much better than those written by Catholics.

Catholic approbation would have been unlikely to bolster Cather's reputation among her critics. In fact, the features Catholics were most likely to admire were probably the ones that did the most to diminish her standing. The deemphasis on the heroism of the lone individual, the individual's reliance on community and tradition, these were Catholic emphases that were shared with much of the literature written and read by women in the nineteenth and early twentieth centuries that was widely popular but nearly written out of American literary history by the end of the 1930s. As the outlines of the category of "American" literature became sharper, they defined an entity discernibly more masculine and more Protestant. Nevertheless, Catholic confidence that the contours of their story amply reflected present as well as past realities only continued to deepen.

Iconoclasm and Orthodoxy

If differing understandings of the relationship between the individual and community were the only or even the main element in the divide between

Catholic and modernist approaches to literature, the divide most likely would not have existed. Catholic insistence that individual and community were mutually defining terms prevented them from agreeing to occupy only one pole of the opposition and produced deft reinterpretations of modernist individualism that reinserted the self back into its thick historical traditional context. Only twenty years after the publication of Joyce's *Portrait of the Artist*, Blanche Mary Kelly was asserting Joyce's fundamental continuity with the community he sought to separate from:

> It is the spiritual element in Joyce's *Portrait*, Stephen Dedalus's struggle with his lower nature, even though he eventually loses the struggle, that gives this book its importance. Despite the fact that the wine of virgins turns to vinegar in the young man's heart, the story has qualities, perceptions, a core of realities that lift it out of the ruck of the current into the permanent. And these qualities are the fruit of an experiential knowledge of the Catholic religion. The book is in a sense a Catholic novel, the story of a soul which has exercised its terrible prerogative of saying NO to the urgency of grace. Only a Catholic could have conceived it, perhaps only an Irish Catholic could have set down this record of a great refusal, this repudiation of a spiritual inheritance.[13]

On other points of philosophic and artistic disagreement, the gap was wider and harder to bridge and the rationales that developed to bridge it were more complex and revealing.

Much of American literary tradition is in consonance with—even directly shaped by—Ralph Waldo Emerson's question in *Nature*, "Why should not we have a poetry and philosophy of insight and not of tradition, and a religion by revelation to us, and not the history of theirs?"[14] This question echoed in the next century in Stephen Dedalus's assuming of his mission "to forge in the smithy of my soul the uncreated conscience of my race." The merging of American romantic individualism with modernist reinvention of the self and of the world posed for Catholic critics the problem of iconoclasm and orthodoxy. For modernists, being bound by received wisdom was evidence of lack of imagination at best and of being in thrall to propaganda at worst. If art did not somehow escape the bounds of tradition, it was not art. For Catholics, insight was available only through tradition, revelation was complete, not ongoing, and art that did not accept its place within tradition was not art.

At the beginning of the century this divide was very wide. Condé Pallen in 1897 identified literary excellence entirely with Christian belief:

"Who lives the truth, will think the truth, and who lives and thinks the truth, will speak it. The fuller and deeper his life in truth the completer and sublimer his thought of truth, and the completer and sublimer his thought, the wider and loftier his expression of truth by the exalted power of the human word. . . . Christendom alone possesses the unitive fullness of the law."[15] Pallen's use of "Christendom" deliberately linked literary excellence with a putative "organic" connection between Christian truth and specific social arrangements ("and Dante writes the 'Divina Comedia'"), a connection which he along with many others saw dissolving around him in the modern world. Many Catholics, convinced that the organic unity of medieval society had produced much of the west's greatest literature, lamented the consequences for art of that unity's disappearance. Absent some fundamental restoration, art, separated from truth by modernity's errors, would remain incomplete.

This rift between literary modernism and Catholic aesthetics was already clear by the time of the 1907 condemnation of theological modernism. *Pascendi* made explicit a point that had been reiterated in earlier papal communications and that has implications for the relationship between literature and truth. One of modernism's errors, according to *Pascendi*, had been the attempt to reformulate doctrine in such a way as to reveal what the reformers believed was the conceptual compatibility between Catholic doctrine and the language and epistemology of science. This the Vatican condemned unequivocally, insisting that the truth of doctrine lay in the precise formulations it had been given. The necessity that literature be anchored in the truth of doctrine, and that doctrine be tied to specific linguistic formulations, helps to explain the great anxiety among some Catholic critics about the experiments in language and form that characterized modernism from its earliest years and became its most identifiable hallmark.

The dilemma of orthodoxy and iconoclasm was even more pressing in the realm of content than in that of form. Catholic doctrinal security is an easy attitude to caricature because it contrasted so markedly with the defining characteristics of twentieth-century sensibility—a sense of alienation, dislocation, fragmentation. Catholic critics not only conceded that literature should assist in the spreading of Catholic truth, they reveled in the mission. "The Apostolate of Books," as Stephen J. M. Brown termed it, involved not only authors but also critics, teachers, librarians, booksellers, and readers in the task of disseminating good books—and preferably good Catholic books—as widely as possible.[16] At the same time they explicitly rejected the idea that this mission limited or distorted literature's purposes; on the contrary, it was the only thing that allowed literature to flourish. By making explicit that reading could and should include works that were not solely Catholic or solely by Catholics—making clear, that is, that the authentic presentation of human experience was literature's heart—they intended to balance their insistence on truth with a comparably intense insistence on the integrity of the resulting art. They had a touching faith in the power of translation, even as the daunting extent of the task presented itself again and again. Daniel Lord described sitting "behind a group of literary Americans one evening while Eugene O'Neill's 'Days Without End' was being presented off-Broadway. I realized with a shock that the phrases and thoughts that were Catholic, including the great central Catholic doctrine of the saving power of Christ's death, were meaningless jargon to even the educated American non-Catholic."[17]

However broadly and inclusively Catholics attempted to define this balance by ingenious interpretation, for many of their contemporaries a commitment to orthodoxy in itself was sufficient to disqualify something as art. Not only that, but insisting that art serve a particular formulation of the truth meant for modernists abandoning art altogether and instead producing propaganda. This charge was damning enough in the years immediately following the Great War, when modernists stood not only against Catholic notions of orthodoxy and tradition but also against the Protestant-secular Anglo-American bourgeois conventions of Victorian literature. As political developments in Europe aroused increasing alarm through the 1920s and into the 1930s, however, Catholic insistence on orthodoxy came to seem even more threatening, carrying as it did a whiff of authoritarianism that looked a little too akin to the unsettling ideologies taking root overseas. Increasingly throughout the 1930s and into the 1940s, U.S. Catholics would feel compelled to demonstrate their commitment to artistic freedom, while attempting to maintain fidelity to their sense that truth was knowable and that art and truth were inseparable in the modern world as in the eras that had preceded it.[18]

Once again, this situation of espousing a view of literature that to most mainstream writers and critics seemed the opposite of literary was not unique to Catholics. The dilemma of Catholic critics in this instance resembles that of the creators and defenders of proletarian literature in the 1920s and 1930s. These writers, who attempted to illustrate the effects of industrial capitalism on the working classes with the express purpose of eventually bringing about the revolution, were influential in shaping the literary culture of the years between the wars, but as the modernist aesthetic became more dominant in American critical life they were increasingly derided as propagandists at worst, naive and sentimental at best. Lawrence F. Hanley notes that by the 1950s the project of proletarian literature had come to seem like an "indiscretion," in contrast to the conviction of many influential critics a generation earlier of its strength and influence.[19] Hanley attributes proletarian literature's "exclusion from literary history" to its "overpowering worldliness": "scored too deeply by the radical politics of the thirties, proletarian texts fail to achieve the transcendence from history that, traditionally and ideologically, defines aesthetic value." Here proletarian literature would seem to part company with Catholic views, which emphasized the timelessness and universality of doctrine and institution. Ironically, however, Catholic commitment to orthodoxy—to some recognition of the sacred grounding of reality as a requirement for literary excellence—was seen as partisan and particular in its assertion of timelessness. In this and in what Kenneth Burke called proletarian literature's "addressedness" ("This literature is written *to* people, or *for* people. It is *addressed*."),[20] there are analogies between what proletarian and Catholic writers and critics did to defend their enterprises against the founding assumptions of modernity in literature.

As proletarian writers defended the "addressedness" of their work on political grounds that explicitly invoked the need for human solidarity, so Catholic writers and critics drew a theological connection between literature and society, insisting that the former help save the latter. The critique of Catholic confidence in doctrine as self-absorbed and disengaged from social reality might be more persuasive were it not for the persistent sense among Catholics writing about literature that Catholicism fully understood—was indeed the answer to—the questions of the modern world. They refused to embrace iconoclasm—the shattering of old images and ideas and the creation of new ones solely for its own sake—not only because it was idolatrous (artists participated in the action of the Creator, but were not themselves capable of creation) but because in their eyes it could never be effective. But this refusal took on a qualitatively different stance in the years after the Great War, one that led them to distinguish themselves from and at the same time claim common ground with both modernists and proletarian writers. "Christian literature is proletarian," *Commonweal's* editors wrote in 1937. "That the proletarian class will surely make the future society of the world is a reasonable and natural, and an undogmatic belief that many Christians subscribe to, but that is not at all the same thing as Christian faith in the triumph of the lowly and the overcoming of the world. This has, indeed, already been accomplished."[21] Condé Pallen's rearguard defense of a disintegrating Christendom had given way by the next generation to the

Catholic revival's energetic conviction that Catholicism could revivify the modern world. The two viewpoints were clearly related, but the distinction between them is important—one lamented a passing order; the other accepted its passing, but called for a transformation of the new order that was emerging. The first was only antimodern—the second was an antimodern plunge into modernity's heart. "If we would preserve our culture, the soul must be Christian again. We need Catholic writers and, especially, Catholic readers."[22] And literature as a prescription for the ills of modernity required attending closely to what would speak to modernity as its inhabitants experienced it.

Although Catholic writers and critics never abandoned orthodoxy in principle, they did gradually become less suspicious of modernism's emphasis on the need for new forms to speak to a new age. The impetus for this shift came from at least two directions. It was clear that modernity in the form of popular culture was indeed speaking to people at many different levels and that unless the Church was willing somehow to engage and inhabit these forms, it risked abandoning all possibility of influencing them. The extent to which this engagement affected how Catholics thought about literature and other art will be examined in detail in Chapter 6. From a different direction, the rapprochement between Catholicism and modernist innovation was probably facilitated greatly by T. S. Eliot's 1927 conversion to Anglicanism. While Eliot's later work was not as stylistically cataclysmic as earlier poems such as "The Love Song of J. Alfred Prufrock," "The Hollow Men," and especially "The Waste Land," it did not reject modernist formal innovations as it explored religious themes in works such as "Ash Wednesday," "Journey of the Magi," and *Four Quartets*. It became ever clearer that iconoclasm in form was not equivalent to heterodoxy in doctrine, that certain aspects of the truth of Catholic habitation of modernity could find best expression—*pace Pascendi*—in fresh formulations.

Innovation and Repetition

The third opposition with which Catholic literary work had to come to grips in the early years of modernist predominance was between innovation and repetition—the belief that art required newness and that attempts to repeat old forms or old themes created something besides art. In many ways modernism defined itself against romanticism, but in this the two look more alike than different: both imagine the artist as a person of genius and vision whose distinctive individual creativity is embodied in unique artifacts that differ profoundly from those that preceded them. Perhaps the most famous example is the modernist icon *Rite of Spring*, Stravinsky's ballet, so innovative it caused a riot at its 1913 Paris premiere. The literal inability of many people in its first audiences to hear it became almost instantaneously a mark of its greatness. The desire that a work of art uniquely and newly express its age and its artist's vision was intense and determinative.

In contrast, objects created to a pattern or a formula could belong to one of two categories, neither of them genuinely "art." They could be folk artifacts, tied to a tradition and bound to a community that decreed their design and their use. Such artifacts could aspire to the level of craft, and played a significant role in the modernist imagination and its fascination with the primitive.[23] Folk art signified connection to a lost sense of authenticity and continuity that haunted modernism. Except in remote and exotic remnant communities (within and outside the United States), it had been irrevocably replaced by the mechanized reproduction of the industrial age, in which the unique work of art witnessed to human creativity in the face of the numbing and impersonal repetition made possible by the machine. In many areas of U.S. life, such replication was in fact becoming a standard feature—literally, a selling point—for emerging consumerist sensibilities, but the consequences for art were generally seen as dire.[24] Folk art was medieval (or at least premodern) and irretrievable as art; popular culture was modern but soullessly commercial.

In one of modernism's more pervasive ironies, despite its concern with immediacy and with revivifying passions deadened by urban industrial commercial life, literature that aimed to replicate reliably for a certain audience a certain set of experiences and feelings could not be art. Popular literature's genre conventions, according to modernist critics, satisfied desires inherently lower and less artistic than did the more complex and difficult modernist text. Seeking repetition of previous artistic experience was a sign of insufficiently developed taste and intellect. Especially dangerous was the capacity of this repetitive appetite to take works of art that should be appreciated fully in their uniqueness and reduce them to commodities capable of being consumed as part of the pursuit of this low and uninteresting satisfaction. Readers, viewers, listeners who could not perceive innovation—and the requisite need to constantly relearn how to read, see, and hear—as constitutive of real artistic experience were at best ignorant but educable, at worst defective receptive devices incapable of appreciating the complexities of their own situation.

Far from being constitutive of their aesthetic, "innovation" was for Catholics a deeply suspect category in the years after the condemnation of theological modernism. In so many words, "innovation" was one of modernism's defining errors—the belief that the modern world required newness, required beliefs, doctrines, and categories to be at least restated, if not wholly rethought, in order to meet the changed situation of the church in the modern world. For Catholics thinking and writing about literature, novelty at best had no inherent value—newness for the sake of newness could be just as easily mistaken or barren as interesting and refreshing. Benjamin Musser, in his 1931 *America* article "The Newness of New Poetry," dismissed the value of "newness" by asserting that conservative and radical had vied with each other since time immemorial. He does concede, though, that "at no time has he [the radical] been more obviously a mirror of the feverish unrest of his day, of the jazz-mad, sensation-mad, sophistication-mad, sex-mad, machine-mad, building-mad, irreligion-mad spirit of the earth earthy, than he is at this moment, a reed shaken in the wind, thinking himself free, thinking himself progressive, yet held indomitably in the gyves of thralldom and controlled by circumstance."[25] At worst, innovation accentuated its departure from the past by rejecting the very truths that gave literature its life, by cutting it off from its own roots and proclaiming the dead shoot more vivid than the living growth.

All this is not to imply that Catholics rejected the possibility of artistic genius or of creative innovation—they did not. But neither did they reject repetition per se. Within their aesthetic scheme innovation and repetition were neutral strategies; their value depended on the ends toward which they were directed. If repetition were solely commercial, aimed at exploiting vulnerabilities or sinful desires, it was worthy of condemnation. If the commercial dimension of repetition was part of the means by which literature could move human hearts to genuine sympathy with others and genuine appreciation of beauty and complexity, could provide genuine entertainment and relaxation for working people whose aspirations were not and would likely never be primarily intellectual, then it was a legitimate category of literary creation and experience. This blurring of the boundaries between the popular and the high, boundaries that modernism and its advocates went to great lengths to tend, was one of the most significant points at which Catholic approaches to literature departed from those of their contemporaries.

The paths of Catholic writers and critics through these waters once again convey the variety in their antimodern appropriations of modernity. In writing about literature, Catholic critics, teachers, editors, librarians—those whose business included guiding the reading experiences of others—framed guidelines that applied to both serious literature and popular literature. This is not to say that no Catholic critic ever derided popular or derivative fiction; far from it—periodicals such as *America, Catholic World,* and *Commonweal* are full of laments about the deplorable taste of the Catholic reading public. Nonetheless, when they talked about literature as a whole, self-consciously Catholic critics were required to take into account everything that would likely enter into the reading experience of the average reader. The imperative for this inclusiveness derived from the all-encompassing scope of theological aesthetics—all art and entertainment, whether high or low, sacred or secular, good or bad, had cosmic implications. Therefore, much Catholic writing about literature ignored the distinctions that much secular criticism took great pains to delineate and police.

Beyond this sense of self-conscious obligation, though, lies an elusive but discernible, characteristically Catholic stance toward the relationship between innovation and repetition as they relate to literary style and, in turn, to modernity. Catholic views of repetition were shaped not solely by the negative reference point of mechanization but also by liturgy. Seen in the light of liturgical repetition, innovation is not its opposite but its companion. Newness consists in the fresh encounter with old forms, old gestures, old texts. This point is elusive because (perhaps surprisingly) Catholic writers talked very little about the effect of liturgy on their literary sensibilities. There are hints of it in a variety of places—in Evelyn Waugh's sanctuary lamp "burning anew among the old stones," in T. S. Eliot's playful self-interrogation, "You say I am repeating / Something I have said before. I shall say it again. / Shall I say it again?"[26] Flannery O'Connor famously said of her retort to Mary McCarthy about the Eucharist being a symbol ("Well, if it's a symbol, to hell with it.") that "this is all I will ever be able to say about it, outside of a story, except that it is the center of existence for me; all the rest of life is expendable."[27] This reticence about the sacramental heart of Catholic life may seem to be counterevidence of the interconnection between the literary and the theological, but its very implicitness instead reveals its centrality. Liturgy's prerogative to enact the eternal in every ordinary parish church, its claim on the past, present, and future, its insistence that repetition is what prepared the ground for the only really real newness—these collapsing distinctions reflect the way Catholic writing and thinking about literature bridged the gaps between popular and high, old and new, American and European, aesthetic and theological. In so doing, they played a tangible role in reconfiguring Catholicism's relationship to modernity and its peculiar embodiment in American culture.

Openness and Closure

The belief that some forms were more expressive of the contemporary situation than others was central to literary and other genres of artistic modernism. Artists who clung to old forms were refusing not just a place among the avant-garde but a more fundamental engagement with the world in which they lived. Folklorist Henry Glassie rendered the story this way: "Once, understanding humankind was easy. There was this omniscient deity who kept the universe in order, winding the spring that drove people and planets in accord. Then a jealous folk, enlightened and inner lit, killed their clock-winding god, and order vanished into millions of separate skulls."[28] Few aspects of intellectual and artistic modernity are as unequivocal as the disintegration of confidence in a shared basis for human meaning.

In myriad ways unsettling, this disintegration powered a phenomenal burst of artistic creativity, as a result of which, among other things, formal and substantive openness—ambiguity, indeterminacy, lack of resolution—became deeply identified with the modern in literature. Literature opened out formally with blank verse, with experiments in stream-of-consciousness and other innovative prose, with lack of closure in plot. Substantively, literary "openness" referred to an inability or refusal to resolve or easily answer certain basic human questions. A broad and long-lived critical consensus emerged conferring approbation on works that emphasized substantive and formal openness.

Opposed to this openness supposedly most characteristic of modernity was formal and substantive closure. Closure could take the form of resolution in plot (Dickens's happy endings compared to Joyce's *Ulysses* beginning and ending apparently arbitrarily midsentence) or of form, rhyme, and meter in poetry (Wordsworth's or Longfellow's metrical stanzas contrasted with Eliot's or Pound's, deliberately ragged and unscannable). From early on, modernists associated closure with the nineteenth-century optimism, confidence, and certainty that had been shattered by the Great War. It was necessary to reject it in order to speak to and from the alienated, fragmented condition of modern humanity.

Modernists embraced openness in literature, then, as a self-conscious means of rejecting the Victorian mores and conventions they believed were no longer tenable. At the same time, however, closure was becoming more rather than less culturally pervasive. It is arguably one of the most important defining features of the popular culture that was becoming central to American life in the early years of the century. A love story that ends with a kiss or a wedding, a gangster story that ends with a cell door clanging, a western that ends with a shoot-out on a dusty street—genre fiction and movies are defined by the expectation of a certain kind of satisfactory resolution. The murderer is revealed, the unfaithful lover is rejected and the faithful lover rewarded, the hero rides off into the sunset. As sales of popular novels and movie tickets skyrocketed in the third and fourth decades of the century, novelists and poets, painters and musicians who saw their work as, by contrast, "serious," sought an increasingly elusive audience whose aesthetic was, as the modernist artists saw it, more in tune with the age.

As popular culture became more dominant and more associated with the urban working classes, a modernist assertion of openness and ambiguity as defining features of art became more insistent. Jazz was more evocative of the undetermined and improvisational quality of American life than the sixteen-bar popular song; cubism a more accurate reflection of the contingency of human perception than magazine illustration and photography. Those who insisted on the uncomplicated resolution, the satisfying happy ending, were indulging rather low desires, experiencing easy pleasure instead of the rigorous and demanding satisfactions of real art. They were also making themselves available for exploitation by commercially driven manipulators of emotion and fantasy, passively consuming whatever numbing prescription was put in front of them. The modernist critique of closure was elitist from two different political angles: from one it looked like the snobbery of the old aristocracy observing the low pleasures of the common people; from the other, like the egalitarian insistence of liberal fellow citizens that the populace resist anything that encouraged mass thinking or discouraged autonomous self-reliance.

In the eyes of the modernists, Catholics were clearly at the closure pole of the spectrum along with the other common people. If, for modernists, artistic closure represented a false sense of order and meaning in a world devoid of both, then reliance on it was at its worst a cowardly capitulation, a refusal to face the harsh reality of the world as it is. Catholics probably reinforced this perception by intervening publicly and frequently on the depredations of popular culture—not in sympathy with the critique of mass thinking, but, apparently, with the sole goal of insisting that movies and novels be more conventional, more wholesome, more reflective of precisely the worldview modernists found so stifling and so stale.

But Catholic affinity for closure had deeper roots than bourgeois convention or Irish social conservatism. The Catholic narrative was, ultimately and existentially, complete. The world had fallen and been redeemed. God had taken on human form, had died and risen, and humanity lived in the knowledge of that fundamental completion. Closure in literature—the restoration of unity and harmony that characterized the *Divine Comedy*—affirmed and expressed this completion.

Therefore, to the extent that modernist openness was more than a formal strategy and somehow represented a worldview, an ontological assertion that the nature and destiny of humanity were still indeterminate, Catholics explicitly opposed it. Defending *vers libre* in 1917, John Bunker urged poets who decide to "sin against accepted canons" to "sin boldly." "Only too often you sin drably, dully, unintelligibly, in a word unmannerly; and for that the world has no forgiveness. Blasphemy is not wit, nor can sound art be reared on rotten foundations. The soul, the very breath of life of poetry is spiritual content. If you have not that, you have nothing."[29] Other critical articulations located the dangers more explicitly in time and space. Stephen J. M. Brown, in *Libraries and Literature from a Catholic Standpoint,* argued that the "moral anarchy" of World War I had created a literature that reflected and pandered to it. At the very least, in Brown's view, the Catholic novel was free of poison, its atmosphere was clean, though it "may or may not be invigorating."[30] In a 1938 talk titled "Training Youth for Authorship," Daniel Lord used the example of a girl who received a grade of 78 on an essay about Edith Wharton because, according to Lord, the professor thought she was too immature to recognize Wharton's value. "I myself read the girl's paper with three rousing cheers. She had been Catholic enough to see that Mrs. Wharton was a hopeless modernist; a pagan of pagans; a woman with a most depressive philosophy of life and a real despair over the characters she created out of the entirely pagan world in which she moved."[31] Dismissal was not the inevitable result of such an assessment, though, as we can see in Blanche Mary Kelly's analysis of T. S. Eliot: "In *The Waste Land* he called attention to a more unutterable despair. This surely was the uttermost woe that man could know, this feeling that had ceased to be feeling, this blind numbness and paralysis of the spirit, this desolation of the flesh. . . . These were the only voices left to that bereft generation for the telling of its woe" (that is, the "complaining voices of the nerves").[32]

While Catholics defended traditional forms in literature and gave them critical praise long after they had fallen out of fashion elsewhere, their praise did not derive from unreflective conservatism, nor did it represent a refusal to confront modernism's dislocations. Catholics, as we have seen, diagnosed the source of modernity's ills quite differently from their contemporaries. Far from rejecting it as outmoded and useless, they saw closure—the affirmation of meaning and fulfillment—as part of the cure. They also accepted that modernist openness could be an aesthetically powerful formal strategy precisely because it so vividly expressed the barrenness of a world that be-

lieved God was dead. This sense of alienation, fragmentation, and dislocation only deepened in the aftermath of the Great War and became something
akin to despair as artists and intellectuals watched the slow spiral toward yet
another war develop in the 1930s.

Closely related to the opposition between orthodoxy and iconoclasm,
the tension between closure and openness was real but subject to reinterpretation through the lens of Catholicism's theological-literary aesthetic. Instead of allowing the oppositions to define their approach to literature,
Catholic writers and critics used their own critical system to reinterpret the
opposition in a way that affirmed their own critical presuppositions. They
would eventually acknowledge and incorporate the great aesthetic achieve-
ments of modernism not by disregarding their own distinctive theological
criteria but by taking them to their farthest possible conclusion.

Literary Work and Communal Accountability

At the century's beginning, the papal condemnation of theological modernism was authoritative, absolute, and unequivocal. Literary modernism
was from one angle an entirely distinct thing and therefore, presumably, not
implicated in the condemnation. It was, though, undeniably part of the
coming to grips with modernity—philosophical, political, economic—that
had preoccupied so much of Western intellectual culture for over a century,
and therefore Catholic literature and writing about literature had to address
and somehow locate it. Especially in the early years of the twentieth century,
Catholics rejected many of the presumptions and defining commitments of
literary modernism, seeing in it many of the errors that characterized its
theological counterpart. But even from these early years, Catholics also refused to truncate the category of the literary by accepting the oppositions
against which modernism and its explicators constructed it. Instead they
used Catholicism's claim to timeless categories and criteria to subsume the
contemporary oppositions and eventually produce a version of the present
that took the whole system into account. By shifting the context within
which it was examined and rationalized, American Catholic writers and
critics incorporated modernism into a larger set of strategies by which they
reinterpreted the context for intellectual and artistic work in the twentieth
century. By continually wrestling in terms that were both literary and theological with ostensibly literary questions about modernism, Catholic writers
and critics were developing theological as well as literary resources. Over the
course of the decades between the 1907 condemnation and the recovery of

the discussion in the wake of the Second Vatican Council, they helped to reconfigure the relationship between religious belief and the narratives that shaped the experience of modernity in ways that prepared the ground for the reencounter with questions that had been deferred generations before.

The peculiar nature of Catholic literary analysis helped to make this reconfiguration possible. Its categories were so far removed from the mainstream of U.S. intellectual and cultural analysis that they have perhaps more often seemed like an obstacle, but close attention to how they were used in practice suggests that they functioned at least as often as means of engagement and rationalization. For example, Catholic literary analysis (in company with much thinking informed by Catholic Action), insisted that premodern insights were precisely the most relevant to the fragmentation and dissociation of modern life. "Perhaps what I am saying," Jesuit William Lynch wrote in 1960, "is that we need a lot more dancing in common before we do any more thinking."[33]

Catholics, when they wrote self-consciously as Catholics about literature, felt (gladly or irritably) an accountability to others that set them apart from many of their literary contemporaries and was largely coded by those contemporaries as unliterary and antimodern. Therefore, the cultural work that Catholic literature and writing about literature did was to articulate and rationalize (that is, provide an available rationale for) the relationship between the individual and the community, the present and the past. These rationales reassured individuals that fidelity to a religious view of the world did not disqualify them from modernity; it made them, in fact, essential to it. Further, these rationales, these rhetorical strategies provided a pathway through territory the culture often proclaimed to be impassable; they provided for a self-consciously matter-of-fact, matter-of-factly self-conscious occupation by Catholics of the landscape of intellectual and artistic modernity.

The sense of being both caught and free, solipsist and social, captures the density of engagement with American modernity available through—not in spite of or alongside of—the most overtly sectarian Catholic experiences. This attempt to aggregate widely varied cultural, artistic, and religious categories and experiences, to draw together elements from multiple aspects of human experience, reflected a basic impulse of Catholic literary culture, one that differentiated it from the literary mainstream. There, from the standpoint of both the market and the academy, delineating and maintaining distinctions became increasingly important over the course of the middle decades of the twentieth century. Although the market was indeed "mass" for the first time in history, it also relied on segmenting and targeting, dividing the population into affinity groups in order to determine how

best to sell different sorts of cultural productions to them.[34] The end of the
nineteenth century had already seen the rise of high culture—symphonic
orchestras, Renaissance "Old Masters" painting as the basis of private and
museum collections, "serious" theater as distinct from vaudeville—as a means
by which the industrial aristocracy could distinguish itself from the immigrant masses of urban America and associate itself with the culture and
social hierarchy of Europe.[35] The emergent category of "middlebrow"
culture depended on a similar sense of distinction for its most basic economic success.[36]

The literary academy was hard at work institutionalizing a number of
these distinctions in the critical strategies and schools that emerged in the
first half of the twentieth century. Scholars recently have argued that modernism was a more kaleidoscopic phenomenon, drawing actively and enthusiastically on the welter of experiences and sources available in early
twentieth-century urban life, than its 1950s New Critical champions would
like to have believed, and they are probably right. But the tendency throughout the first half of the century and well into the postwar period was to
separate the work of literary art from its social and cultural context, and to
attempt to judge it on aesthetic terms alone. Eventually judgment became
almost entirely attenuated and was suspended altogether in favor of interpretation.[37] Fewer and fewer works of art became worthy of such attention,
and by the 1950s it was not clear that anything but the works of the metaphysical poets, a few of their modernist heirs, and about a dozen mid-
nineteenth-century American writers really fulfilled the notion of the
"literary" at all.[38] In contrast to such a rarefied refining of the category, the
apparently indiscriminate Catholic approach was easily dismissed. Trying to
reconcile what others consider irreconcilable can elicit accusations of bad
faith, even insanity.

The answer to why so many Catholic writers and critics continued
working so assiduously to sustain their alternative network of literary institutions and practices has to do with James Fisher's insight that, as he puts it,
Catholicism *is* popular culture. For early twentieth-century urban Catholics, "Pluralism was a creative fact of life rather than a theory in need of
justification. Precisely at the moment when 'Americanism' was drawing
condemnation as a theological premise, it was being mastered in practice by
the urban laity with little apparent spiritual damage. . . . While [modernism's]
condemnation by Pope Pius X as the 'synthesis of all heresies' may well
have dampened academic theology for decades, in the broader culture such
Catholics as Eugene O'Neill and F. Scott Fitzgerald helped shape the contours of 'the modern.' "[39] Fisher develops the point in relation to popular

culture per se, but it also applies in the realm where modernism and urban life, academic study, Catholicism, and commercial activity all came together, in American Catholic literary culture and its debates and wrangling over what was Catholic, what was literary, and what was American about American Catholic literature.

Within these debates, Catholic literary culture performed a variety of cultural work: clearing a space within which to work out an adaptation to modernity on Catholicism's own terms, which included claiming ground as legitimately American and clearly Catholic; providing rationales for the eventual reconciliation and appropriation of literary modernism within the scope of Catholic literature, and even of modern theological work within the scope of Catholic theology. The system of ideas that animated Catholic literary culture and the structures and institutions that facilitated its functioning made this job of cultural work—earning Catholics a place in the American landscape as both American and Catholic—both possible and difficult.

CHAPTER 4

The History and Function of Catholic Censorship, as Told to the Twentieth Century

Nothing could be clearer about U.S. Catholic literary culture in the years after the Great War than its interdependence with theology and philosophy in defining and evaluating literature. The resulting literary aesthetic drew multiple aspects of Catholic thought and experience into a powerful and flexible imaginative framework that operated in an extensive network of literary institutions. These institutions in turn functioned in the context of a church polity and a tradition of ecclesiastical law that encompassed literary activity within its jurisdiction. People involved in Catholic literary work were imagined by church authority not as solitary artists or disinterested scholars but as believers with a high calling and a grave obligation to the truth, and those obligations were spelled out formally in canon law. In the literary and artistic climate of the early to mid-twentieth century, these legal specifications and the dilemma they posed for Catholics involved in literary and print culture could serve as Exhibit A in a trial by which Catholics were found to be, as John McGreevy put it, "heretics from what Arthur Schlesinger Jr. called 'the democratic faith,' one in which 'theology and ritual . . . hierarchy and demonology' would step aside for 'intellectual freedom and unrestricted inquiry.'"[1]

The philosophical framework underlying Catholic literary culture might have been assimilable within Schlesinger's dichotomy had its proponents derived it independently and espoused it voluntarily as a response to its intellectual appeal. But key elements of Catholic views of literature were given, not invented; prescribed, not voluntary; they were legislated. For four centuries Catholic relationships to print culture had been codified in canon law (the official law of the church). Compiled primarily as a response to the spread of the ideas of the Protestant Reformation, these laws concerning reading and publication originated in the impulse to suppress one of the phenomena most deeply associated with the definition of the modern. As a result, their existence into the twentieth century posed a significant dilemma for Catholics confident that their views of literature could speak effectively to the modern situation. The most potent symbol of this dilemma was the *Index Librorum Prohibitorum*—the Index of Forbidden Books, a list compiled and published by the Vatican, begun in 1564, remaining in effect until 1966, consisting of books that Catholics could read only with permission. The Index and the system that undergirded it were, in the eyes of critics, irreformably part of the premodern.

It is difficult, perhaps impossible, to write about the Index as anything other than an anachronism. Established in the heat of Counter-Reformation anxiety about the spread of Protestantism by means of the newly invented printing press, in the middle of the twentieth century it stood, at best, as an anomaly—evidence either that the Counter-Reformation, Tridentine church was desperately out of step with the intellectual culture of the modern West or that it was toothless and on its way out.[2] Either way, its reason for being ran so clearly counter to the main intellectual currents of the century that anything other than an edifyingly teleological account of its demise seems almost impossible (and perhaps undesirable).

But twentieth-century Catholic intellectuals had to render such an account; that is, they had to develop a coherent rationale by which they could observe apparently incompatible commitments. If they believed that Catholic literary work presumed a dense web of accountability, mutual obligation, and community, then simply ignoring or rejecting the Index and the system of laws it represented was not a viable option. If at the same time they wanted to be clearly and firmly part of American culture—and especially of American intellectual life—they needed terms in which to understand their obligations that would explain to both themselves and their compatriots how it was possible to respect the spirit of inquiry around which American intellectual life in the twentieth century centered. As Catholic critics writing about literary modernism rewrote the story of modernity to maintain a continuous Catholic presence on the stage, Catholic critics and teachers explaining the Index of Forbidden Books to their students and compatriots had to construct an account of the emergence of intellectual and philosophical modernity in which Catholic tradition retained its centrality.

This task was necessary, and its scope extensive, because the history of intellectual modernity, as conventional academic wisdom construed it for much of the twentieth century, featured as its chief antagonist, even its chief villain, the Roman Catholic Church. Beginning with the scientific revolution and the Renaissance, the Church (in the persons most often of the Vatican hierarchy) figured as an opponent of intellectual freedom and scholarly progress, intent on preserving its own authority and prerogatives at the expense even of truth. In the sixteenth and seventeenth centuries, the locus of Western intellectual life shifted north, to Germany and England, leaving the unreformed lands of Italy and Spain behind as liberalism rose and Enlightenment intellectual autonomy prevailed. Via the growth of the research model in German universities of the nineteenth century, the scientific revolution and Enlightenment philosophy together shaped the creation of the modern university, with Schlesinger's "intellectual freedom and unrestricted inquiry" as its organizing principles.[3]

In the early acts of this drama the Index and its curial enforcers played a starring role.[4] The curial congregation that originally produced the Index was the Holy Office, also known as the Inquisition. Although administration of the Index was moved to a separate, eponymous congregation in 1572, the Index retained its association with the repressive, authoritarian mythos of the Holy Office and the Inquisition throughout its lifespan and beyond. The myth of the Inquisition as "the great enemy of the human spirit" was tempered somewhat in the last quarter of the nineteenth century by the first important modern historical works on the subject.[5] The most prominent of these in the United States were by Henry Charles Lea, the self-taught, extremely prolific historian of (among other things) the medieval (three volumes) and Spanish (four volumes) Inquisitions.[6] Lea believed himself, and was judged by his contemporaries, to be operating by strictly objective and neutral premises and methods, but his very reputation as a scientific chronicler lent authority to his judgment as to the Inquisition's inherent backwardness and immorality.[7] Thus in specific and timely ways was the very idea of the Inquisition entangled both with the origins of the modern profession of history and with the idea of the Roman Catholic Church as a hopelessly corrupt obstacle to human progress. The commonly held view of the Inquisition in early twentieth-century American intellectual culture had not only long-standing anti-Catholicism to back it up but also the full authority of the scientific methodology that had come to predominate in fields outside the natural sciences.[8]

For American Catholic intellectuals who wanted to lay claim both to the intellectual tradition of Catholicism and to the freedom of inquiry and democratic ethos of twentieth-century American intellectual life, navigating this unfriendly territory was daunting. For one thing, one reason the conventional wisdom had become conventional was that a fair amount of evidence existed to support it. But defining contemporary scholarly inquiry largely against Roman Catholicism both oversimplified the intellectual history of the eighteenth and nineteenth centuries and created a needlessly stark dichotomy for U.S. Catholics seeking to understand the role of Catholicism and Catholic intellectual work in the modern world. They had to construct an intellectual history of modernity that would accommodate their commitment both to many of the ideals of scholarly inquiry that had emerged since the Reformation and to their religious tradition and the continuing vitality of its distinctive intellectual claims. One key site within which they constructed this alternative history was the explanation, translation, and justification of the Index and the parts of canon law related to reading and publication that Catholic writers and teachers developed for a wide variety of audiences. Catholics involved in literary work retold the story of modernity in order to rediscover themselves as continuing characters in the drama, and in so doing helped to change the story. From 1917 on, they used the language of the Code of Canon Law approved in that year as their starting point, which gave their accounts a notable consistency throughout the end of World War II and into the 1950s. What had changed significantly by the postwar years were the roles in which Catholic writers and critics cast themselves and their fellow American Catholics.

The Index of Forbidden Books looms larger in the imagination of twentieth-century Catholicism than it did in practice. But the process by which it went from being an accepted element of Catholic regulation of reading and publication (in the reforms of Leo XIII at the beginning of the twentieth century) to its quiet abrogation in the year following the close of the Second Vatican Council reflects the larger process by which Catholic literary and intellectual culture both resisted and accommodated to modernity more broadly. It became a focal point and a symbol of the struggle over the intellectual legacy of Reformation and Counter-Reformation that formed a significant part of twentieth-century intellectual life both in the United States and in Europe. The histories of the Index and associated canon law, the explanations of the obligations it imposed on ordinary readers, and the rationales by which Catholics attempted to explain it to themselves and their compatriots all laid claim to this legacy and in so doing claimed as their own the deep intellectual history of Catholic tradition and the energetic intellectual ferment of the twentieth-century United States.

Histories of the Index

Where the narrative of church regulation of reading and publication begins depends on the motives that power the narrative. Historians of early modern Europe tend to see it as one of the clearest institutional manifestations of Counter-Reformation, an attempt by the Vatican to stop the spread of Protestant ideas and to control the unruly intellectual energies unleashed by the invention of movable type. As historians of early modern Europe seem to agree,[9] histories of the Counter-Reformation are inevitably implicated in current debates over issues sometimes far removed from historiography. Accounts of the era are often starkly formulated, with a cast of heroes and villains. Which is which depends to a certain extent on what current situation the historian hopes implicitly or explicitly to justify. Even as one strives, in the spirit of William Hudon's advice, to avoid "heroic or demonic commonplaces we should seek to leave behind," it is safe to say that among academics, historians included, the Index and its creators and enforcers, the Holy Office of the Inquisition, have occupied the heroic role less frequently than have their opponents.[10]

Roman Catholic historians of Roman Catholicism, especially those writing in the middle of the twentieth century, had always as part of their task to explain and rationalize the existence of censorship in the context of twentieth-century intellectual work. In writing the history of the Index, then, they were looking, if not for heroes, then at least for an intellectual tradition defensible in their own time. They cast their nets backward through the centuries before the fifteenth and sixteenth in order to assert an unbroken history of concern, dating from the early Church, for the orthodoxy of written material. Thus P. W. Browne in *The Sign* in 1934: "The present-day legislation of the Church regarding pernicious books has always existed in its essential features, though there were no written decrees regarding the condemnation of books until a comparatively recent period."[11] This desire and search for continuity reflect the concern for unity and coherence that characterized Catholic literary culture as a whole; they reflect, as well, the confident placing of Catholicism in the center of the intellectual tradition of the West.

Given the array of conflicting agendas and the current unsettled state of the question, it will be necessary to be as clear as possible about which aspects of the history of censorship served and therefore were championed by historians from different perspectives. This brief survey looks at three periods: before the invention of movable type, a long period of readjustment to the technological implications of print culture (roughly the mid-fifteenth through mid-eighteenth centuries), and a modern period, in which censorship regulation functioned in the context of a well-developed print culture.

Even to assert the existence of this first period is in some ways to construct a Catholic narrative of Counter-Reformation regulation of reading and publication; that is, it is really only to Catholic historians that the continuity with the early years of the Church and particularly with scripture is at all important. Texts written to explain the Index and censorship in terms understandable to contemporary readers, such as J. M. Pernicone's *Ecclesiastical Prohibition of Books*, commonly construct a historical narrative that begins in apostolic times. Pernicone finds the earliest concern for the connection between writing and orthodoxy in the Acts of the Apostles, when Paul's effect on the Christian converts at Ephesus leads "a good many of those who formerly practised magic" to "collect their books and burn . . . them publicly" (Acts 19:19).[12] The practice of burning heretical works would be praised by numerous historians of censorship (up to and including Daniel Lord's 1930 pamphlet, *I Can Read Anything: All Right! Then Read This*) as a bold sign of commitment to the truth.

Scripture plays a role in the narrative of the history of Catholic censorship not only by including a precedent and therefore warrant for condemning and destroying heretical works but also because the formation of the scriptural canon itself was a process of deciding which writings were authoritative and which should be excluded (and therefore forbidden).[13] The connection between scripture and other forms of writing and publishing was central for the entire history of the Index and censorship. Once the canon was more or less set, the questions did not end—the advisability and legitimacy of scriptural translations continued to be a focus of debate. Most common were arguments over, and a variety of policies concerning, vernacular translations of scripture. Before the Reformation era per se, various reformers argued that making scripture available to ordinary readers in their own languages was essential to the lived reality of Christian communities. As they would in the succeeding centuries, objections had to do with the dangers involved in mistranslation and unguided individual interpretation. Vernacular translations were not forbidden in all times and places; like so much of this history, the question was variable and contested.

In addition to the emphasis on the earliest Christian centuries and on scripture, accounts of the history of censorship also focus on the condemnation of heresy. The points of greatest contention within the history of Christian tradition are nearly all marked with the condemnation—and sometimes the burning—of the writings of their principal actors: among others were Arius (250–336), Origen, Pelagius, the Nestorians, Berengarius of Tours (ca. 999–1088; disputes over the Eucharist), Abelard (1079–1142), John Wycliffe (1324–84), and Jan Hus (1369–1415). In addition to the writings of Christians judged to be unorthodox, the core writings of other religious traditions were also sometimes proscribed. Most frequently specified was the Talmud; though the proscription was never universal, it was enforced with great severity in certain times and places.[14] The 1913 *Catholic Encyclopedia* discerned a fundamental consistency and continuity in the attitude taken by Church authorities toward control of texts and reading: "Thus at the beginning of the Middle Ages, there existed, in all its essentials, though without specified clauses, a prohibition and censorship of books throughout the Catholic Church. Popes as well as councils, bishops no less than synods, considered it then, as always, their most sacred duty to safeguard the purity of faith and to protect the souls of the faithful by condemning and forbidding any dangerous book."[15]

In constructing this narrative, this history of Catholic regulation of reading and publication, sources emphasize the Church's duty to preserve the truth of revelation and the close connection between that obligation and the written word. This dual emphasis serves such accounts well when they come to the second of the three periods in the history of the Index—the era during which the ideas of the Protestant Reformation and the invention of movable type helped to transform the intellectual landscape of Europe. The Gutenberg revolution led to a much more sustained and systematic effort on the part of the Vatican to control publication and reading. At the very moment when control of publication began to become literally impossible, the Church asserted the obligation of publishers, booksellers, and others involved in the process to obtain permission before publication.

The *Index Librorum Prohibitorum* is most closely associated with the Council of Trent, but precedents existed well before that. There were "lists"—the literal translation of "index"—of prohibited books published as early as the fifth century; Pope Gelasius I's (d. 496) "celebrated catalogue of the authentic writings of the Fathers, together with a list of apocryphal and interpolated works, as well as the proscribed books of the heretics" is often cited as the earliest known papal attempt to compile a list of forbidden works.[16]

Soon after the invention of movable type in the 1450s, the Church made control over the spread of printing an urgent priority. Not all initiatives originated at Rome: by the 1470s the university at Cologne was asking for and being granted rights to censor books being printed and sold in its jurisdiction. In 1486 Innocent VIII issued *Inter multiplices*, the initial ambition of which was very wide—it stated that *all* works could be published only with the permission of the Church. Its prescribed mechanism, though, was the local bishop, meaning that there was not as yet any overall centralized attempt at control by Rome. *Inter multiplices* was never enforced,[17] and it would be thirty years before the next significant legislation emerged from Rome. In the meantime bishops issued various local decrees, and the pressure points and incipient conflicts on the issue emerged. For example, Alexander VI encountered protest from the printers of Cologne when he decreed in 1501 that nontheological as well as theological works required censorship before publication.[18] This example reflects two aspects of the early struggles over what Church censorship should look like: whether it should extend to all works or only those explicitly religious and theological, and whether it should apply primarily to authors and readers or should also include printers and booksellers. The historical moment in which the answer was "all of the above" was brief indeed.

Julius II called the Fifth Lateran Council in 1512 after much wrangling with bishops who thought he was reneging on his promise to hold a council. Some bishops, impatient with waiting, had convened their own, schismatic, council at Pisa in 1511. The Lateran Council lasted longer than Julius did, and was continued by his successor, Leo X, who in 1515 issued *Inter sollicitudines*, "the first general decree of censorship which was universally accepted." It ordered that all works be censored, aiming primarily at printers, excommunicating and fining them for infractions as well as confiscating and burning the offending books.[19]

This list of precedents notwithstanding, the history of Church censorship was permanently altered by the conflict with Martin Luther. It seemed to the opponents of the Reformation to clarify and render urgent the right and duty of the Church to censor, but it also and more fundamentally made clear that the technological wonder of the spread of print was inextricably historically bound up with the widening rift in Christendom. Texts, the control of texts, and a deeply visceral response to the very material existence of texts permeate the events of the early Reformation. In July 1520, Leo X's bull excommunicating Martin Luther, *Exsurge, Domine*, also condemned his writings, ordered those already published to be destroyed, and forbade the publication or reading of all of his future writings as well. The

1913 *Catholic Encyclopedia* suggests that the destruction of offending texts was a powerful stratagem and metaphor on both sides: "The Bull itself became the object of shocking indignities. . . . The crowning dishonour awaited it at Wittenberg, where . . . the university students assembled at the Elster Gate, and amid the jeering chant of 'Te Deum laudamus,' and 'Requiem aeternam,' interspersed with ribald drinking songs, Luther in person consigned it to the flames." The *Encyclopedia* also quotes Luther several months earlier as saying, "I despise alike the favour and fury of Rome; I do not wish to be reconciled with her, or ever to hold any communion with her. Let her condemn and burn my books; I, in turn, unless I can find no fire, will condemn and publicly burn the whole pontifical law, that swamp of heresies."[20]

The history of Catholic regulation of reading and publication is inextricable from the context of reform but not limited to the reaction against Protestantism. Instead, Protestant reformers were only one of many elements catalyzing reform in many areas of sixteenth-century society, most of which had some connection to the emerging print culture and therefore some connection to the development of modern structures for censorship. The Church's system of censorship surely emerged in large part as a reaction against the spread of Protestant ideas. Elizabeth Eisenstein says that the Index "transformed advocacy of Copernicanism into a patriotic Protestant cause."[21] But the need to assure authenticity in scriptural and liturgical texts in light of the technological changes wrought by the invention of print also played a major role. These two motivations and others ensured that control of print was a central element of the agenda of the Council of Trent and a key aspect of the implementation of the Council's reforms for each succeeding pontificate. In addition to stopping the spread of heresy, control of print was seen as central to spiritual renewal and liturgical reform, to the maintaining of church discipline, and to the reorganizing of the curial bureaucracy.

Fear of the spread of the Reformation into Italy was behind Paul III's reorganization in 1542 of the Roman Inquisition as the Congregation of the Holy Office. Originally established in the twelfth century by Innocent III, the sixteenth-century Holy Office was intended to have universal authority. Because of the key role books and printing played in the spread of Reformation ideas, the Congregation was assigned responsibility for censorship, evidence that censorship was seen as intimately connected to the protection of doctrinal integrity. The assumption of this relationship was such a sixteenth-century commonplace that the establishment of a separate Congregation of the Index (planned by Pius V in 1571 and implemented by his successor, Gregory XIII, in the following year) should be seen not so much as the intensifying of a crackdown on intellectual freedom as a part of bureaucratizing reform as papal administration grew more complex. As Cardinal Ugo Buoncompagni, Gregory XIII had been head of the Holy Office under Paul IV and saw the regularizing of censorship structures and procedures as a routine part of the overall implementation of Tridentine reform.[22]

The regularization of procedures and centralization of authority in Rome that characterized so much of Tridentine reform during and after the Council gave rise to two elements of the control of print that would remain prominent into the twentieth century. The first was the preparation and issuance of a "Roman" Index of Forbidden Books; that is, an Index intended to be comprehensive and applicable universally. The first such Index, commissioned by Paul IV in 1557 and issued by him in 1559, was considered from the first unworkably harsh (two examples: it condemned all of the works of Erasmus, and also forbade not only prohibited works themselves but all future works printed by any printer of a forbidden work). This Index was never accepted or enforced, but was followed soon after by the product of the deliberations of the Council of Trent, which from its opening session had had control of print on its agenda. Work on the issue continued after the close of the Council, which decreed in 1562 that "the fathers [bishops] elected for this examination of censures and books should consider what needs to be done and report back in their own time." In 1564, a year after the Council ended, Pius IV issued the so-called "Tridentine" Index.

The Tridentine Index was the first to feature a list of general rules about forbidden books—that is, to describe classes of materials that were forbidden whether or not they had ever been specifically condemned by title by the Congregation.[23] These rules, which would exist largely unaltered into the twentieth century, were a concession to the impossibility of ever keeping up with the vast flood of print unleashed by movable type. They reflected a crucial shift that began almost at the moment that Counter-Reformation-era procedures for the control of print were established. Initially the Church attempted to control print by controlling the mechanisms of production. Such control, in which figured not only the ecclesiastical penalty of excommunication but civil penalties such as fines and confiscation of merchandise, would have required a seamless wielding of temporal authority that the Church never possessed and certainly was only less likely to possess in the aftermath of the Reformation. As the divisions within Christianity became permanent and as separation between church and state became a defining feature of the modern nation-state, the emphasis shifted from public to private control—away from the Church's ability to intervene in the economic processes of printing and bookselling to the obligation of individual readers to form their consciences about what to read in light of Church teaching.

With the exception of a significant revision undertaken by Benedict XIV in the middle of the eighteenth century, the structures for censorship developed and implemented between 1450 and 1600 remained in most important features unchanged through the twentieth century. That is not to say there were not developments and conflicts, a number of them persistent and recurring. New Indexes were issued with some regularity to keep up with changing ideas that posed new threats to orthodoxy, and also to correct errors that crept in over the years. Revisions in regulations grappled with how to balance the local and the universal—that is, how papal authority interacted with the authority of a bishop in his own diocese. Whether the Church had the obligation or the right to censor nontheological works as well as theological remained a persistent theme, though over the long term the latter became the clear conventional wisdom. Hilgers in the 1913 *Catholic Encyclopedia* described the shifts as occurring "quite spontaneously" and being "assented to first tacitly, then also indirectly by other ecclesiastical enactments." Similarly, early edicts forbidding the publication of writing in the vernacular—on the grounds that scholarly Latin would have a more limited circulation and therefore run less risk of affecting the doctrinal soundness of the beliefs of large numbers of people—gave way gradually to the inexorability of the dominance of the vernacular.

Prior censorship—the obligation to submit writings to church authorities for approval before publication—coexisted, sometimes uneasily, with prohibition after publication. Church authority waxed and waned depending on the century and the country, but the shift away from control of print at the point of publication was steady and long-term. It was also accompanied by its own ironies: As early as Kepler, people believed that condemning a book could be good for business, making more people interested in obtaining and reading it.[24] Giordano Bruno's works were published in London between 1583 and 1585 by a Protestant printer, who deliberately falsified the imprints of Paris and Venice to take "advantage of free publicity provided by the Index."[25] That is, the notoriety of a work that defied its condemnation in the Catholic-controlled cities of Paris and Venice could give it a perceived commercial advantage in Protestant London.

Though implementation and oversight were inconsistent enough that generalizations are difficult, it seems reasonably clear that the censorship system that had emerged by the end of the sixteenth century was variable and fragmentary. Is it enough simply to assert the complexity of the record and move on to the next topic? Or does the historian have an obligation to make some more substantive statement about the overall effect and effectiveness of church regulation of reading and publication? Paul Grendler in his study of sixteenth-century Venice concludes that censorship was most effective (to some extent only effective) when civil authorities took enforcement seriously and were not in competition with the papacy. In addition he notes that at any given moment there were enough loopholes in the system even when it was being strenuously enforced that anyone with enough money and determination could get hold of banned books if they wanted them.[26] Sometimes these loopholes functioned with something close to authoritative approval—German Protestant students at the University of Padua had access to prohibited texts despite the papacy's objections because the government of Venice thought the benefits of the students' presence outweighed their defiance of the Inquisition's rules.[27]

To complicate the picture further, almost every post-Tridentine pope (the Council ended in 1563) involved in revising or elaborating censorship regulation was also a serious patron of the arts and learning. Pius V established the Congregation of the Index and completed the construction of Santa Maria degli Angeli with Michelangelo as chief architect; Gregory XIII furthered the implementation of the Index and established the Collegio Romano, which would become the university that today bears his name, the Gregorianum, as well as donating his personal library to the Vatican Library and opening its collections to scholars; Paul V oversaw the condemnation of Copernicus's *De Revolutionibus* and the trial of Galileo, and established the Vatican archives and completed St. Peter's Basilica.[28] To be sure, such patronage was linked to aggrandizement of the office and in many cases the self of the pontiff, or to addressing issues of distinctive importance to the Church.[29] It was also, however, driven at least intermittently by a genuine interest in fostering artistic talent and new learning, including extending tolerance and official protection to new ideas and methods while the questions of how and whether they might cohere with Catholic tradition worked themselves slowly out.

This combination of motives and actions was still operative a century and a half after Trent during the papacy of Benedict XIV (r. 1740–58), the pope responsible for the only thorough reform of the Index and censorship regulation between the end of the Council and the end of the nineteenth century. From his days as archbishop of Bologna, Prospero Lambertini had been deeply interested in medical and experimental science. He encouraged the careers of several women scientists. As pope, he oversaw the hiring of an experimental physicist to fill a vacant chair at La Sapienza (University of

Rome) and established a School of Surgery at the University of Bologna. He somewhat notoriously maintained a correspondence with Voltaire, accepting the dedication of Voltaire's play *Mahomet* to him and sending a gold medal as a token of thanks. In response to the criticism he received on this account, he asserted the necessity of maintaining contact with the *philosophes* as a way of preserving their connection to the Church—even while eventually conceding that certain of Voltaire's works did belong on the Index. As pope, he became convinced that the Congregation of the Index was becoming capricious in condemning books; the ambiguity and disarray surrounding the eventual condemnation of Montesquieu's *L'Esprit des Lois* was one of the factors that led Benedict to initiate the largest-scale reform of the Index undertaken between the beginning of the seventeenth century and the end of the nineteenth.[30]

The bull published to accompany the reforms of the Index and its procedures, *Sollicita ac Provida* (1753), reflects the sensibility of someone who, while not questioning the right and duty of censorship, wants it to limit intellectual freedom as little as possible. It included numerous provisions to ensure fairness and impartiality in the examination of questionable writings. It specified that a book had to be denounced first by someone not in the Holy Office and in a position to make such a judgment; that is, the Congregation of the Index could not seek books out in order to condemn them. It spelled out procedures that ensured multiple levels of review, ending in a final condemnation only by the pope himself. In addition the bull specified that only qualified readers do the evaluating, that passages not be taken out of context, that authors be able to defend their work, that the Congregation's work be kept confidential to protect an author's reputation, that the consultors not present their own ideas as official doctrine, even that the tone of the Congregation's report not be scolding or abusive.[31]

Prescribing impartiality and fairness does not ensure their delivery, of course, nor does it answer deeper questions about the wisdom of censorship as a mechanism of control. But it does reflect an attempt to continue to grapple with changing intellectual and cultural conditions, an attempt that was largely derailed by the upheavals of the century and a half after Benedict's death in 1758.

According to much of the conventional historiography of the early modern era, the effect of post-Trent censorship and the general attitude of the church hierarchy toward the scientific revolution and the ideas of the Protestant Reformation was very nearly unequivocal. "From that beginning [i.e., Sarpi's *Istoria del Concilio Tridentino* (1619)], Italian culture in the later sixteenth and seventeenth centuries came to be characterized with one

word: decline."[32] The Index has long been associated with a generally repressive intellectual context to which was attributed, from as early as the
beginning of the seventeenth century, a long and permanent cultural decline especially apparent in those lands where the Church was most dominant. Eisenstein quotes a 1965 history of *Science and Civil Life*: "Everything
vital and new that had been produced during a century and half of cultural
effort was now being mutilated and suppressed."[33] That "everything" is both
inaccurate and instructive. The evidence is clear that, although the mutila-
tion and suppression were real phenomena, at the same time a number of
"vital and new" things were supported and encouraged. But the sweeping
nature of the assertion ("everything vital and new") suggests that at some
point the complexity of the evidence and the possible stories to be constructed from it were flattened out into a univocal narrative in which the vital
and the new were by definition not only not Catholic but actively opposed by
church authorities.

Among historians of the early modern era, this univocal narrative became dominant in the nineteenth century. In response as much to the political upheavals of the age of revolutions as to the philosophical challenges
of the Enlightenment, the Church by the middle of the century stood quite
clearly (if perhaps somewhat understandably) against the major intellectual
currents of the century. At precisely the time that the modern research university was defining itself in the United States, Roman Catholicism and the
Roman Catholic Church seemed ever more tangibly to be the opponent of
progress and the new. The immediate background for U.S. Catholic intellectual work in the twentieth century, then, was the most antiliberal moment in Catholic history.[34] Instead of the variability and flexibility that had
at least intermittently characterized Catholic responses to earlier intellectual
revolutions, the nineteenth century saw the Syllabus of Errors and the definition of papal infallibility. The same convulsive changes that gave rise to
the intellectual stance that resulted in the condemnation of modernism in
1907 ensured that censorship remained front and center—for much of the
nineteenth century less a delicately applied last resort than a blunt instrument ready at hand. Questions about censorship were prevalent enough by
the middle of the nineteenth century that a number of bishops, particularly
from Germany and France, pressed the First Vatican Council (1869–70) to
include some "mitigation of the ecclesiastical laws" as part of the Council's
agenda, but that did not happen. Apparently as a result, Pius IX's successor,
Leo XIII, considered reform of the censorship legislation to be part of his
responsibility on taking office in 1878. Leo's reform produced the system
that would remain in place for most of the twentieth century and in light of

which U.S. Catholic scholars and artists had to determine their sense of themselves and their work.

By the middle of the nineteenth century and increasingly into the first two decades of the twentieth, U.S. Catholic scholars and intellectuals had to navigate a rocky course. U.S. scholars narrating their own intellectual history looked back over the preceding centuries and saw intellectual movement and energy in precisely those areas where Protestantism had been most successful (England, Netherlands, northern Germany) and intellectual and cultural decline in areas that remained predominantly Catholic (Italy, Spain, southern Germany), and this narrative played into nationalist-cultural self-definition among the U.S. intellectuals and academics seeking a native intellectual tradition consistent with WASP hegemony of American cultural life.[35] By the twentieth century, most Catholic accounts of the history of church censorship were explicit counternarratives to the belief that an incontrovertible decline of Catholic European intellectual culture was directly traceable to the intellectually repressive atmosphere and procedures of the Tridentine and post-Tridentine Church. Twentieth-century Catholics writing about censorship, then, had to construct a counternarrative that would bear the full historiographic weight of an entire profession and three centuries.

Twentieth-Century Regulation of Reading and Publication

In 1897 Leo XIII issued a new apostolic constitution on censorship, *Officiorum ac munerum*, and in 1900 approved the revisions of the Index (the first new one to be published since Benedict XIV) and of the Congregation's procedures.[36] The revised Index dropped all titles dating from before 1600, with the explicit warning that the force of their condemnation still applied—the Church was not changing its mind or its principles, but recognizing that changed circumstances meant that certain debates and arguments no longer retained their controversial force. The reforms also removed a long-standing prohibition on a variety of medieval, early church, and classical titles, though again maintaining the caution that readers should take seriously the reasons for the earlier condemnation and guard against any threat the works might pose to an individual reader's faith. In this revision, as in Benedict XIV's, a guiding principle was whether a rule regarding reading and publication had been observed; if it had widely fallen by the wayside, that was taken as evidence for abandoning it. This is, for example, how the

limiting of the scope of censorship only to matters of faith and morals became an explicit part of the law, because while a wider scope was prescribed
it was never enforced or observed.

The constitution *Officiorum ac munerum* identifies "the uncurbed freedom
of writing and publishing noxious literature" as the "most perilous" of all
the "stratagems and hurtful devices of the enemy" in the modern warfare
necessary to defend Christian faith and morals from constant attack.[37] As
does almost every explanation and justification for censorship, the constitution rehearses the history of censorship from St. Paul to the First Vatican
Council and goes on to say that the current revision was aimed primarily at
making the rules "somewhat milder, so that it cannot be difficult or irksome
for any person of goodwill to obey them" (411). It reiterates the right and
obligation of the church to condemn heretical, superstitious, and immoral
books; books insulting to Catholicism or crucial elements of it (such as
Mary and the saints); and books or images related to scripture, and to liturgical and devotional practice, that had not been approved before publication. It concludes by specifying the rules governing the Index—who has
the power to enforce it, how to gain exemptions from its obligations, etc.,
and by specifying regulations for previous censorship.

Leo's 1900 revision of the Index, along with the 1897 *Officiorum ac
munerum* and Benedict's 1753 *Sollicita ac Provida*, was incorporated into the
1917 revision of the Code of Canon Law and remained the relevant ecclesiastical legislation for most of the twentieth century. They should be understood within the context of the 1907 condemnation of modernism, as
the encyclical announcing the condemnation, *Pascendi dominici gregis*, emphasized the role books played in spreading modernist ideas. *Pascendi* attempted to counter this spread by reiterating the requirement that every
diocese appoint a censor to review books before they were published
(para. 52).

The relevant sections of the 1917 Code of Canon Law were canons
1384–1405, translation and explication of which formed the core of most
works on censorship, short or long, scholarly or pastoral, in the twentieth
century. These canons fell within the section of the 1917 Code concerned
with the teaching mission of the church, reflecting once again the close
connection between control of print and orthodoxy in doctrine. Canon
1384 asserts the right of the church to prevent the faithful from publishing
books not previously approved, as well as to prohibit those already published. Sections 1385 through 1394 detail the categories of published work
requiring previous censorship (*censura praevia*)—examination by ecclesiastical authorities and formal permission to publish. Works requiring prior

censorship included editions of scripture intended for a Catholic readership (including scriptural commentaries), theological works, devotional works, works generally concerned with religion and theology, and devotional images. Permission to publish was to be sought from the local bishop or from the superior for members of religious orders or congregations. Clergy and religious were required to obtain permission before publishing anything on any subject; laity, while required to obtain ecclesiastical permission only to publish works on faith and morals, were admonished not to write for publications that attacked Catholicism or faith and morals. Translations of liturgical and devotional texts required new approval.

The Code also specified that every diocese was to have a designated censor, who should be a mature person of learning and judgment, able to steer a middle course in a dispute (Canon 1393, §3: *qui in doctrinis probandis improbandisque medio tutoque itinere eant*).[38] The censor was required to give his opinion of a work submitted for review in writing, along with the verdict of *nihil obstat* if there was "nothing objectionable" in the work in question. The bishop was to grant an *imprimatur* ("it may be printed") as permission to publish.

Canons 1395 through 1405 dealt with the prohibition of books already published. They clarified who had the power to prohibit books—any "ordinary" (someone with episcopal authority over a given community; in practice the term usually refers to a bishop in a diocese), plus abbots and religious superiors. The pope could prohibit a book for the whole church everywhere. Canon 1397 also includes the *obligation* to denounce books believed to be pernicious, an obligation that applied to all the faithful but especially to those with authority; that is, priests and bishops. "Prohibited" was defined to mean that a work could not be published, read, sold, kept, translated, or communicated in any way.

Canon 1399 was a centerpiece of the works that explained and translated canon law for ordinary readers, because by its enumeration of the *classes* of prohibited books it most explicitly laid out the obligations of canon law regarding reading and publication for someone not connected with the hierarchy or the book trade. The following twelve classes of works were prohibited to Catholic readers: all versions of scripture published by non-Catholics; works defending heresy or schism, or undermining religion; works attacking religion or good morals; books written on religion by non-Catholics, unless it was certain they contained nothing contrary to Catholic doctrine; any version of scripture (including notes and commentary) and any works claiming to document new revelations or miracles, unless they were submitted for prior censorship; works that disparaged or ridiculed Catholic dogma or practice; works that encouraged superstition, spiritism, or magic; works that defended dueling, suicide, divorce, or Freemasonry; books that were *ex professo* [as their main purpose] obscene; liturgical books in which any changes from the officially approved form had been made; works of spurious or revoked indulgences; sacred images not in keeping with the "meaning and decrees" of the Church.

The remaining sections of canon law devoted to the regulation of reading and publication detail first how prohibitions applied to various classes of people. Theology students, for example, were exempt from the prohibition related to scripture (they could read vernacular translations and versions in original languages without prior censorship), and cardinals and bishops were exempt from the prohibition of books but not from prior censorship. The remaining sections outline who had the authority to grant permission to read forbidden books, what that permission covered and what it did not, and the obligations of Catholic booksellers. Canon 1405 in conclusion reasserted the precedence of natural law—even official permission to read a prohibited book did not exempt someone from the obligation not to read something that would lead them into sin. Those in positions of authority were once again reminded of their obligation to warn others of the dangers inherent in reading bad books (*librorum pravorum*).

The machinery of the Index—the rules for its procedures and functioning—was not part of canon law, but was instead codified in the apostolic constitutions and carried out by the Congregation of the Holy Office, then by the Congregation for the Index (from 1571 to 1917), then again by the Congregation of the Holy Office. A book recommended or denounced to the Congregation of the Holy Office was sent first to one individual (consultor, censor, qualificator—usually a cardinal, always a member of the clergy) to examine and render an opinion. That initial report then went to all the consultors appointed by the congregation, who voted whether to recommend that the book be forbidden, and then forwarded their recommendation to the cardinals who made up the Congregation. Their vote and report were then in turn to be passed on to the Pope for the final word. The recommendation could specify that a book should not be listed on the Index, that it should be forbidden unless read in an expurgated edition (*donec expurgator*) or until corrected (*donec corrigatur*), or that it merited condemnation. If the author of a book were Catholic, the agreement of two censors that a book should be condemned was required before the consultors sent the recommendation on to the cardinals. The rules specified that the censors and consultors be "men of virtue and of learning, of ma-

ture judgment and of absolute impartiality" and "have a very good knowledge of the subject treated in it, acquired through years of labor and study."[39]

The procedures as regularized by Benedict XIV in the mid-eighteenth
century were still those in place in 1917; they remained largely unchanged
until the next major revision of canon law, which was promulgated in 1983.
As such, they were part of the landscape for those engaged in Catholic print
culture. For example, the "Chronicle" section of a 1924 issue of the *Catholic Historical Review* might include a brief item noting that a "well-known
Catholic newspaper" had erroneously announced that a *Manuel Biblique* often used in U.S. seminary study had been placed on the Index of Forbidden
Books, and clarifying which volume actually was involved.[40] And one of
the very earliest issues of *The Catholic Library World* (when it was still mimeo-
graphed rather than printed) included an article intended to help reference
librarians answer questions such as "Is such a book on the Index? If so, why?
What books are placed on the Index?"—which, the author (Catholic University of America librarian H. Joseph Schneider) notes, "Any librarian
knows by experience . . . are asked quite frequently."[41] Even in the denser
and more coherent subculture that characterized much of interwar U.S.
Catholic life, this system of regulation was so arcane and foreign that it
required constant translation and explanation, and frequent correction of
misunderstandings and misapplications, even for those—writers, readers,
publishers, editors, librarians, and others—most involved with Catholic
print culture in the twentieth century.

CHAPTER 5

Censorship in the Land of "Thinking on One's Own"

Despite the various attempts at revising and modernizing the mechanisms and legal framework of censorship, by the time the 1917 Code of Canon Law was promulgated, even to many contemporaries censorship was an anachronism. Nevertheless, readers, writers, and other participants in the print culture of U.S. Catholicism were officially bound by it, and needed ways of navigating it within the cultural, intellectual, and commercial context of the United States. The system of Roman Catholic censorship had to be translated and rationalized for internal and external audiences, a project undertaken by a wide variety of participants in Catholic print culture. These translations and rationales not only deal with the complexities of print culture, but extend into popular media more generally and beyond that into discussions about the place of Catholicism in twentieth-century American life.

To continue to function in the twentieth-century United States, the Index had to be translated in a variety of senses. The Latin that still constituted the language of official church documentation needed to be translated into English (at the same time that certain English-based neologisms were being added to Latin in order to talk about things that it did not have words for). The legal terminology of canon law (the legal code and system by which Roman Catholicism regulated itself as a polity) needed to be translated into straightforward obligations applicable to the lives of ordinary believers as readers and writers. And most broadly, the presumptions about human relationships and obligations underlying canon law's ecclesiastical language and its philosophical and theological reasoning needed to be translated culturally into a language, a set of ideas, and a repertoire of rhetorical strategies that were defensibly modern and defensibly American.

The Work of Translation

This translation and transmission happened in part in the classroom. John Bonn includes in his lecture notes entitled "The Moral Effect of Literature" these fairly technical specifications about the obligations imposed by the Index on ordinary readers: "The Index forbids the reading of books not condemned by the natural law, only without permission and for valid reason. Such permission may be obtained from a confessor with faculties. If one confessor refuses another may be approached."[1] Immediately qualifying the Index's prohibitory function with the assurance that anyone who had a valid reason to read a book on it was a standard feature of these explanations, emphasizing the compatibility of the existence of the Index with legitimate scholarly work. While students may have been likely to learn of the existence and purpose of the Index as part of undergraduate education, it seems to have had an effect on the work and consciousness primarily of those who went on to pursue graduate work.

The classroom was far from the only site within which the Index was presented and explained to Catholic readers. Translating the Index literally and figuratively for an American audience produced a distinct subgenre in U.S. Catholic print culture. The four most widely cited book-length works were Francis Betten's *The Roman Index of Forbidden Books Briefly Explained* (originally published in 1909, revised and republished until at least 1940), Joseph Maria Pernicone's *Ecclesiastical Prohibition of Books* (a 1932 canon law thesis at the Catholic University of America), Redmond A. Burke's *What Is the Index?* (originally a 1948 thesis in library science at the University of Chicago, published as a book in 1952 and currently held by 536 libraries, according to WorldCat), and *The Catholic Viewpoint on Censorship* by Harold C. Gardiner, SJ (reviewed in the *New York Times Book Review* in 1958). In addition, the entries in the 1913 *Catholic Encyclopedia* on "Censorship of Books" and "Index of Prohibited Books" are important out of proportion to a typical reference work entry, partly because of the prominence of the *Encyclopedia* and partly because of their author. Joseph Hilgers, a German Jesuit who participated in the revision of censorship legislation under

Leo XIII, was the author of *Der Index der Verbotenen Bucher*, the most extensive and most recent account of the Index available during the time under
study here.[2] The book-length work was never translated into English, but
Hilger's *Catholic Encyclopedia* entries made at least the broad outlines of his
scholarship and his narrative of the history of censorship widely available.

All these works were well known and widely cited in both Catholic and
secular publications. Although they ranged over time and differed somewhat
in intended audience, they had a number of crucial features in common:
their authors were all priests (who had close to a monopoly on theological
education for much of the twentieth century), and the main source and rationale for their analyses lay in the canon law of the Church. As a result, the
histories and justifications they presented for church regulation of reading
and publication were very similar. Other publications relied heavily on these
book-length analyses, so there is a great deal of commonality and consistency in the explanations and rationales for censorship in Catholic print
culture in the first half of the twentieth century.

Even sources with a popular or pedagogical focus rely on and seek to
impart a working knowledge of key philosophical notions. A 1939 study
outline entitled "The Index," published in the *Journal of Religious Instruction*,
suggested beginning with "The Natural Moral Law and Limitations on
Reading."[3] Explaining a believer's obligations under canon law required
distinguishing it from and relating it to natural law. That is, a believer acquired by baptism the obligation to obey canon law, because it reflected the
teaching authority of the church. But canon law was not coextensive
with the natural moral law that Thomistic philosophy argued applied to
all human beings, whether baptized Roman Catholic or not, because, as the
Church maintained, of the way God created the world. These distinctions
were important because they became the basis for extended and sophisticated discussions of the role of conscience and the possibility of collaboration and solidarity with people of other faiths. The distinctions could become
narrowly technical; for example, the specialized pages of the *American Ecclesiastical Review* or the *Homiletic and Pastoral Review*, directly primarily at clergy,
included extended examination of legal questions such as the precise definition of "keeping" a forbidden book—in what sense did it apply to librarians?
bookbinders? servants? Could one keep a book that had lost its relevance as
an argument and become more of an art object or historical artifact?[4] Did
the prohibition on a forbidden book also apply to a movie made from the
book?[5] At the same time, the fineness of these distinctions and the precision
of the categories reflected a notable respect for the philosophical capacity of
the ordinary believer.

The translation and explanation of the technicalities of canon law appeared not only in publications directed toward the clergy. Similar questions were as likely to appear and be seriously addressed for a different audience in pastoral or popular periodicals such as *Our Sunday Visitor* or *Ave Maria*. Information about the Index and other aspects of censorship appeared at some point in virtually every Catholic periodical. Editors of publications directed to both popular and scholarly Catholic audiences saw the need at some point to explain the Church's system of censorship—or at least some particular confusion or obstacle—to their readers. In order to understand, explain, and abide by the Church's laws and institutions, the faithful needed good information about what was and was not required, and how the mechanisms that guarded the faith were intended to function. In order to "avoid bad books," readers had to have a reasonably clear idea of what the term was meant to convey.

While the Index loomed large in any discussion or explanation of church law on censorship, it was not the most important factor in most individuals' reading. Most explanatory accounts of censorship regulations emphasize the point that the vast majority of works on the Index were philosophical and theological treatises, of interest only to scholars. William Kerrigan chattily advised readers of the Davenport, Iowa, *Catholic Messenger* (and, a few weeks later, of the *Catholic Digest*): "If someone tells you that some popular book is on the Index, ask him whether he saw it there with his own eyes. If he didn't, bet a thousand to one that it's not there at all."[6] By virtue of both church teaching and natural law, however, believers had the obligation to learn to recognize and seek out good books—or, at the very least, books that were not harmful—and the more general regulations of canon law existed to that end.

Time and again the explanatory works referred readers to Canon 1399, which enumerated the twelve classes of prohibited books, in order to be clear about the obligations most likely to affect the ordinary reader. Many of these were relatively straightforward (such as reading only approved translations of the Bible), but most commentators spent some time explicating the prohibition of books that were "*ex professo*"—as their main or major purpose for existing—obscene. These explications cut two ways. Some were attempting to check excessively moralistic interpretations by making clear that the prohibition was not against any depictions of the complexity of human life or the existence of evil. Others, though, emphasized the sentinel role that knowledge of canon law could play for those easily tempted by the pleasures of fiction to ignore or minimize the Church's moral law. "Don't waste your time reading things like *Forever Amber*," Kerrigan goes on to say, "but don't judge rashly all the people who have read it, either, nor let anybody think that the Church dignifies such books by putting them on the Index."[7] The larger point in most such admonitions was that knowing and loving good literature was the best safeguard against not only aesthetically but morally inferior work. Although these explanations of ordinary readers' obligations under canon law were grounded in fairly heady metaphysics, in stance and tone they most often stayed in the realm of common sense and the matter-of-fact. They downplayed the strangeness of the Index, and indicated that the vast majority of what obedience to canon law required was what reasonable and respectable people would want for themselves anyway.

Censorship and Catholic Scholars

By contrast, the argument that the Index and canon law regarding reading and publication would have little effect on their work was inadequate reassurance to the subset of believing readers who were also scholars and intellectuals. As they sought credibility and recognition within U.S. intellectual and academic culture, while at the same time acknowledging the Church's obligation and authority to preserve the integrity of doctrine, Catholic scholars could not escape the fact that many, if not most, of the greatest hits of philosophical modernity were prominently—some thought scandalously— included on the Index. Francis Bacon, Thomas Hobbes, René Descartes, John Locke, François Voltaire, David Hume, Denis Diderot, Immanuel Kant, Jeremy Bentham, John Stuart Mill—it is probably difficult to exaggerate the sense of frustration and displacement Catholic intellectuals expressed when they observed the disconnect between the roster of modern philosophical achievement and their own self-understanding of the Church as one of the historic guardians and cultivators of philosophical greatness.

The nonphilosophical works on the Index increased this sense of distance. Literature never formed a large percentage of condemned works but contributed to the impression that the church was intractably opposed to the modern because of the increased pace with which contemporary fiction was condemned during the nineteenth century: Samuel Richardson, Stendhal, Honoré de Balzac, Victor Hugo, Alexandre Dumas *père* and *fils*, George Sand, Gustave Flaubert, Émile Zola, and Anatole France.[8] (Only a small percentage of books on the Index were in English; there were no American novels.) In addition, the tendency to condemn the very things that defined the modern in art and in thought had an internecine dimension that was difficult to explain—among condemned works were ones by Descartes,

Blaise Pascal (*The Provincial Letters*) and Lord Acton (*History of the Vatican Council*). Theological modernism probably intensified this phenomenon; it seemed as if those Catholics most sincerely engaged with sorting out how Catholicism might relate effectively to modernity were precisely those most vulnerable to condemnation. Both externally and internally, observers could not escape the sense that the Church's most interesting minds could not be both creative and faithful in engaging contemporary issues.

The procedures by which the Index operated served to make the distance seem even more unbridgeable. The reasons for a book's being placed on the Index were never made public, nor were the arguments made in the reports submitted by the consultors. What would be announced in Latin in *Acta Apostolicae Sedes* and reprinted shortly thereafter in English in *Homiletic and Pastoral Review* were the fact of the condemnation and under which canon it was being made. The stated reason for keeping the Congregation's deliberation secret was to protect the reputation of the author, though the vacuum left by the absence of an explanation allowed speculation to flourish without counter.

These provisions presume a certain portrait of the Catholic scholar and vision of the scholarly life in which regulation regarding reading and publication can fit seamlessly and without conflict. First, virtually every account of censorship regulations included the assurance that anyone with a valid reason to read a forbidden book could readily obtain permission to do so. Scholars and advanced students could obtain permission, sometimes virtually blanket permission, to read works on the Index. Canon law contained some complexities about certain kinds of condemnations for which only the pope could grant exceptions, but ordinarily someone's confessor could grant the permission. One interviewee believed that the faculty and administration at her small Catholic women's college in the 1950s had blanket permission from the local bishop to assign any work in their classes.[9] Index apologists explained these provisions in a mild expository tone, reassuring readers that the Church's regulation of reading and publication could never be an obstacle to scholarship or any other legitimate professional necessity.

What remained a stumbling block from the standpoint of American conceptions of intellectual work was the question of what might constitute a valid reason. For explicators of Catholics' obligations under canon law, reading forbidden works was limited primarily to those who would refute the arguments they contained. Simple intellectual curiosity or the desire to be familiar with current controversy was not sufficient reason. Time and again the explanatory works emphasized that even the oldest and wisest, most educated, most devout Catholic was not exempt from this provision.

Freedom of inquiry was never and for no one exempt from the obligation to take the laws of the Church into account. Perhaps here as nowhere else the gulf between Catholic conceptions of intellectual and artistic autonomy and those of their compatriots and contemporaries becomes apparent. Even simply characterizing the Catholic views as "intellectual" requires a significant redefinition of the idea of intellectual work and the intellectual life, and of the person and psyche of the intellectual.

One means by which this redefinition took place was in the telling of exemplary stories about scholars who observed, and did not observe, the church's admonitions in their approach to works listed on the Index. These parables included Francis Betten's tale "of a priest, who was in every way a model man. He suddenly fell away from the Church, married, and died as a foremost champion in the ranks of the enemy. His apostasy is, not without reason, attributed to the reading of infidel books, though no doubt he had the necessary dispensation." Betten continues, "There was another priest who has meanwhile died the death of the just, a celebrated author and art critic. In writing a work on Voltaire he had to study the books of that arch-agnostic. He obtained the requisite permission, but, while perusing Voltaire's writings, he was on his knees to implore, as it were, by this humble posture, the protection of God against the wicked influence to which he was exposed."[10] Reported accounts of contemporary cases need to be taken with a grain of salt, but they often exhorted a similar attitude. *America* in 1936 told the story of Luis G. Alonso Getino, OP, who found out while reading the evening paper that a book of his had been placed on the Index.[11] His reaction: "At once . . . I went to the chapel to cast myself at the feet of Our Lord in the Blessed Sacrament (in whose honor I had written the book), and made at once an act of submission to the Holy See." He then, according to this account, took steps to make sure an amended version would not be published before review by the Holy Office. "People may say of me that I have made many mistakes; but I trust that no one will ever say that I disobeyed even one single time the supreme authority of the Church." *America*'s "Pilgrim" noted approvingly, "Such conduct is not a matter of human calculation nor of human origin. It rests upon a Divine Faith in the authority of the Church as conveying the authority of the God-Man who founded it."[12]

Here is the crux of the difference—and distance—between Catholic understandings of scholarly work and those of their compatriots. Instead of an autonomous seeking after the unknown, Catholics envisioned service to the truth as the highest, and freest, calling. This view places humility—understood thickly and historically as an intellectual virtue—at the center of scholarly inquiry. The often exasperated Bakewell Morrison, charged with reading the work of the very prolific Daniel Lord, amended one report with the almost involuntary concession, "I am really moved by Father Lord's intellectual humility. I withdraw my objections and so judge that the pamphlet may be printed."[13] Catholic scholars defined humility in this context not as mindless obedience to authority regardless of truth, but as the necessary submission of the intellect to reality and to truth. Within emerging contemporary intellectual frameworks that questioned the possibility or desirability of certainty in knowing truth, and that considered such ambivalence the requisite stance for a democratic citizenry, such submission placed someone beyond the boundaries of intellectual work.[14] But for a number of Catholic scholars writing about this dilemma, it was a key source of something like serenity. The search for truth, intellectual integrity, even academic freedom, was possible precisely *because* of the belief that reality would push back; honest scholars could therefore explore fearlessly.

The explanatory works also told real-life cautionary tales of what could happen if the appropriate attitude were missing. Will Durant's life in particular was presented as an example of the dangers of forbidden reading, as he admitted publicly that he had lost his faith through reading a wide range of works, regardless of whether they had been approved by the Church. "My curiosity," Durant wrote in *Transition: A Sentimental Story of One Mind and One Era*, "continued to prove greater than my respect for my immortal soul. . . . I concluded that almost every independent spirit of the nineteenth century had been an agnostic or an infidel."[15] Daniel Lord held up Durant's experience as an example in his 1930 pamphlet "I Can Read Anything! All Right. Then Read This," in which Father Hall reminds the teenage Dick and Sue that Durant was a "Catholic-college graduate" who "No doubt . . . was quite sure at the beginning that he knew the answer to every difficulty that could arise. . . . Yet within a matter of months he was tortured by doubts, then stripped of belief, and finally was left utterly without faith in anything supernatural."[16] In response to Dick's objection that it was necessary to see "two sides to every question," Father Hall reassures him that any Catholic work would give a full and fair account of the opposing position before effectively refuting it. In his 1955 autobiography, *Played by Ear*, Lord attributed his own temporary (*circa* 1906) loss of faith to indiscriminate reading, his return to reading a "long series of Catholic books which have presented our side of the question and made such a defense of God, Christ, the Church, and Christian morality that the other side seems fireworks, froth on the beer, icing on the cake and veritable moonshine."[17] Joseph Pernicone also invoked Durant's fate early in *The Ecclesiastical Prohibition of Books* in order to establish the enduring need for the Church's vigilance over reading.[18] For scholars as much as, and even more than, for ordinary readers, preserving one's faith took precedence over every other intellectual obligation, and any intellectual path that put it in jeopardy was barred. In both the rationales they constructed and the stories they told, Catholic defenders of the Church's system of regulation of reading and publication maintained that this commitment put no meaningful limits on intellectual freedom, because all legitimate paths of inquiry were open to scholars and to travel on barred paths was by definition not to be free.

The portrait of the reading life that emerges from these explanations and defenses is eminently orderly—the imagined reader is a believer aware of the purpose and end of the universe, capable of the self-control necessary to keep one's mind always on things of ultimate importance while not neglecting the joys of the created world, attentive and obedient to the loving command of the Church but also intellectually mature and independent of judgment. How did this aspirational vision of harmony among life, belief, and art play out in the lives of readers, writers, publishers, scholars—and censors? Did the Church's program for the control of reading and publication actually work?

Censorship in Practice

Although prescriptive evidence for censorship's functioning abounds, evidence demonstrating how prescriptions functioned in the lives of readers and writers is fragmentary and largely unrepresentative. Especially from the standpoint of the cultural historian, this question may not even be the most fruitful one to ask—it is worth pausing to examine assumptions about what compliance or lack thereof might actually indicate. Would 100 percent compliance with the Church's law regulating reading and publication be good news or bad news? Either perspective could yield a dreary morality tale devoid of historical insight.

U.S. Catholic censorship in the early and mid-twentieth century reflected the features of the literary and ecclesiastical culture that produced it. In practice it structured relationships among those involved in literary production and other intellectual activity in such a way as to bridge the gulfs it had helped to create. In having to make something so inescapably premodern compatible with modernity—at least in the de facto sense that people living in the modern era sought to find a way to function within the system—Catholics bridged a gap that was supposedly unbridgeable. It might have been a makeshift, temporary and somewhat shaky bridge, but it functioned well enough to get some key minds across to a spot where they could take up the work waiting for them on the other side.

The relationships structured by censorship in practice were hierarchical, but the dynamic of authority and obedience, dominance and subordination, was not their sole nor even their most salient characteristic. Because, it can be argued, the relationship between hierarchy and faithful within Roman Catholic polity is by definition never *not* hierarchical, what is important is how hierarchy manifests itself and what results from its form and stance in a given situation. In practice, censorship regulation in the United States was highly decentralized, allowing for a flourishing rhetoric of individual responsibility and communal solidarity that helped to bridge the gap between Counter-Reformation church discipline and modern American understandings of the mature ethical self.

Decentralized hierarchy seems oxymoronic, but it is a distinctive feature of Roman Catholic polity. Within the defined limits of canon law, a bishop's authority in his diocese is paramount. He is accountable not through a chain of command of archbishops and cardinals and nuncios and curial secretaries, but directly and only to the pope. As a result, the structures for Church censorship in the United States seem to have varied considerably over time and place. For example, the requirement, specified in *Pascendi dominici gregis* and incorporated into the 1917 Code of Canon Law, that every diocese appoint an official censor seems to have been variably implemented. Whereas "one authority has suggested that there should be at least six censors in every diocese, so that no author would be able to determine the identity of the one chosen to examine and approve his manuscript,"[19] evidence from the *Catholic Directory* suggests that outside the very largest dioceses there were seldom more than two censors officially appointed. A number of dioceses list no censors for at least some of the years investigated.[20] In most cases, censors held other offices in the diocese simultaneously; many remained in the position for more than a decade. This variation makes a great deal of pragmatic sense—dioceses that included within their boundaries many universities, or cities that were centers for publishing, would need an efficiently functioning censorship system in order to keep up with the volume. In dioceses where the demand was less the position could be part-time, perhaps even ad hoc (though strictly speaking that would not be in keeping with the specifics of canon law).

Other day-to-day ambiguities about what canon law actually required make clear that the system was far from monolithic. For example, an inquiry from the secretary of the indefatigable Daniel Lord, Marian Prendergast, to

Lord's provincial, Rev. William J. Fitzgerald, SJ, went as follows: "So far the children's books published by Mr. Lowe have carried the imprimatur of the Archbishop of New York but have not had the imprimi potest of Father Provincial. Do you think this should be added to books in the future or would you think cum permissu superiorum would be sufficient." A reply typewritten below on the same sheet, "'Cum permissu Superiorum' O.K.," answers the question, but then a new paragraph goes on to ask, "I have no record of any of these books. Have someone in the office send me a notice as each one goes to press." Prendergast responded with a list of works and the names of the relevant censors.[21]

This example also makes clear another feature of the relationships that were structured by censorship in practice—their multiplicity. Writer and longtime secretary, Jesuit priest and provincial superior, religious superior and bishop (of the diocese in which the books were published, not that in which the author resided), secular publisher and religious community. Far from a simplistic one-way vector of authority-submission between bishop and writer, in practice the requirement of censorship could create (and strain) relationships within which a variety of simultaneous commitments were negotiated and refined. These relationships were not solely structured by hierarchical authority, but were also animated by a sense of solidarity in being engaged in the same enterprise. This solidarity could manifest as mundane tending to administrative procedure or as urgent exhortation to the protection and defense of truth, but in every guise it reflected the Catholic insistence on the interdependence of art, intellectual work, and beliefs about the ultimate nature of reality.

Thus, although censorship was frequently a flashpoint of controversy over the position of the Church in the twentieth-century United States, in the background was a matter-of-fact system of implementation within which censorship existed as one of many administrative responsibilities of a diocese. Interview evidence suggests that for many people as students, readers, and teachers, it was simply one feature of a varied landscape. One interviewee noted explicitly that he and others realized at the time and were quite aware in retrospect that censorship was considered by some both inside and outside of the church laughable and intellectually suspect. His reaction to this attitude was a kind of bemused resignation—he understood it, but he also saw the Church's position as complicated. The responsibility to protect doctrine was real, there were things in the world that could genuinely threaten belief, and how to design a system by which all of the various needs were respected was a complicated question. And many people were inclined to trust the Church in deciding how to approach these complexities.[22]

Solidarity did not guarantee harmony. In the case of E. Boyd-Barrett, author of a series of articles on the "New Psychology" in *America* magazine in 1924–25, there was conflict at the levels of both ideas and structure. Barrett's confidence in the potential of the New Psychology was so great that he presented it with almost no caveats, which apparently alarmed some of his confreres. Four articles in Barrett's announced series had appeared when his provincial sent a letter to the editor of *America*, Rev. Richard H. Tierney, asking, "Kindly let me have all future contributions of Father Boyd Barrett for censorship."[23] Kelly's request touched off a dispute both about the substance of the articles and about where the authority for censorship lay. To *America*'s editors, the problem was twofold—on the issue of authority, as one of their number, Joseph Husslein, SJ, wrote, no one except the "Moderator [editor]" was required to be consulted about censorship, although "any single Provincial" was free to "express his views to the Moderator."

The deeper, more neuralgic problem seemed to be over the extent to which new ideas could be examined before running up against the boundaries of orthodoxy. Husslein follows his judgment about where censorship authority lay in canon law with an additional editorial comment: "In regard to the subject of the New Psychology, I may add, that members of the AMERICA staff have given deep and long study to it, while on the other hand, their carefully weighted judgment is impugned, without citing any specific instances, by men who may be far less qualified to judge in this particular matter." An additional report, from Peter M. Dunne, SJ, concurs: "Concerning Father Barrett's articles and the objections raised against them, it is my opinion that the criticisms are another example of scholars taking alarm without sufficient objective reasons. Sometimes certain scholars, not abreast of modern thought, confuse what is new with what is unorthodox, and what may not be in their view Scholastic with what is not Catholic."

One additional response, from Francis X. Talbot, SJ, suggests the substance of the orthodoxy being questioned: "If the articles are 'offensive' in a general way—either through subject matter, through a harmful tendency, through a too frank expression or exposition, through suggestiveness, or through the possibility of being misunderstood—then the critics of the articles must state clearly their objections, and substantiate them."[24] Talbot's delineation of likely objections helps explain the subtle shifts in Barrett's articles as they appear. The first three give almost no indication that they are appearing in a Catholic periodical. The fourth, titled "Normal and Abnormal Impulses," includes the following disclaimer, "Without delaying to deal with this point of view, let us say *en passant* that no impulses have 'moral' quality, they do not spring from man's rational nature, nor from his deliberate will. They are amoral. They are neither morally good nor bad."[25] This article announces five more to complete the series: "wanderlust, cleptomania and pyromania, narcotomania, dipsomania and gamble-lust." The articles on "Wanderlust" and "Cleptomania" (which also treats pyromania) also include disclaimers that make clear the potential distance between "impulses" as understood in the New Psychology and the tradition of Catholic moral reasoning. "Wanderlust" concludes with a religious finish notably out of keeping with the preceding articles. "In good Christians the yearning for a higher and better world so possesses the heart, and the impatience to be on their way to God so stirs them, that they are often drawn impulsively to go on pilgrimages or to visit shrines. Their *wanderlust* is a sacred urge that impels them forward even on foot towards heaven." And "Cleptomania" similarly takes pains to locate the disorder within a Catholic moral framework. "In fine it must be emphasized that from a moral point of view, the strong impulse to commit theft, from whatever source it may ultimately be derived, does not necessarily destroy the accountability of the agent, but may merely lessen it, as is the case with any other violent impulse."[26] Both articles also switch to using the term "sensuous impulse" instead of the blunter "sex instinct"; probably responding to the objection Talbot characterizes as "too frank expression or exposition."

There does not seem to be any response or follow-up letter to this flurry of reports in the *America* magazine archives. But E. Boyd-Barrett's proposed articles on "narcotomania, dipsomania, and gamble-lust" did not appear in *America*.

A less fraught but equally complicated set of issues and relationships surrounded censorship in the case of Daniel Lord. As a Jesuit, Lord was required to submit everything he wrote to his superiors for censorship before it was submitted to the diocesan censors. Finding censors was a perennial task, as Lord's productivity was so great that reading and commenting on his writing required a great deal of time from many different people. Lord's prodigious output and his wide-ranging interests generated a certain amount of exasperation on the part of his censors. Deep and vehement differences in literary, theological, and political sensibility emerge in censor's reports and in Lord's responses to them, written to his superior. Lord's style, especially, came in for significant criticism—it was described at various times as "overwrought," "shallow," "cheap," "melodramatic," "undignified," and "insufferably priggish and mealymouthed." What is most likely revealed here is the disdain for popularizers (which Lord most assuredly was) held by those to whom a more refined literary sensibility was important. Most of these descriptions were nonetheless accompanied by a recommendation that the piece in question be published, as the censor's sole job was to identify any deviations from doctrine—they threw in the literary criticism for free.

Bakewell Morrison (b. 1894), himself a well-known writer on education, the sacraments, and the relationship between Catholicism and modernity, became over time a trusted commentator on Lord's writings, though he offered his share of devastating critique. Morrison's attitude seems to have softened over time, as he repeatedly found Lord to be remarkably "docile" and "humble" intellectually. His comments gradually become more personally addressed, apparently no longer anonymous. Among other things, he constantly exhorted Lord to refer to, quote from, or make some use of the encyclicals of Pius XII; for instance: "I am very anxious that the author add to his own authority and increase his value to the reader by adverting to the papal insistences."[27] Morrison consistently expressed a mix of exasperation at Lord's characteristic shortcomings (pleading at one point, "PLEASE, DAN, FIX IT UP. I've had too much trouble IN CLASS with the points I note to allow them to reach the general public in a careless form.") and appreciation for the value of Lord's topics and his approach to them.[28]

The case of Daniel Lord is atypical in numerous ways, and the dynamic of these particular relationships emerges largely from the distinctive setting of a religious order, in this case the Jesuits. But these relationships share key elements that characterized Catholic literary culture as a whole. Foremost was the dynamic of mutual accountability, the claims that community and authority made on intellectual freedom and autonomy. Those in positions of authority (religious superior, bishop, teacher) had a responsibility for the welfare of those in their charge; those under the authority of others had the responsibility of obedience, but of *mindful* obedience, the ability to see the reasonableness of what is required and to assent to it freely.[29] The role of individual conscience included as well the obligations articulated in Canon 1405 regarding natural law—no matter who permitted or even recommended a book, if it endangered a reader's faith it was not permitted. Whether as reader or writer, teacher or student, clerical or lay, intellectual or popularizer, Catholic literary culture required from its participants an awareness of and responsibility for how an individual's own behavior affected others. Those who wrote about censorship and control of print, like those who wrote about the nature and function of literature, had to do their best to take everybody into account—all classes, all stages of life, popular and serious, scholar and dilettante, teachers, librarians, servants, booksellers. The result is an extremely thoroughly imagined set of relationships among the participants in Catholic literary culture.

In practice this affirmed solidarity frayed with some frequency under the pressure of controversy and in the absence of relationships as sustained as that of Morrison and Lord. The same obligations, the ties that bound members of a community to each other, also deepened a variety of fissures. These divisions were particularly clear in the case of controverted issues. Censorship could be a blunt weapon ready at hand for those who saw need of it and had the power to employ it—this seems to be the primary way it functioned in the modernism controversy and other analogous struggles between the Church hierarchy and scholars exploring the relationship between Catholicism and modernity. A high percentage of the books (few, if any, of them by Americans) placed on the Index in the twentieth century were outgrowths in one way or another of the modernism controversy. Indeed, a key component of modernism's effect on twentieth-century U.S. Catholic intellectual history is the effect it had on what could be written and published.[30] From the perspective especially of the history of theology in the twentieth century, the Church's censorship system was a primary obstacle to many important avenues of theological scholarship.

Not surprisingly, interactions having to do with increasingly controverted teachings on sexual morality reflected the increasing controversy. Though the strain on the relationships that bound participants in Catholic print culture showed, in many cases the system remained malleable enough to accommodate a variety of interests. An example is the case of Dr. Leo Latz, who through his 1932 *The Rhythm of Sterility and Fertility in Women* was responsible for first publicizing the rhythm method of birth control for American audiences. Latz sought and received an imprimatur from the Archdiocese of Chicago, but was eventually asked by the chancery to change the title page of the book so as to moderate the endorsement. The reason for the request seems to have been complaints to the chancery about the prominent featuring of the imprimatur in an advertising pamphlet for the book. The change from the "imprimatur," which carried the name of the approving bishop, to the more generic "with ecclesiastical approval," would deflect the criticism directed at the diocese while still indicating that the book contained nothing contrary to Catholic doctrine.

Latz emphasized that he had sought and followed expert advice: "I had been cautioned by a friend of mine who has a great deal of experience with priests and especially with books destined for them, that it was of the utmost importance to be able to tell them that the book had the Imprimatur of diocesan authorities. There was danger that otherwise they would pay no attention to the book. And rightly so." At the same time he also made clear that he "had the title page in the three thousand copies of the first edition of my book 'The Rhythm' ripped out and a new title page with reading on the reverse side printed and pasted in." "The extra expense entailed," he continued, "will come close to one hundred dollars."[31] Including notice of an imprimatur was very common in advertising Catholic books to Catholic audiences, so the extra sensitivity here on both sides, as well as the bumpier road to approval and publication, likely derived from the extrasensitive nature of the topic.[32]

Latz's compliance reflected his apparent desire to retain ecclesiastical approval, motivated by a pragmatic concern for reaching the audience he sought. Luis Getino's more dramatic submission reflected his more drastic and personal situation. Not all conflicts over the Church's censorship mechanism were stories of immediate compliance or submission, however. Michael Williams in his weekly *Commonweal* "Views and Reviews" column recounted the predicament of Alfred Noyes, convert to Catholicism and recent biographer of Voltaire. Noyes was asked by the Holy Office via a letter to his archbishop to revise his work on Voltaire or face having it condemned. Noyes made the correspondence public along with his refusal on the grounds that "he would feel himself traitor to one of the greatest English traditions if he were to shrink from saying it."[33] While noting that encountering "ecclesiastical authority of such a summary character" was unfortunate ("It may readily be anticipated how anti-religious as well as anti-Catholic critics and journalists will seize upon the episode hungrily"), Williams criticized Noyes's reaction on the grounds that it placed "English traditions, or customs, or habits," before the authority of the Church.

This was not a new complaint. A generation earlier, biologist George Mivart had written to Cardinal Andreas Steinhuber, prefect of the Congregation of the Index, complaining that his articles on Hell were included in the new Index, despite his submission to the decree. "I need hardly point out to you, My Lord Cardinal, that the mode in which my condemnation (like that of others) was effected, is a mode profoundly abhorrent to us Englishmen, to Americans also and indeed to all English-speaking people."[34] The assertion of a special Anglo-American exemption to Roman procedure is interesting in light of the cultural situation of American Catholics in the years following World War I. This English tradition had long defined itself largely against Roman Catholicism, but it was precisely the one American Catholics were attempting to lay claim to in the third and fourth decades of the twentieth century. The decline of Protestant hegemony and the increasing prominence of Catholics in American political and economic life foregrounded and intensified the need to make a case for the consonance between Catholic tradition and American polity. For a while this became a kind of cottage industry within U.S. Catholicism, as a number of writers argued that there had been a direct influence on the ideas of the U.S. founders by Catholic thinkers such as Robert Bellarmine.[35] The evidence for this line of argument was always diffuse at best, but the effort reflects an explicit attempt by Catholics to write themselves back into the history of U.S. Catholicism and show themselves not just heirs but bequeathers of the nation's deepest traditions.

As usual, censorship presented a particular dilemma, as its incompatibility with foundational American tenets such as those embodied in the First Amendment seemed intuitively apparent. Significantly, the case increasingly had to be made not only to non-Catholics but to Catholics as well: as the percentage of native-born Catholics grew and immigration declined, those who were inheritors of the Anglo-American culture grew in numbers and had to be socialized into Catholic culture. U.S. Catholics charged with explaining how censorship (as they defined it) could nonetheless be seen as not only compatible with but essential to American freedoms understood the distance between this position and what American culture presumed about intellectual autonomy and freedom of individual judgment. Nonetheless, they cleared a significant swath of common ground.

The centerpiece of their argument was an appeal to natural law, often recast as simple common sense. All people of good will, Catholic explicators of censorship pointed out, instinctively understood the need to protect society, and especially children, from ideas and beliefs that were genuinely harmful, that destroyed a belief in and commitment to the truth. Therefore, the need for some kind of control of print was evident through reason to all people of good will, and did not solely reflect the imposition of clerical authority on a sectarian community. This argument was more plausible before the Second World War than it would be after. There is considerable evidence that "censorship" (defined as a variety of formal and informal controls exercised by institutions other than the federal government over what could be printed and read) was in the early decades of the twentieth century seen as part of the responsibility of a number of cultural institutions, not solely as a distinguishing feature of the Catholic Church. Catholic commentators could therefore argue that it was part of the necessary duties of authority. They could also argue, though, that if their compatriots agreed that the duty of censorship was best not left to government, then other cultural authorities had to approach it effectively and in a unified manner.

At the same time, Catholic defenders of censorship did point to the actions of the U.S. government to demonstrate that censorship was not in practice incompatible with American commitments, especially to the extent that those commitments came under serious threat. They noted frequently that the government refused second-class mailing privileges to materials deemed obscene, and that wartime censorship had been a critical element of maintaining citizen support for the Great War. As late as 1946, Edward Mahoney, OSB, head librarian of St. Bede College Library in Peru, Illinois, introduced a *Catholic Library World* article on the Index by asserting that in his comment to Harriet Beecher Stowe about *Uncle Tom's Cabin* ("so this is the little lady who started the great war") "the wise Lincoln paid fitting tribute to the power of the printed word." Mahoney then goes on to say, "Nations at all times have feared the danger of bad books and have taken some kind of measures to prevent their subjects from reading them. Our United States government refuses second-class mail privileges to the publishers of lascivious and obscene books."[36] The example of refusal of second-class mail privileges was clearly intended as an irrefutable example.

Making this case remained possible throughout the 1930s and beyond because censorship had not yet taken on an entirely negative connotation—that would happen with Cold War polarization in the years after World War II. In the 1930s Catholics still could and did argue that censorship—in the sense of regard for a real protection for the truth—was necessary to the defense of democracy, because only the abandonment of belief in truth could allow distorting ideologies such as communism to flourish.

Throughout the end of the 1930s, therefore, appeals to the consonance between censorship and core American commitments relied heavily on appeals to the urgency of the contemporary situation. These appeals relied on a shared, world-historical narrative in which everyone, from the highest place to the lowest, played a crucial role in the oncoming battle. And a battle it was, or was imagined to be. After the Great War as never before the U.S. church felt the weight of countermodernity—of defending and enlivening structures with roots in premodern centuries. Explanations and defenses of censorship are full of images that convey a sense of urgency—the modern world is threatened by contagion, epidemic, poison. Whether directed at Catholic canonist or high school teacher, Protestant magazine editor or Jewish neighbor, these explanations took on the historiographical burden of demonstrating why a sixteenth-century bureaucracy was still useful in the century of mass culture, why and how these structures were necessary to neutralize the poison, to halt the spread of the epidemic, for the health of the republic at large, not just its Catholic citizens.

Making this argument required some deft intellectual maneuvering, to elide two fundamental disconnects: U.S. Catholics identified deeply with the increasing nationalism of the interwar period, while simultaneously sustaining the transnational and supranational identification inherent in belonging to a self-consciously universal church; and they continued to insist on the essential continuity between past and present in a culture long intent on celebrating self-invention, innovation, and freedom from history. Even the briefest one-page question-and-answer columns on censorship in pastoral periodicals reached back through time and constructed a rapid narrative in which the burning of the books of magic at Ephesus, the triumph over Arius, the essential completeness of the church's system of censorship before the conflict with Luther—all these elements make regular appearances. Among other functions, this history reminded twentieth-century American Catholics that their solidarity with others in the past served as a brake on their immediate and complete identification with the innovations of the present.

Over the course of the 1930s the public rationale for and defense of censorship narrowed its focus from modernity generally to the more immediate urgencies of the international political situation. For Catholics censorship was so explicitly tied to defense of the truth—regulation of reading and publication being cornerstones of protecting sound doctrine—that they could argue that commitment to democracy a fortiori required admitting that censorship had a role in protecting what society most treasured. That argument would be stood on its head in the decades following World War II, when censorship became inextricably identified with Soviet communism and the rejection of basic human freedoms, a shift that had extensive repercussions for American Catholic defenses of censorship. But while world events would prompt much of the coming change in how Catholics understood censorship, at least as volatile a catalyst was the creative, capitalistic ferment of American popular culture.

CHAPTER 6

Art and Freedom in the Era
of "The Church of Your Choice"

Censorship—the elaborate system of laws and institutional structures surrounding the regulation of publication and reading—reflected for better and worse the worldview that grounded Catholic literary culture and aesthetics. Because salvation, and therefore doctrinal truth and fidelity, were the highest goods, everything else achieved goodness to the extent that it was in harmony with them. Seen from within the tradition, this assertion did not put unacceptable limits on art and artists. In fact, its strongest proponents insisted that the only limits it imposed were constitutive of art; art was not possible without those limits. For those drawn to and animated by the vision of Catholic literary culture— the grounding of art in the ultimate, the awesome possibilities for writer and reader of participating in the work of creation and incarnation— censorship was a necessary check. The censor's impulse had to be kept in its place, but it was not by its nature inimical to art.

Catholics were not talking only to themselves on these issues, especially in the early decades of the twentieth century. The *New York Times* on February 25, 1917, reported on a meeting of the Republican Club in which the topic of "free expression" was explored by Rev. Dr. John Barlow of the Memorial Presbyterian Church, Brooklyn; Henry Morelli of Paterson, New Jersey, "who was the attorney for the IWW and other strikers in the 1913 silk mill strike"; Grenville S. McFarland, editor of the *Boston American*; and

Congressman Frederick W. Dallinger of Massachusetts. Father Joseph H. McMahon of the Catholic Library Association "opened and closed" the meeting, "explained the Catholic belief in censorship of morals, founded on the Decalogue," and "answered 'God forbid' to Dr. Barlow's suggestion of a supreme censorship [of] motion pictures by a board of mothers and fathers, saying we had had enough of that sort of mawkish sentimentality and needed experts for such work if it should be undertaken." Even the brief, terse *Times* account indicates something less than agreement on the issues under discussion (McFarland, it notes, "gave a scholarly review of the history of censorship and pleaded against it," while Barlow argued strenuously for censorship not only of motion pictures but of newspapers), reflects the complexity of the political, religious, and economic context, and, strikingly, highlights the matter-of-factness with which Catholics approached censorship as a clear duty for which the Church had, at this point, centuries of "expert" experience to call on.[1]

From outside the Catholic Church and its intellectual and artistic tradition, the view was different. For those, Catholics and others, who stood outside the coherent framework of Catholic aesthetics, even momentarily, Catholicism's view of art and artistic creation was distorting—deforming, even—of art, limiting the necessary freedom of the artist to question and hold up in a new light every tradition, without limitation. Modernism elevated this belief to its own constitutive aesthetic principle; capitalism in this instance reinforced it. The book or movie or play or comic book able to be published was the book or movie or play or comic book able to be sold.

For believers and nonbelievers alike, though, there was real distance between Catholic views of the place of literary art and intellectual freedom in the world and those fostered by American culture. Even (perhaps especially) those who most fully embraced the holistic vision of a Catholic aesthetic needed a rationale by which its communal and activist dimensions could be reconciled with the individualist and capitalist dimensions of American artistic life and thought. Regulation of reading and publication generated an extensive companion literature, intended both to explicate for Catholics the obligations the Church's law imposed on them and to construct a history and a rationale by which writers, scholars, and intellectuals could see themselves as both American and Catholic. As censorship came more and more to be seen as a relic of the premodern past and to be associated with the totalitarian movements of the twentieth century, this rationale became more urgent. It remained, however, primarily the province of scholars and others laboring in the fields of print culture. This was not, increasingly, where large segments of the U.S. Catholic population could be most readily encountered.

Catholics and Popular Culture

Even a brief examination of what Catholics wrote about literature and reading reveals that by the 1920s they could not help but see books in the context of the other media, particularly movies and radio, rapidly burgeoning around them. With a speed and matter-of-factness that could perhaps characterize only an institution confident that it had dealt effectively with that earlier technological innovation, the printing press, the Church applied its centuries of aesthetic-theological reflection to D. W. Griffith, Al Jolson, and Mae West. The result in the United States was an unprecedented level of Catholic involvement and influence in a central institution in American life.

As James T. Fisher has observed, "Unlike the nation's civil and ecclesiastical traditions, there are few creation narratives for American popular culture that exclude a Catholic presence."[2] Catholics were never not at home in popular culture, because they were responsible for creating so much of it. The urban immigrant localities within which the popular culture of the twentieth century was first produced and disseminated were home to a disproportionate number of Catholics, who were both creators and consumers from popular culture's earliest days. Fisher and others have explored the connections and affinity between the color and pageantry and multimedia appeal of European devotional Catholicism and the color and pageantry and multimedia appeal of vaudeville and movies.

Being at home with popular culture did not mean being uncritical of it. Few thoughtful observers at the time (and in this Catholic bishops shared with people of impeccably Progressive lineage such as Jane Addams) marveled at motion pictures' possibilities without also expressing some trepidation about their power. What stands out sometimes in looking at what Catholics said about popular culture is that it is by early twenty-first-century standards distastefully Olympian (in a pastorally Thomist kind of way). Considered, though, from the standpoint of the times, the deep involvement of these particular people in such new things prompts a more complicated analysis: popular culture propelled Catholicism inexorably into the orbit of the modern in a way that sometimes invited ridicule and objection but that also shaped not only Catholicism but also American life.

Even though Roman Catholic responses to print culture and popular culture were officially and historically distinct from each other, they were deeply associated in the cultural imagination of American Catholics. In interviews people commonly conflated the Index of Forbidden Books with other official and unofficial Catholic responses to high-profile authors, works, and movies. In response to a question about the Index, one interviewee said that she did not remember anything specifically about it, but that she knew *Gone with the Wind* had been banned in Ireland—which it may have been, but condemnation of a work by a local bishop was canonically distinct from its being placed on the Index. Another response to the question "What do you remember about the Index?" was, "Joyce was full square on it," which he was not, although his works, too, were banned in a number of places, by both civil and religious authorities. Another interviewee began to reminisce about seeing "The Moon Is Blue," which generated controversy upon its release as a motion picture in 1953, as a stage play.[3] Thus is the historian concerned with definitions of literature and censorship of print culture led inexorably into the world of motion pictures, pulp magazines, comic books, and paperback novels.

Documentary as well as oral sources tend to move seamlessly from literature and print culture to other forms of popular media, conflating the Index and canon law regarding reading and publication with various other elements of official and unofficial ecclesiastical controversy and censure. In an English course lecture titled "The Moral Effect of Literature," John Bonn of Boston College noted that the idea that literature as a whole has a moral effect "has been disputed only by the 19th [and] 20th century naturalists and aesthetes." "There is an obligation to judge literature according to its moral effects: a. on the part of the state: Censorship b. on the part of the Church: the Index c: on the part of the Critic: Correct evaluation; labeling d. on the part of the Individual: subjective factors." On the reverse of these typewritten lecture notes is a handwritten outline entitled "Internal and Extrinsic Morality of Hollywood," in which Bonn considers the "lives of actors" and "their product: the cinema," the "Effects of violence in comic books and TV," followed by "Legion of Decency." Bonn seems to have presumed that the principles of moral evaluation he was attempting to convey needed a context that included not just literature but other forms of media as well.[4]

Because its practical relevance was much more to scholars than to the general reader, the Index was linked in the cultural imagination of U.S. Catholicism with the more prominent and, to most people, more relevant public debates over the morality of popular culture touched off by phenomena such as *Gone with the Wind*. Within the cultural history of Catholic literature, this association is not to be dismissed lightly. The rationales necessary to make cultural sense of the *Index Librorum Prohibitorum* in the twentieth-century United States looked backward, renarrating the intellectual history of modernity to make the Catholic Reformation an equal forebear of the American experience. The rationales that energized and defended Catholic involvement in the control of popular culture looked forward, asserting the relevance of Catholic aesthetics in that most modern and commercial of realms.

The public rationales Catholics developed to justify their involvement in the control of popular media reveal a fully articulated understanding of the relationship of Catholicism with American culture and, by extension, with modernity. Catholics could explain to themselves and others the imperatives of their tradition and ecclesiastical polity that necessitated their engagement, their drawing of connections between ideas and institutions that their compatriots often preferred to separate.

Their rationales were not entirely persuasive; indeed, they probably provoked as much anxiety as they alleviated. While print censorship was often seen as a sign of the disconnect between Catholicism and American culture and identity, by even its most vociferous critics it was viewed as an issue internal to Catholicism—the problems it posed externally related to what censorship suggested about how U.S. Catholics approached other issues with public implications, and possibly to the effect on the personality of Catholics who also had to function as autonomous citizens. Catholic interventions in popular culture, however, provoked in respectable venues comparison with the century's worst villains. So it is all the more remarkable that a system of censorship largely conceived, motivated, and staffed by Catholics played a key role in the formative popular culture of the twentieth century—motion pictures. Both things are true: Catholics were some of the most influential shapers of twentieth-century popular culture generally, and were also attacked as un-American for exercising that influence.

The attacks were most often directed at the Legion of Decency and the National Organization for Decent Literature (NODL). Better known than the NODL, the Legion of Decency ranks just below the Baltimore Catechism and fish on Fridays as a marker of mid-twentieth-century U.S. Catholic identity. Both organizations were created in a historical moment when the emergent national self-consciousness of the U.S. Catholic hierarchy confronted the emergent power of mass media. Both evoked criticism that questioned their consonance with foundational American principles. And both prompted self-reflection on the part of postwar Catholics that led to significant rethinking of the relationship among Catholicism, art, and modernity.[5]

In the years after about 1890, the explosive growth of popular media elicited anxieties from a wide variety of sectors. Dime novels, sheet music, recorded music, motion pictures, radio, pulp magazines, and other media reached unprecedentedly large audiences by means of the same communication and transportation revolutions that fueled the broader transformations of the preceding century. Popular culture in the form of parlor organs and sheet music was effectively nationalized even before the growth of the motion pictures, by means of the railroad and mail-order catalogs such as Montgomery Ward and Sears, Roebuck. For many groups in addition to U.S. Catholics, this unmediated access to the large majority of the population seemed to herald a crisis of authority. The anxieties provoked by the explosive growth of the motion picture and other popular culture industries were not limited to Catholics, but Catholics had a prominence in the debate that stemmed from two distinctive features of their situation: their concentration in large numbers in urban areas and the widespread perception of their unhesitating and monolithic obedience in response to clerical command. A larger-than-average percentage of the population consisted of those foreign-born and native-born of foreign parents. Popular culture was an avenue toward Americanization. Catholics were in the audience and on stage, behind and in front of the cameras. The cities in which Catholic populations were most concentrated were where the changes happened first and were perceived as most transformative (and therefore most threatening). The anxieties evoked by popular culture were inextricable from those evoked by the changes in American identity foreshadowed in the burgeoning immigrant populations of the cities.

If popular culture had produced only anxiety, it probably would not have lasted very long. It also produced large audiences and large profits, employment opportunities, and just plain entertainment. Virtually no one wanted to eliminate it, even if that had been within the realm of possibility. Many of its most vocal critics were also fans, hoping to see its vast potential put to the task of enriching human flourishing instead of pandering to the worst human instincts. Aware of the changes in the landscape of leisure activities available to members of their flocks, Catholic priests and bishops took account of which aspects of popular culture served to reinforce their overall religious message and which seemed to undercut it. This concern was not solely a one-way street: complaints over the possible negative effects of popular culture often originated with the laity, and clergy acted in response to lay pressure.

Out of this combination of enthusiasm and anxiety emerged the organization most closely linked in Catholic minds with censorship and the Index, the Legion of Decency. Along with its analogous but less-well-known counterpart, the NODL, the Legion was the popular-culture face of Catholic censorship—a system and a set of guidelines intended to make compatible the twin goals of salvation and entertainment. Like the Index and the system of control of reading and publication it represented, the Legion and the NODL elicited derision and outright attack from those who saw them as incompatible with the marketplace and/or the First Amendment. The Legion of Decency originated first and was by far the better known and more influential of the two groups, but the NODL is important in demonstrating both the connections and the disjunctions between movies and print media as the twentieth century progressed.

Movies, the PCA, and the Legion

The Legion of Decency was established in 1934 by the U.S. bishops at the end of a decades-long wrangle with the motion picture industry over the increasing sensationalism of its offerings. The Catholic Church was not the only participant in the fray. Protestant clergy, government officials, civic organizations, and ethnic heritage associations all expressed concern over the content of films and often exerted pressure to affect that content.[6] The motion picture industry wanted to increase the moviegoing audience as much as possible while avoiding federal censorship. It had adopted several reform measures during the 1920s in an attempt to maintain this balance, including establishing in 1922 the Motion Picture Producers and Distributors of America, with the impeccably midwestern, Republican, and Presbyterian Will Hays at its head. It became clear soon, however, that Hays's office had little real power over the content of movies, and the protests continued to grow (as did the audiences). Eventually the studios agreed to adopt and abide by the Motion Picture Production Code (MPPC), in itself a remarkable story of the involvement of American Catholics in the control of popular media.[7]

Adopted in 1930, the MPPC lacked an enforcement mechanism, so it gained the studios some short-term goodwill but had little effect on the content of motion pictures. Protests continued, but little muscle might ever have been put behind the industry's attempts at self-regulation had the U.S. bishops not been persuaded by Catholic layman and *Motion Picture Herald* owner Martin Quigley to put the issue of movie decency on the agenda for their meeting in November 1933, at which they appointed a four-member Episcopal Committee for Motion Pictures (ECOMP). In the spring of 1934 the committee announced the formation of the Legion of Decency, a Catholic group intended to mobilize the population in pursuit of decency in motion pictures. The committee's work was propelled (somewhat against their wishes) into the public eye by the highly publicized boycott of the movies in Philadelphia called on May 23 by its cardinal (and ECOMP member), Dennis Dougherty. The reaction to the boycott, both for and against, was intense and ensured that the Legion was launched squarely in the public eye.[8]

Membership in the Legion was gained through taking the Legion's pledge, administered in churches around the country, usually after the sermon at Sunday Mass. The pledge read, in part, "I acknowledge my obligation to form a right conscience about pictures that are dangerous to my moral life. As a member of the Legion of Decency, I pledge myself to remain away from them." Parishioners were asked also to sign two copies of the pledge; the parishioner kept one copy and the other was sent to the diocese as confirmation of membership. By the summer of 1934, Legion organizers were claiming that nearly two million people had signed the Legion pledge.

Why did the establishment of the Legion of Decency have an effect on the motion picture industry when so many earlier reform efforts had not? Part of the reason had to do with movie studio finances in the depths of the Depression. Most studios were heavily mortgaged because of the investments in technology necessary to implement the shift to sound pictures only a few years earlier. But probably the decisive factor was a combination of the demographics and the prevailing stereotypes of American Catholics. Demographically, because the Catholic population was concentrated in the cities, as were the large majority of movie theaters, studio owners worried that any episcopally mandated boycott would have a devastating effect on movie attendance and revenue at a time when the industry could least afford it. The stereotype lay in the presumption that such boycotts, once called, would *have* such an extreme effect. That is, the studio heads were paralyzed by the idea of U.S. bishops forbidding U.S. Catholics to attend movies, because they assumed that Catholics would comply unquestioningly and in large numbers.

America magazine announced the Legion's advent this way: "A relatively small group of ignorant and wilful men"—Hollywood producers—"are engaged in creating entertainment for the public which outrages every dictate of Christian morality. When the public's patience is exhausted, it can wreak a terrible vengeance. It has been exhausted."[9] Whether the public's patience really was exhausted is hard to tell; what is clear is that those interested in greater control over movie content saw the moment as opportune. The result was the Production Code Administration (PCA), an office set up in Hollywood and headed by Joseph Breen, who for the better part of three decades would have more control over the content of Hollywood movies than any other individual. The PCA achieved compliance where other mechanisms had failed by requiring that scripts be submitted for approval before production began. Breen's office reviewed the script and prepared reports about what might present problems in light of the MPPC. Negotiations often ensued in which producers and directors vied for concessions from the PCA that would allow them to implement their original plans. At stake was the Production Code "seal," without which a movie could not be shown in most U.S. theaters (since the studios also owned most of them).[10]

These negotiations and their results and effects, like the debates over censorship, can be construed simplistically from either direction. From the standpoint of the moral guardians, producers and directors trying to evade the Code were cynically maneuvering to ensure that their films were as sensational as possible, their only motive maximizing profits. From the standpoint of the champions of artistic freedom, the PCA was charged with implementing a truncated vision that prevented artists from the mature artistic use of film as a medium. The two views are nearly irreconcilable. The moral guardians' assessment has difficulty accounting for the undeniably circumscribed views of life and society imposed on filmmakers in the PCA negotiating process—insisting, for example, that the 1938 film *Blockade*, ostensibly set in the Spanish Civil War, remove any dialogue or symbols that would identify the location of or the sides in the conflict.[11] The champions of artistic freedom, conversely, have to deal with one of the century's great artistic ironies. As Tom Doherty puts it, "To . . . look back over the first full century of the moving image, is to suspect that the most vivid and compelling motion pictures—glorious as art, momentous as texts—were created under the most severe and narrow-minded censorship ever inflicted upon American cinema."[12]

This history of competing morality tales has helped to obscure interesting questions about how Catholics came to be so central to the story. The most easily available answers depend again on old stereotypes—because, as a number of critics did not hesitate to charge, the mentality of Catholics predisposed them to censorship. A more complicated answer rejects the easy stereotype but looks straightforwardly at what might be some truth about its origin: a Catholic theological aesthetic sees censorship as a last resort but will prefer it to the dominance of solely commercial values or to any bed-rock confidence in the untrammeled taste and judgment of the viewing public. It is important to emphasize that although censorship is an entirely accurate term for what the PCA did, it was an explicit and preferred alter-native to government (especially federal) censorship, which also had its ad-vocates in the early thirties. One of the reasons the studio owners eventually agreed to the establishment of the PCA was the proliferation of state-level governmental censorship, which had been wildly arbitrary, often resulting in different cuts of the same film showing in different states. Federal censor-ship would have solved the problem of inconsistency, but it was a solution all of the constituents involved wanted to avoid. The PCA was the product of a complicated set of relationships and negotiations both in its origin and in its relatively long period of effectiveness. "Never before in the history of American commercial culture," as R. Laurence Moore wrote, "despite the steady efforts of Protestant moralists, had the entrepreneurs of an entertain-ment industry accepted such a formal declaration of moral obligation or bowed to pressure to encode explicit restrictions. The document was writ-ten by a Catholic theologian. And those who pledged compliance were Jewish."[13]

Though not officially a part of the mechanisms of the Production Code Administration, the Legion of Decency remained for decades integral to its functioning. Because motion picture producers feared that a "C" or "con-demned" rating from the Legion (meaning that Catholics who had taken the Legion's pledge would promise to stay away from seeing it) would result in a drastic decline in attendance for a particular movie, they acquiesced in an unofficial review process by which the Legion screened a film before the PCA had made a final decision about whether to award it the Production Code seal. If the early word was that the screened version was going to be rated "C," producers usually would reluctantly make further changes in the film in order to ensure at least a "B."

This system was possible because the Legion had found a workable so-lution for one of the most intractable problems facing any group that wanted to exercise some control over the content of popular culture—how to establish a review body that would produce timely and reliably consistent assessments of which movies were potentially "dangerous to one's moral life." The Legion drew on the work of the Motion Picture Bureau of the New York City chapter of the International Federation of Catholic Alum-nae (IFCA), members of which had been screening and rating films for some twelve years as a voluntary service. Catholic newspapers and commentators nationwide had drawn on their ratings for years, so they already had established credibility. In addition, as the place where most movies played first, New York City could claim a legitimate primacy as the market and audience where the Legion's judgment would have the first and greatest impact.[14]

The Legion's creators and supporters pointed out early and often that box-office attendance increased dramatically in the years immediately following its establishment. Because these were also the years in which the country was struggling out of the Great Depression, it is unclear where one cause left off and the other took over. What is clear is that the Legion was perceived as extremely powerful for much of the golden age of Hollywood, and its opinions had tangible effects on what made it into the movie theaters even before a picture was released.

By 1936 Pope Pius XI could look at the first two years of the Legion of Decency's existence and comment on the movies in terms both retrograde and contemporary: "Recreation, in its manifold varieties, has become a necessity for people who work under the fatiguing conditions of modern industry, but it must be worthy of the rational nature of man and therefore must be morally healthy. It must be elevated to the rank of a positive factor for good and must seek to arouse noble sentiments. A people who, in time of repose, give themselves to diversions which violate decency, honour, or morality, to recreations which, especially to the young, constitute occasions of sin, are in grave danger of losing their greatness and even their national power."[15]

That this system ever came into being, much less functioned effectively for more than two decades, is remarkable. The absence of any one of a number of factors could have changed the outcome. Motion pictures did not have First Amendment protection until 1952, which meant the actions of the PCA could not be opposed via the legal system. The movie industry was dramatically concentrated: eight studios produced about 95 percent of all the movies released annually, so that a handful of executives in a room could come to an agreement that transformed an entire industry. The family of Martin Quigley, owners of the influential trade paper the *Motion Picture Herald*, were Catholic laity with credibility and influence both in Hollywood and among the U.S. Catholic hierarchy, giving Quigley unique status as a broker. Cardinal George Mundelein, archbishop of Chicago, had an intense personal interest in the movies and a relentless commitment to seeing them morally improved, along with considerable power within the 1930s bishops' councils. He could draw on the enthusiasm of Daniel Lord, a Chicago native and every bit as much a movie lover as he was a prolific pamphlet writer and cultural commentator. Supremely and buoyantly confident about the relationship between Catholicism and popular culture, Lord wrote most of the 1930 Motion Picture Production Code, though he agreed that his involvement be kept secret so as not to diminish its public credibility.[16] IFCA contributed a deft national leader and spokeswoman in Rita McGoldrick as well as a ready-made mechanism for evaluation. And at the center of the PCA was Catholic layman and St. Joseph's University alumnus Joseph Breen, an indefatigable and implacable negotiator impervious both to the blustering threats and to the artistic integrity of the movie directors and producers with whom he dealt for over twenty years. Criticism and conflict were endemic, but as Frank Walsh notes, "despite the Legion's assertion that it was simply advising Catholics on what films they should avoid, the result was a national classification system that affected what all Americans saw and didn't see on the screen."[17]

Pulp Magazines and the NODL

Movies were not the only area of popular culture causing increased anxiety in the 1930s. All-fiction "pulp" magazines (so-called because they were printed on cheap paper made from wood pulp) escalated in number of titles, sales, and popularity in the early years of the century and were at their most popular in the early 1930s.[18] They combined some of the familiar features of soap opera and reality television—aimed at wide popular audiences, appealing to an interest in "real-life" drama and intrigue, ranging from sentimental to provocatively sensational. Sold at newsdealers and drugstores everywhere for pennies, they existed in targeted genres: detective and spy stories, romance and "true confession" dramas, "girlie" magazines, westerns. Critics objected to the pulps on many of the same grounds as to the motion pictures (and even more so, as print could then as now often be more explicit than movies): depictions of bumbling police ineptly pursuing glamorous and sophisticated gangsters, explorations of marital infidelity and illegitimate pregnancies, suggestive photos and cartoons and a persistent fascination with women undressing.

And so the Legion of Decency's counterpart, "a Legion for decent literature," appeared in 1938 when the U.S. bishops established the NODL, headed by Bishop John F. Noll of Fort Wayne, Indiana. The differences between the movie and magazine industries meant that the strategy the NODL developed was different—and less clearly effective. The bishops involved agreed to take responsibility for reviewing a number of magazine titles, primarily by designating priests within their dioceses to do the reviewing. The reviewers prepared reports on which magazines violated the

NODL "code," written by Bishop Noll, and lists of magazines guilty of such a violation were circulated to members of NODL local chapters, who were then encouraged to visit local newsstands and drugstores where the magazines were sold and to alert the owners to the presence of titles un-acceptable to those interested in decent literature. If the owners refused to remove the offending titles, local NODL members would publicize the re-fusal and encourage fellow churchmembers and citizens not to patronize the stores involved.

The Legion of Decency succeeded—at least in the sense that it was per-ceived to have considerable influence—because the movie industry was so highly centralized. In contrast, pulp magazines were published by dozens, if not hundreds, of small, fly-by-night publishers who could dissolve and regroup with little effort and less notice. One company often published a number of different magazines, so that if one title came under heavy attack the company could drop it with little effect on their profits, then restart it under a different name and wait for the NODL's list to catch up.

Even saying this is probably implying a little more credit than the NODL deserved. While it did organize in some respects nationally, and intensively in some local areas, it had nothing like the nationwide reach and popular awareness achieved by the Legion. Part of the reason was the logistics—bishops interested in the project had to divvy up long lists of suspect maga-zines among already overworked priests, who then were responsible for getting hold of copies of the magazines and evaluating them according to the criteria contained in the NODL "code." The code, formulated by Bishop Noll, defined as indecent any publication that "1 - glorifies crime and the criminal; 2 - is predominantly 'sexy'; 3 - features illicit love; 4 - contains indecent or objectionable pictures; 5 - carries disreputable advertisements."[19] Noll was very particular about the NODL asserting only that a given maga-zine did not fit with the NODL code. Any further assertion that a publica-tion was "indecent" or "obscene" invoked a legally definable term that could result in litigation.

A typical report contained story summaries and extended quotations to document a publication's violation of the NODL code. In his report on the April 1941 issue of *Personal Romances Monthly Magazine*, reviewer John G. O'Connor completed his summary of the story "Too Young for Love" with the following lines: "'I'm not too young for love. Ray—please.' I felt him tremble. Tenderly his lips sought mine and in that moment of ecstasy I felt that I was truly a woman now. Ray was my man. I wanted him, as a woman wants the man she loves." Without further comment, O'Connor signed the report.[20] From the NODL's point of view, the problems in romance magazines tended to come from the stories' depictions of "illicit love," while "girlie" magazines were most likely to offend by publishing objectionable photos and cartoons (reviewer E. W. Mahoney noted that the front cover of the September 1941 issue of *Peek* magazine "shows a girl barely covered with ribbon lying on a haystack").[21]

The NODL became more centralized over time, centering much of the coordination after 1942 in the office of the National Council of Catholic Men, at the National Catholic Welfare Conference in Washington, DC.[22] The reviewing, however, was still delegated—partly because of how many different publications had to be reviewed regularly, partly because of the lack of funds to pay to have it done centrally. Organizers were reluctant to create full-time reviewing positions, because of the effect reading too much indecent literature might have on anyone who had to do so much of it. As the NODL developed, it became in response to repeated requests also concerned with, first, comic books,[23] and then with paperbound books, the popularity of which exploded in the 1950s.[24] As the NODL's scope expanded, its methods seemed less effective—the scale of what it was attempting was too great for it to have much more than symbolic impact, apart from local, atypical cases. Its influence is perhaps most apparent in the regular appearance it made in the national media as the subject of controversy. In fact, both the Legion of Decency and the National Organization for Decent Literature are illuminated at least as much in the opposition and criticisms of their opponents as they are by their creators and defenders. Though the criticism they elicited echoed that raised against Catholic print censorship, the Legion and the NODL raised more-urgent issues about U.S. Catholic public presence, and prompted more immediately political objections. The Index was a troubling symptom of the persistence of premodern pathologies, but not as immediate a threat to a democratic ethos as the Legion and the NODL.

Criticism and Controversy

The Legion and the NODL were both founded in the mid- to late 1930s; both were institutionally transformed nearly beyond recognition by the mid-1960s. In between, both functioned for most of the time below the radar, emerging into public consciousness at infrequent intervals via criticism of their motives, leadership, or tactics. The terms in which they were criticized and defended reveal a sustained conversation about the terms on which Roman Catholicism could and should accommodate to American modernity. The conversation makes clear that modernity, by the postwar period, included the conflation between democratic political ideals and attitudes and corporate-consumer capitalism.

From its inception and continuing throughout its existence, the Legion of Decency provoked criticism from those alarmed at the thought of the Catholic hierarchy pronouncing judgment on the content of popular culture. "What we want to know, the majority of us, is what mangy assortment of tails is trying to wag this majority dog," film critic and reviewer Otis Ferguson wrote in *The New Republic* in 1941. "I have seen the Catholic ladies at screenings," he continues, "and I can report that they compose a congregation of horrors that no good Catholic would have any business with if he had any business at all. Yet they are part of the organization which is going to tell us what we may see for the next ten years."[25] The Legion also seemed like twentieth-century evidence for the old nineteenth-century belief that Catholics' habit of obedience to clerical authority raised serious doubts about their autonomy as citizens of a modern democracy. At other times these criticisms were carefully limited to the hierarchy, avowing confidence in the good sense of American Catholics to reject un-American circumscriptions of their freedom.

Nonetheless, despite the initial and continuing unease with Catholic influence over the movie industry, the Legion of Decency became part of the woodwork, so to speak—one part of a familiar mechanism that had troubling aspects but functioned as part of a spectacularly successful industry. Although when the Legion was founded, it was criticized in the liberal press in the harshest terms, including comparisons to Hitler and Stalin, it was operating in a constitutional environment that made its position legally unassailable. Movies did not in the 1930s enjoy First Amendment protection—the Supreme Court in 1915 had explicitly withheld it on the grounds that "the exhibition of moving pictures is a business, pure and simple, originated and conducted for profit like other spectacles, and not to be regarded as part of the press of the country or as organs of public opinion within the meaning of freedom of speech and publication guaranteed by the constitution of Ohio."[26] Thus, while the PCA and the Legion (and the collaboration between them) raised liberal hackles, it was to the motion picture industry a temporarily preferable alternative to governmental censorship.

In contrast, the NODL from its inception in 1938 was dealing with material that clearly was covered by the First Amendment. The material generated so much anxiety, however, partly because in its scale and pace of production, breadth of distribution, and low cost it seemed as pervasive and innovative as the movies. Pulp magazines, comic books, and paperbound books with

1940s illustrations on their covers all may seem quaint in the era of the internet, but they profoundly changed the print context into which they were introduced. The abundance of their proliferation, the deliberateness with which they identified and targeted different audiences and markets, their low cost—all made clear that they targeted popular tastes in order to make money, with few pretensions to uplift, education, or culture. While trade publications for paperbound books did highlight the advantages of having the "classics" easily accessible in inexpensive editions, these editions were often marketed with covers that made them indistinguishable from thrillers and detective stories.

Thus the NODL's dilemma—attempt to respond to something genuinely new and unquestionably ancient in the world of print culture. The tactics of its founder and its participants were both subtle and unsubtle. John Noll, as already noted, planned the NODL with a clear-eyed awareness of its potential critics and the legal circumscriptions on its tactics and effectiveness. At the same time he conceived of and encouraged strategies that contained an indisputable element of deception, such as the use of staged "protest dramas" in which NODL members, without identifying themselves as such, might enter a business that sold publications on the NODL list and pretend dismay at discovering them, lamenting that this would prevent them from shopping there in future.

Noll's tactics extended to taking advantage of allies where he found them, such as the confidence he expressed in a 1941 letter: "The new Postmaster General has been cooperating with me splendidly. I have sent him the names and addresses of houses sending out nude pictures and other indecent things, and the Postmaster General makes immediate investigation and prosecution has resulted in five or six cases during the last month."[27] The PG Noll referred to was Frank Walker. Walker was a Notre Dame alumnus who grew up in Montana and eventually practiced law in New York City, where he reconnected with Franklin Delano Roosevelt, whom he had met in Butte in 1920. Walker played a significant role in Roosevelt's first administration as head of his Executive Council and of his National Emergency Council, before leaving to return to his family's law practice. When FDR's postmaster general resigned at the beginning of FDR's third term, he offered Walker the position.[28] Walker's particular usefulness in the NODL campaign was his power to deny second-class mailing privileges to publications that, "in his view . . . did not contribute to the public welfare," a strategy Noll fervently supported. Walker's use of this strategy against *Esquire* magazine in 1943 was a definitive overreach—*Esquire* sued, the case went to the Supreme Court, and Walker lost.[29]

The *Esquire* case attracted high-profile attention when *Washington Post* columnist Drew Pearson criticized Walker's action in a 1943 column: "Efficient Postmaster General Frank Walker has got himself into a situation whereby certain zealots of the church to which he belongs have become unofficial censors of American magazines. And Frank is playing into their hands."[30] Walker denied being influenced by members of his church, but the NODL happily claimed him publicly (in their magazine, the *Acolyte*) and privately. (Noll contentedly affirmed in a letter that "He [Walker] has raided a number of places for me and closed up some of them.")[31] Anyone disposed to see signs of Catholic conspiracy in American public life could take such observations as evidence.

Postwar Transformation

Until the beginning of World War II (only three years after the NODL's founding), confidence in the obligation and right of U.S. Catholics to develop effective (but also legal and ethical) tactics for insuring "decency" in popular culture was on the increase. After the war, even among Catholics, beliefs about public control of popular entertainment—and deeper beliefs about individual rights and the free market that underlay them—had changed enough that both the Legion of Decency and the NODL changed, eventually beyond recognition. Groups that in the 1930s had appealed confidently to Catholic Action and to the obligation natural law imposed on "all people of good will" were by the late 1940s not so much less confident as they were reliant on other rationales to describe how Catholics should orient themselves in debates over the place of popular culture in American life. This shift reflects both a growing internalization of American norms for public discussion and the role of conscience, and also a distinctively Catholic self-understanding rooted in the unique circumstances of the dense postwar Catholic subculture, which was being transformed by exponentially increasing education and affluence.

The Legion of Decency was affected by changes that were largely external; that is, what affected the motion picture industry in general in the 1950s necessarily influenced the Legion's role in monitoring it. As with so much else in the 1950s United States, however, the role of American Catholics was not offstage even in these broader developments. The uneasy collaboration among the movie studios, the Production Code Administration, and the Legion's New York reviewers, which had functioned effectively, if contentiously, for most of two decades, had begun by the early 1950s to show clear signs of deterioration. In both the changes that led to the deterioration and the attempts to forestall it, Catholic themes, Catholic pressure groups, and their relationships with civil authority were at the center of crucial disputes.

In December 1950, *The Miracle*, a short film by Roberto Rossellini, began to play in New York City as part of a trilogy of foreign films. Rossellini had by the time of the movie's release already generated outrage among American Catholics on account of his affair with (and eventual marriage to) Ingrid Bergman. Bergman was not herself Catholic but had become an icon of U.S. Catholicism a few years earlier as Sister Mary Benedict in *The Bells of St. Mary's*, the sequel to the iconic *Going My Way*. For those predisposed to see in Hollywood a disregard for all things sacred, especially when it came to explorations of sexuality and belief, *The Miracle* seemed like a flagrant insult. It told the story of a mentally disturbed Italian peasant woman who, after being seduced by a stranger she thinks is St. Joseph, believes her ensuing pregnancy to be miraculous. She is ostracized and driven out of town by her neighbors and gives birth at the movie's end to a baby she believes to be the Christ child.

Foreign films were exempt from the Production Code; they could be exhibited in the United States without prior screening as long as they passed a customs inspection that determined they were not obscene. They were, though, limited to being shown in independent art theatres, outside the PCA-controlled chains. *The Miracle* had been passed not once but twice by the New York state censors, but shortly after it began its run at the Paris Theater on December 12, 1950, it was closed down by Edward T. McClafferty, New York City's commissioner of licenses (and former state commander of the Catholic War Veterans) on the grounds that it was sacrilegious.[32] Condemnation by Cardinal Spellman and picketing by Catholic War Veterans and Holy Name Society members were accompanied by legal action challenging the commissioner's ban. In May 1952 the Supreme Court rejected sacrilege as legitimate grounds for governmental censorship (without yet extending full First Amendment protection to motion pictures).

Although Catholic opinion on the decision was divided, and most observers today might not go so far as the *Albany Evangelist* in declaring the decision "a victory 'for the forces of paganistic secularism' and 'tragic in its implication,'" nonetheless it represents a significant turning point in the history of the relationship among art, religion, and governmental authority in the United States.[33] If sacrilege no longer could provide grounds for legal prohibition of a work of art, then what it meant for religious groups to make a public case about the relationship between a work of art and a consensus on public standards had changed fundamentally. The religious revival that characterized postwar culture coincided with an increasingly explicit public sense that civic issues could not be negotiated based on the particular claims of any religious tradition, including the ones in which much of American society considered itself to be grounded. Controversies over art and entertainment were a crucial venue within which this sense was articulated and made explicit, with Catholics as key protagonists.

Partly as a result of the *Miracle* and subsequent court decisions, the influence of the PCA continued to decline. Joe Breen, who had attempted to retire once, finally left the office permanently. His personality had been crucial to the functioning of the system from the beginning; his successor, Geoff Shurlock, seemed neither able nor inclined to achieve the same results.[34] Ironically, one of the factors in the decline of the PCA was the Legion of Decency, which was increasingly reluctant to be as assiduous in applying the Production Code as it had once been. Time and again the Legion granted significant latitude to films that more conservative segments of the Catholic population would have preferred to see condemned. When in 1960 the Legion refused to condemn *La Dolce Vita*, placing it instead in its "Separate Classification" category, the rough if tenuous critical consensus that had sustained the collaboration was near collapse. In 1966 the PCA was dissolved into the Motion Picture Producers of America (MPPA), which adopted a new system, still in use (and which the movie industry and the Church had actively opposed since the 1930s), in which movies are assigned ratings that determine who can attend them. For some a victory, for others a depressing capitulation, it was regardless an abandonment, once again, of the belief in a societal consensus. It freed art in one way, by eliminating the necessity of adhering to a "code," but arguably at the same time surrounded art with an inescapable aura of restriction—abandoning the ideal that every movie can be attended by anyone surrounds every movie with suspicion as to whether everyone can attend it. Whether the overall effect was positive or negative, a victory to the "party of exposure" or a defeat to the "party of reticence," it was a watershed.[35]

A year before the dissolution of the PCA, the Legion of Decency had reorganized itself to adapt to the changing situation. In 1965 it renamed itself the National Catholic Office for Motion Pictures (NCOMP), and took as its revised task making its ratings available for use by members of the public, who could then form their consciences and inform their decisions about which movies to attend. No annual public pledge, no movie industry influence, no signed pledges returned to the bishop. These changes, too, could be construed as capitulation, the abandonment of any public Catholic attempt to influence popular culture, leaving the internalization of essentially consumerist values (masked and served by the language of liberal autonomy) as the only means for navigating mass media. A look at the parallel situation of the NODL suggests that the story is more complex.

In contrast to the Legion of Decency, the NODL never managed to overcome the limitations of its own methods, which were not capable of keeping pace with the fluidity and proliferation of postwar popular culture. It had a limited effect in some local areas, where well-organized chapters conducted sustained campaigns. Some of the tactics employed by at least a small number of local chapters were primarily effective at generating high-profile headlines. One particularly troublesome maneuver was to turn over the NODL-generated list of indecent magazines to the police and ask police assistance in preventing their sale. Even for many strong supporters of the NODL's basic goals, this crossed the line from legitimate pressure-group strategy into outright censorship.

The NODL was on the radar of the American Civil Liberties Union at least as early as 1953, but it made national news four years later when the ACLU issued a "Statement on Censorship Activity by Private Organizations and the National Organization for Decent Literature."[36] The ACLU statement followed an October 1956 editorial, "The Harm Good People Do," by the editor of *Harper's Magazine*, John Fischer, which had been answered in November 1956 by John Courtney Murray in a response entitled "The Bad Arguments Intelligent Men Make."[37] The ACLU and *Harper's* critiques were not formally connected, but they served to bring anxieties about the NODL under national scrutiny and to elicit reflection from Catholic explicators that illustrated how the understanding of a Catholic stance in American public life was shifting. The ACLU's 1957 "Statement" acknowledged the NODL's right to speak to Roman Catholics, or even to the general public about the morality of their reading material, but objected to the use of NODL lists by local police and prosecutors and also to using the threat of boycott or negative publicity to discourage newsstands and other stores from carrying listed publications.

The public Catholic response was somewhat subdued and apparently unified, unlike the sharp divergence over the *Miracle* decision only a few years before. Those Catholics who responded in print to the controversy asserted the right of the NODL to issue its list and rejected the idea that boycott was somehow un-American. But they also sharply disassociated themselves from the entanglement of the NODL's procedures with those of civil authority. In doing so, they reinforced and likely accelerated the reorganization of the NODL along the same lines as the Legion of

Decency—in 1955 the NODL had renamed itself the National Office for Decent Literature and, like the Legion, by the mid-1960s had dropped its most distinctive interventionist tactics in favor of providing information on various publications for individuals to form their own opinions.[38]

Two responses to these public challenges, by Jesuits John Courtney Murray and Harold C. Gardiner, illuminate both the context of the NODL's decision to reorient itself beyond recognition and a generational watershed in American Catholic intellectual and cultural life. The two were drawn into the controversy by the way it unfolded. Murray, a theologian on the faculty of the Jesuit Woodstock College, responded to the *Harper's* critique of the NODL because it mentioned him. He elaborated his critique further as one chapter of four "Unfinished Arguments" in his best-known work, *We Hold These Truths: Catholic Reflections on the American Proposition* (1960), "Should There Be a Law? The Question of Censorship." Gardiner, the literary editor of *America* since 1940, was invited by editor John J. Delaney at Hanover House (a Doubleday imprint) to write a book on censorship as part of their "Catholic Viewpoint" series. The result was *Catholic Viewpoint on Censorship*, published in 1958 and reviewed in the *New York Times Book Review*.[39]

On many fronts Gardiner and Murray represent a significant transition in American Catholic cultural life. This transition is especially clear when the two are compared with NODL founder John F. Noll, bishop of Fort Wayne, Indiana. Noll's involvement in the early years of the Legion of Decency (through his membership on the Episcopal Committee on Motion Pictures) and his founding and leadership of NODL were textbook examples of Catholic Action, the diffuse but all-pervasive midcentury Catholic movement and philosophy in which laity participated in the work of the hierarchy to "bring all things to Christ." Though both groups were initiated and authorized by the hierarchy, and validated explicitly and repeatedly by successive popes, neither the Legion nor the NODL could have existed or functioned effectively without extensive and sustained lay collaboration. In addition, their founding philosophy assumed widely shared community standards and the possibility and necessity of widespread collaboration among people from all faith traditions. Their locus was primarily the parish, their origins were midwestern (the Legion in Chicago, the NODL in Fort Wayne), and much of their activity was local and presumed the responsibility of people for their local community and the efficacy of such action in effecting change.

The year in which the *Harper's* NODL controversy occurred, 1956, was also the year John Noll died. Born in 1875, Noll was a generation older than Murray and Gardiner, both born in 1904. Gardiner and Murray were both primarily identified with the East Coast. Both held doctoral degrees, Gardiner's in English literature from Cambridge, Murray's in theology from the Gregorianum in Rome—in short, the main participants in the discussion were no longer the hierarchy urging local activism, but intellectuals advocating reasoned debate. Both had to grapple with a media context in which the possibility of effective local action and confidence in shared community standards had largely eroded. Though both were clerics, as members of a religious congregation they were not officially part of the hierarchy. These shifts in social location were accompanied by an increasing prominence for lay voices as well.

In the history of U.S. Catholic intellectual life, it is an understatement to say that John Courtney Murray is better known than Harold C. Gardiner. Murray's story is more spectacular, but Gardiner's influence was equally consequential. Murray is justifiably famous as the person most responsible for formulating an accommodation between Catholicism and U.S. culture that prepared the way for the Second Vatican Council's document on religious liberty (much of which was written by Murray), a decisive theoretical break with the nineteenth-century European formulations of the relationship between church and state that had emerged from antiliberal reactions to that century's revolutions. In the 1950s, however, the ideas that would guarantee Murray's fame a decade later put him under a cloud of suspicion and led to his being required not to publish on the topic.

In Murray's response to the *Harper's* piece, he split the difference, in a sense, between the NODL and Fischer—he was sharply critical of the NODL's crossing the line between acting as a legitimate interest group and collaborating with coercive governmental authority; he also was unenthusiastic about the use of the boycott as a tactic, though he criticized it on the grounds of prudence, not of right. He insisted on the importance of what he identified as NODL's distinctive task, stated first in cool sociological terms: "to represent, soberly and honestly, the principle of voluntary reform, to be accomplished on the basis of social cooperation." By the end of the same paragraph, however, the stakes were considerably higher: "to inject the Catholic tradition of rationality into a mass democracy that is rapidly slipping its moorings in reason."[40]

Key elements of this analysis reappeared more fully elaborated in *We Hold These Truths*. Murray framed his analysis as a response to what he saw as a persistent flaw in "Protestant moral theory"—a conflation between law and morality that led to the inability to distinguish between private and public morality. (In a neat reversal of the typical critiques of Catholic censorship, Murray identified the chief culprit not as Rome but as Comstock-ery.) Acknowledging that governments have always claimed the right to censor for the good of the community, he argued that restrictions on free-dom must serve the purpose of increasing freedom, that the procedures for such restriction (whether by government or through voluntary association) should be "juridical," and that their aim should be, and eventual effect likely will be, very limited—"no society should expect very much in the way of moral uplift from its censorship statutes."[41] He does not mention the NODL by name, but argues that it is "incongruous" for a voluntary association to use any methods that seem coercive (among which he includes boycotts) as a means of persuading fellow citizens concerning issues of "morality in lit-erature or on the screen," appealing to the virtue of prudence in identifying as the "chief danger" that "the Church itself be identified in the public mind as a power-association."[42]

Murray noted that censorship "itself is not of major importance in American society. What is important is that so much bad argument gets into the discussion of it"; and, later, that "our chief problem, of course, is not literary censorship, but literary creation."[43] While perhaps not the chief problem, censorship was prominent enough to merit a place in his analysis (as one of four specific issues) alongside the most high-profile intellectual issue for midcentury U.S. Catholics, religious liberty. It was his reformula-tion of this latter problem that brought him to the attention of the main-stream, practically the only Catholic intellectual to make it there, but he was part of a larger group whose concerns were more broadly cultural and whose work has received much less attention.

Murray's path into the censorship issue was through political theory and questions about the place of minority groups in a democratic society. Harold Gardiner came via the literary route. After receiving a flood of critical reader mail in response to his positive 1942 *America* review of *A Tree Grows in Brooklyn*, Gardiner took upon himself the task of educating the Catholic reading public about criticism. The series of articles he wrote for *America* became a widely influential book entitled *Norms for the Novel*. This work brought him to Delaney's attention at Doubleday and thence into the censorship debate.

What Harold Gardiner says about censorship in *Catholic Viewpoint* is similar to what Murray says in *We Hold These Truths*—not remarkable, given that they knew each other and relied on each other's work. Because Gardiner comes at the issue from an explicitly literary perspective, his analysis in-cludes most of the elements common to discussions of Catholic censor-ship from 1917 on, such as a description of the Index and canon law regarding censorship (including a history that begins with Acts 19:19), an explication of the processes by which a book was censored prior to publication and by which books were placed on the Index, and a refutation of the charge that Church regulation of reading and publication limited the intellectual freedom of Catholics by referencing the ability of Catholics to obtain permission to read any book they have a good reason to read. In addition, Gardiner's analysis contains a critique of liberalism as part of a defense of true freedom; he devotes fully half the book to "The Censorship Controversy in the United States," including descriptions of the Legion of Decency and of the NODL along with primary documents from the public controversies surrounding the NODL. His great plea, like Murray's, is for rational discussion of the complexities of the issues. This overlap between Gardiner's analysis and Murray's is significant because it reveals once again the consequences of the holistic literary and artistic aesthetic that characterized twentieth-century U.S. Catholicism. Murray's concern with the place of Catholicism within the contemporary U.S. context led him to include censorship as an issue of clear concern; Gardiner's concern with censorship led him inevitably to a concern with the place of Catholicism within the contemporary U.S. context.

Both Gardiner and Murray were sketching out a nuanced alternative view of American life that represented the genuine accommodation with intellectual modernity Catholicism had been seeking for nearly two centuries—genuine in the sense that both modernity and Catholicism were accepted as having a role on the stage, rather than one trying to rule the other out or to redefine it beyond recognition. Genuine, too, in the etymological sense of "accommodation" as creating room for things to coexist or cohabit. Neither Gardiner nor Murray, nor their fellow postwar Catholic intellectuals who wrestled with aspects of the same questions, were uncritical of modernity. But they knew it to be the world they inhabited, for better and worse, and the rationales they developed by which Catholicism and Catholics could navigate in it on their own terms were a key aspect of the preparation for the Second Vatican Council before anyone knew there was going to be one.

Gardiner, Murray, and others worked out a rationale by which Catholic polity was compatible with democracy and the American system. Theirs was more than a religious liberty/separation of church and state argument. Though Murray's contributions in that area cannot be underestimated, what he worked out was primarily an internal accommodation—he devised philosophical grounds on which American Catholics could assent to post-Enlightenment, contemporary notions of religious liberty without believing they were conceding anything fundamental. Murray's formulations had real consequences for U.S. Catholicism's reputation and for the self-understanding of Catholics, but in some ways it was not the most notable part of what people like Murray, Gardiner, and a number of others did. They again and again asserted and aimed to demonstrate that Catholicism was also actively beneficial to the American system. And that the modern world needed it—literally—to survive. Thus Murray and Gardiner's fellow Jesuit, the understudied and unjustly neglected William F. Lynch, applauded the emerging impulse to avoid the "ghetto" in political matters, but he nonetheless insisted that U.S. Catholics yet had reason to question, especially in artistic matters, whether the mainstream was clearly their home. "This kind of concern," he writes in *The Image Industries*, "must never be allowed to mount to the stage where we are afraid to be completely ourselves and completely Catholic in those areas where the national culture would be most helped by our being ourselves, and by fearlessly tapping the expressive resources in art which beyond cavil have always been at the command of the Catholic imagination. And this would not be an act of ghettoism but a sheer act of national mercy."[44]

Catholic thinking and writing about popular culture, as about art more broadly defined, drew on a constellation of ideas, distinctively configured—aesthetics, theology, the American civil context, economic justice, the inescapable connection between low and high art in human society, the situatedness of art and community in history. The body of analysis that developed over the course of the twentieth century brought together things usually kept apart and left Catholics poised in the 1950s to participate in the debate over mass culture and high art, especially the fate of artistic modernism, in a way that reflected this polymathic synthesis.

The Stakes

Catholic commentators on the role Catholicism could and should play in American popular culture saw the stakes involved as cosmically, eschatologically high. They saw in Catholicism resources to sustain democracy and to protect it against the things that threatened it—an authentic understanding of freedom, a tradition of rational dispute, a rich understanding of the human person and human community that could help democracy withstand the corrosion of the market. At the same time the qualities they saw as essential to the future of the United States continued to alarm non-Catholic observers, because the distinctive features of Catholic polity did not disappear: obedience, censorship, authority, hierarchy. At each point these Catholic critics held fast to both ends and attempted to retie the knot, turning to a distinctive combination of Catholic philosophy and American rhetoric. They claimed a place on the American landscape that looked Catholic, but they rejected the association between that look and medieval stereotypes that all agreed were incompatible with democratic citizenship.

What resulted was a public rationale for Catholic involvement in the creation and control of popular media that can be translated as an understanding of the relationship between Catholicism and American culture and, by extension, with modernity. This rationale drew on two different versions of where Catholicism entered the stage play of American history. It was simultaneously the eldest and youngest (non-native) American. On the one hand, Catholicism was self-consciously a tradition that predated the founding of the United States; Catholic critics and intellectuals in the 1940s and 1950s increasingly retold the nation's story by emphasizing the continuity of the Western tradition instead of the dramatic eighteenth-century break of the Enlightenment/revolutionary U.S. founding narrative, highlighting the Church's role in preserving that continuity and developing the resources out of which the Enlightenment could emerge. Still deeper in the American past, Catholics could point to Columbus and the early Spanish settlements and bring them back into the origin narratives, countering the influential midcentury emphasis on the Puritans as the most genuine source of American life and thought.

In other key ways Catholicism was the youngest American, reentering the scene in large, transformative numbers after the political framework was already in place, only within the century or so preceding the commentaries of the 1950s. The close of immigration in the 1920s brought about a self-conscious stabilization of the assimilation process—assimilation to American culture became much more of a cohort phenomenon, because there was no longer a continuous influx of new immigrants. Assimilation became more associated with generational difference; the widespread shared experience of the Great Depression and World War II intensified the association, the idea that the assimilation of Catholicism to America was a onetime process that once completed did not have to be repeated in subsequent years. The unique circumstances of early and mid twentieth-century U.S. Catholic immigration and assimilation have given to the two or three generations involved an iconic quality that is only beginning to be put in a wider and deeper historical context.[45]

What ideas comprised the rationale developed during these decades for the role Catholic views of art should play in shaping American popular culture? Like the cultural work of Catholic literature and Catholic justifications of the right and duty of censorship, this rationale both drew on long-standing tradition and adapted to the exigencies of the present age. First, the rationale rested on the presumption of fundamental—and essentially premodern—continuity between art and religion. The public face of this presumption was suitably modern: it did not insist overtly that art and entertainment had no autonomous role apart from worship. It did, however, rule out of bounds any contention that artistic creation—including that done primarily for commercial purposes—could be essentially separated from the purposes for which humanity had been created. Because one of those purposes was communal, a second fundamental continuity existed, this one between high art and popular art. Just as Catholic literary critics engaged not only serious novelists and high modernist poets, but also detective fiction and comic books, so movies, pulp magazines, radio, and television had to be accounted for by any comprehensively Catholic notion of the relationship between art and public life. The intent was not to erase distinctions in artistic value but to be more precise about their basis and significance by incorporating criteria beyond the purely formal. Catholic intellectuals faced the task of fleshing out these criteria in ways both pragmatically useful to the religious communities to which they were accountable and also intellectually plausible to their academic colleagues outside the Catholic community. The result was a stance unique among postwar American intellectuals.

Presuming these fundamental continuities had an additional consequence: it made necessary reflection on and eventual intervention in the structures and authorities that shaped art. If beauty and leisure were tied up with salvation, then the stakes were too high for individual preference and commercial values to predominate. As with print censorship, opinions about the extent and manner of intervention varied dramatically, but Catholics concerned with popular culture thought not only about the artifacts themselves but about the structures and relationships that produced and distributed them. The recurring attempts by Catholics to influence these structures and relationships were grounded in a presumption that they could act as Catholics and as Americans—sometimes in ways that were perceived as coercive, but often through persuasion, cooperation, and voluntarism. In the 1950s the sense that Catholicism was, finally, a product of the native American soil, that "it is now part of the American Way of Life," seemed to be on the increase. "It is because it has become one of the three great 'religions of democracy,'" Will Herberg wrote, "and not because of its claim to speak as the Universal Church, that American Catholicism is today listened to with such respect and attention by the American people."[46]

Catholics themselves made their case in terms that appealed less to natural law and Catholic Action and more to shared assumptions about personality and psychological motivation. In a 1957 *Catholic Digest* column a questioner asked, "Shouldn't people have the right to choose between good and evil (using as a standard the teachings of the Bible) instead of acting as robots, blindly obeying commands?" The column author, J. D. Conway, replied, "Do you really know any Catholic robots, Mrs. Burke? Mind and heart are essential to a good Catholic, and a robot has neither. The Church wants no blind obedience to her commands; she expects and she generally receives a free and intelligent obedience, which is prompted by love and based on sound reasons."[47] The language here is still discernibly Catholic, but the appeal to freedom and reason seems deliberately crafted to resonate with "an organic structure of ideas, values, and beliefs that constitute a faith common to Americans and genuinely operative in their lives."[48]

Indeed, the prominence of Catholics in U.S. popular culture in the decades following the Second World War could suggest that this organic harmony—assimilation accompanied by a distinctive identity and presence—had been accomplished. Everywhere on the landscape of popular culture were Catholic creators and performers who were fantastically successful and iconically American—Bing Crosby, Frank Sinatra, John Ford, Ed Sullivan, Frank Capra. All media, apparently, scrambled for the combination of prestige and sales that came from telling and selling Catholic stories and characters: Ingrid Bergman's Sister Mary Benedict and Audrey Hepburn's Sister Luke; Fulton Sheen in full regalia; the centenary of Lourdes photographed by Alfred Eisenstaedt for *Life* magazine; full-blown, reverent Hollywood treatment for "The Miracle of Our Lady of Fatima"; the process of canonization as high melodrama in Morris West's fiction; the 1960 Buick-Electra Playhouse TV dramatization of Hemingway's story "The Gambler, the Nun and the Radio."

Why then, in this peaceable popular culture kingdom, did the NODL and the Legion of Decency choose such an adversarial stance and evoke such intensifying criticism, internally and externally? The answer has two facets, and both illuminate points at which the changing culture of the postwar U.S. posed fresh challenges to Catholic aesthetics and its rationale for intervention in the control of popular culture.

First, the cultural climate had shifted so that almost any attempt to control popular media came to be defined as "censorship." Before the war, Catholics sought and found models and collaborators among mainline Protestants, who saw the guardianship of public morals—including some control over the content of popular media—as part of the responsibility of the upper classes. But as the Cold War deepened, "censorship" came to be defined not narrowly as federal legal intervention but as any attempt to limit, however informally and unofficially, the scope of artistic creation and dissemination. Supreme Court decisions such as the *Miracle* case cemented this shift in ethos. The result was a cultural climate in which Catholics found themselves, not allied with Protestant reformers as guardians of democracy, but lumped in with Soviet totalitarians as enemies of freedom.

Second, Catholic involvement in the control of popular media became increasingly suspect as the equation of democracy and the "free market" or "free enterprise" became ever more central to definitions of American culture. One consequence of this equation—which had been forming at least since the 1930s but came into full flower in the sun of postwar prosperity and Cold War polarization—was an implicit acceptance of popularity as the primary relevant criterion for success in popular art. If individual preference in the market was to be the equivalent of an individual vote in the political realm, then it was equivalently sacrosanct. The trend of Supreme Court decisions reinforced this shift in cultural ethos away from elite control and toward individual choice, away from widely shared social standards and toward First Amendment maximalism and commercial freedom. The shift is further reflected in the increasingly sharp criticism of Catholic use of boycott as an organizing tool. From one angle, a boycott is an eminently democratic mechanism—it operates outside the realm of political authority in the usually admirable precincts of grassroots citizen action, and involves the collective effect of freely made individual decisions about consumption. But calls for boycott elicited howls of protest and charges of un-American activity that revealed starkly just how deeply the "freedom" of the market had become intertwined with political freedoms and with the ethos of postwar American culture. In the charges leveled against occasional Catholic boycotts of popular culture we can hear echoes of what John Murray Cuddihy identified as "civil religion and Protestant taste," updated for the era of postwar prosperity.[49] Cuddihy's argument that as the price of assimilation, U.S. Catholics (along with Jews) were required to adopt the demeanor of a denomination and to adhere to an "etiquette" that eschewed the effrontery of any claim to being the "one true Church" (or "God's chosen people"), applies also by the 1950s to a deferential stance toward the "free market" as an essential component of a free society.

Catholic engagement with popular culture was a de facto acknowledgment that modernity happened. Its kaleidoscopic, energetic creative ferment cultivated the notion that modernity had advantages as well as disadvantages. In Catholic justifications for the persistence of print censorship into the twentieth century, the continual renarration of the history of intellectual modernity required that Catholics acknowledge their church's resistance to some of what turned out to be truth. The burden of this acknowledgment led some Catholic intellectuals well along the path to accepting a characterization of their tradition as irreformably premodern and in need of discarding. Others, though, staked out a new section of the landscape, one on which the church could engage the modern on the church's own terms, conscious of its past, frank about its failures, confident in its sustained commitments. Part of the capacity to do this came from knitting together the disparate intellectual strands necessary to bring ancient traditions concerning beauty and doctrinal integrity to bear on the sound and light show that was American popular culture. The resulting theoretical framework reflected an internalization of American norms for public discussion and the role of conscience, melded with the Catholic self-understanding necessary to begin to make sense of the postwar circumstances of a dense immigrant and postimmigrant subculture being transformed by exponentially increasing education and affluence. Apprehending this framework is essential to the intellectual history of twentieth-century U.S. Catholicism.

The Catholic critique of popular culture, embodied in writing and in activism, helped hold together what the centrifugal forces of the century kept forcing apart. It made and maintained a crucial connection between the exalted and the mundane. It refused to let the entertainer and the entertained forget about the existence of high art, and it refused to let the intellectual and the serious artist forget about the legitimacy of the human need to be distracted, refreshed, and captivated. Popular culture is the most modern of things, and the extensive Catholic engagement with it forged a continuity between U.S. Catholicism's sense of itself as progenitor of Western art and as active agent on the twentieth-century cultural front that assisted in eliding the distance between Catholicism, modernism, and modernity.

CHAPTER 7

Reclaiming the Modernists, Reclaiming the Modern

In 1948 the novelist Harry Sylvester published an article in the *Atlantic Monthly* entitled "Problems of the Catholic Writer." Among these problems was the obligation that Catholics had to marry and raise a large family, depriving the writer of the solitude and silence necessary for writing, and requiring him to earn enough money to support them all, usually through means other than writing. Sylvester also lamented the Church's prohibition of divorce, as successful writers typically divorced a first wife and married a second, younger woman who could be instrumental in managing the writer's life and career while he concentrated on continuing to write. Sylvester's diagnosis of these problems reflected a deep alienation from what he described as "our American Catholic Bingo Culture" and its emasculating effect on U.S. Catholic men, a diagnosis developed in his novel *Golden Girl*. That novel's Hemingway-esque plot centers on a young Irish American Catholic in Peru coming to the realization that his virginity had kept him trapped in immaturity. His desperate attempts to seduce the "Golden Girl" of the novel's title end in tragedy, reflecting Sylvester's increasing despair over the possibility of American Catholicism's attaining the kind of sexual maturity he thought it lacked. Eventually Sylvester did divorce his first wife (who had struggled for years with mental illness) and subsequently left the Church and remarried. He seemed in that process to achieve a peace of mind that had eluded him for decades when he was striving to become a significant American Catholic writer.[1]

Sylvester's good friend, novelist Richard Sullivan, was milder in temper and more generous in his assessment of the contemporary situation. Nonetheless he also wrestled with finding a place and a voice in the postwar landscape of U.S. Catholic literary culture and American literary life in general. From his position in the English Department at Notre Dame, he wrote and published six novels that never broke through to real sales, and into his old age he puzzled about why. For a while in the early postwar years he attributed his lack of success to a certain "softness" in his subject matter and style, but he could not pull off the harder, "Sam-Spade" approach he experimented with for a while after the war, and eventually he reverted to his customary style. As far as his extant correspondence reveals, he never attributed his personal or professional trials to the church or to Catholic culture, though he sympathized with Sylvester's struggles and frequently asserted substantial agreement with his criticisms.[2]

Different as they were temperamentally, Sylvester and Sullivan struggled with dilemmas characteristic of Catholic writers of their generation. Well before the calling of the Second Vatican Council in 1959, Catholic scholars and intellectuals knew the Church was facing an era of profound change, change manifest in intellectual life and many other areas by the end of the 1960s. This story has often been told as a Catholic American *bildungsroman*, a coming-of-age narrative within which the things of childhood are put away and the things of adulthood embraced. What is embraced are the prosperity and affluence of postwar American consumer society, and, within a few years, the Enlightenment intellectual stance that had come to ground intellectual modernity. The distinctiveness of midcentury Catholic intellectual life, when not overtly rejected, became vaguely embarrassing, something people were happy to see behind them in the rearview mirror as they headed down the Vatican II highway. The intellectual history of U.S. Catholicism has also largely been told as an ancillary narrative—the real story of U.S. Catholic history focuses on politics and sociology (both within the Church and outside it). Accounts that examine intellectual and cultural history at all presume that theology and philosophy compose the central narrative thread.

Literature as Intellectual History

In the history of twentieth-century U.S. Catholic intellectual life, literature has often been treated as though its story is entirely distinct. There are very good works on Catholic writers, but their work often seems to be analyzed as though it happens in parallel with the development of American Catholic intellectual life. In this, Catholic literary history is not far different from its secular counterparts, because this separation is itself an artifact of modernism, which helped to define the literary realm and the literary work as set apart from the contingencies and variability of history and politics. But literary history is also intellectual history, and the picture of the past is richer and more complete in including it. Catholic writers and critics were not only writing and interpreting literature, but participating in an elaborate evaluative system, highly self-consciousness about their philosophical premises. In addition they were acutely aware of a pastoral imperative to think about serious literature in a context that included other forms of art, including popular culture. The result was a distinctively configured understanding of the role of art and literature that elides much of the distance between modernism and the Catholic imagination in realms well beyond the literary.

This consequential elision depended on three distinctive ways Catholics involved in literary work approached their task. The first was their intellectually unfashionable insistence on a connection between art and religion. One effect of the rise of science as a standard for knowledge in the nineteenth century had been the separation of philosophy from theology as academic disciplines. Over the course of that century, philosophy sought and found a place in the secular academy, while theology was relegated to the realm of the partisan and the unscientific. A related but distinct separation took place between religion and art. Among other effects, this separation established the framework within which U.S. Catholics came to see themselves as both eldest and youngest—excluded from the higher ranks of American intellectual life on account of immigrant culture and prejudice, but also supremely confident that the Romantics, including the American Transcendentalists, could not have indulged in their artistic rejections and reinventions if not for what they had inherited from the longer tradition against which they defined themselves. One area in which this reconfiguration most tangibly affected intellectual culture was in the mid-nineteenth-century invention of "Western civilization" as central to university education. Within this newly articulated narrative of the history of the West, culture was borne by art, which was increasingly redefined against the religious context out of which it had originally emerged.[3] The greatness of Western art was achieved in spite of the Church, not on account of it. Art therefore carried into the twentieth century the weight of cultural meaning-making— adding back into intellectual life the dimension that science could not supply—that was being removed from religion, and especially from the historical, hierarchical, sacramentally centered religion represented most emphatically by Roman Catholicism.

Second, in addition to maintaining a conceptual connection between art and religion, U.S. Catholics also asserted the continuity between high and popular art, which required a continuous effort to balance the commercial and noncommercial values at stake, as well as to negotiate the divide between a hierarchical, tradition-centered church and an individualistic, capitalist-democratic political culture. Though much of this engagement was carried on by activists rather than scholars, the extent to which awareness of the Index, movie censorship, and the NODL is apparent in the work of literary academics is striking—the continuity across the divide between popular and high is in many ways contained within single lives and careers, not solely in the culture viewed as a whole.

These first two consequential aspects of Catholic literary work reflect ways in which those involved differed from their compatriots in the secular academy; the third reflects a key difference from their co-religionists. The job description of Catholic writers, teachers, and critics included, in some fashion, a continuing involvement with "modernism" of the literary type. Because they had to deal with modernism in literature, which was distinct but not completely dissociated from theological modernism, they were in conversation with ideas that were officially off-limits to theology for much of the century.

Taken together, these three characteristics represent a conceptual extension across almost every conceivable disciplinary boundary. As a result, Catholics engaged in literary work were uniquely sited to address the postwar moment when modernism's tenuousness as a stance that could withstand the century's tragedies was revealed—ironically, not solely by the century's apocalyptic cruelties, but by the mundanely corrosive powers of commodification. At the moment when it became most apparent that "all that is solid melts into air," a range of voices emerged from Catholic literary culture with a newly synthetic view of art and history. One of the most important of these was Walter J. Ong, SJ. A scholar of English literature and Renaissance and early modern intellectual culture, Ong brought his expansive vision to bear on the situation of postwar Catholicism in his 1959 *American Catholic Crossroads: Religious-Secular Encounters in the Modern World.* The introduction blithely locates the origins of modern science, or at least of science's attitude toward the cosmos, in the medieval "tradition of studying logic and physics." Ong then goes considerably further, asserting that the Church's fundamental doctrines—the Incarnation, the role of Mary, the sacraments, and especially the Eucharist, "where the relationship of

Jesus Christ, Who is God, to the here and now is most spectacularly shown forth"—evince the Church's collaboration in the "development of a greater respect for the material cosmos."[4] Ong's wide-ranging training and expertise distinguish him from his contemporaries in a number of ways, but in his ability to execute a double-reverse baptismal reclamation of secular history and the contemporary world (with a triple flip), he is more like than unlike them. He was one of the first and most accomplished of a generation of Catholic scholars born after 1900, scholars who had no adult role in the Great War, for whom modernism, literary and theological, was the world within which they came to intellectual and artistic maturity. Their ability to assimilate divergences that the preceding generation had been able to experience primarily as fractures made literature and thinking about literature a distinctively powerful resource for Catholic intellectuals in the postwar world.

All this may sound a bit grandiose. But it took place in unassuming and incremental form, through years of interaction and relationship and scrutiny. One key area in which U.S. Catholics involved in literary work developed the intellectual resources necessary to a genuine accommodation with modernity was in their continuing encounter with modernist writers, nearly all of whom by the 1950s had in some sense been brought back within the fold, whether they asked to be or not.

Reclaiming the Modernists

One of the most striking changes in the "content" of Catholic literary culture by the 1950s was the reclaiming of major modernist writers as Catholics, most especially James Joyce and Graham Greene. Early twentieth-century Catholic literary critics tended to define Catholic approaches *against* literary modernism, for reasons of both content and form. In content, modernism rejected bourgeois convention, including religious belief and institutions, depicting them as stifling individual freedom and breeding repression and hypocrisy. Even the strongest advocates among Catholic critics for open and "realistic" depiction of all aspects of human experience at some level parted company with modernism's most scathing depictions of the Church. In form, modernism also rejected convention, seeking fresh, unmediated expression through stylistic experiment and innovation. The earlier generation of conservative Catholic critics, such as Condé Pallen, had read the rejection of order in literary form as a reflection of the rejection of divine order in the cosmic realm.

For much of the century James Joyce most exemplified the dilemma literary modernism posed for Catholic Americans, in his brilliant, excoriating depiction of the stifled, truncated lives led by the thoroughly Catholic characters in his novels and stories. Early in Joyce's career, as he was becoming synonymous with modernism as a literary movement, Catholic critics and readers read and evaluated his work through a conflicted prism of loyalties. Not only did the reviewer for the *Catholic World* implausibly sum up *Portrait of the Artist as a Young Man* as a "story of a young Irishman's loss of faith," but he went on to compare *Portrait* unfavorably to Victorian novelist Robert Hugh Benson's 1914 *Initiation*, implying that Benson's novel accomplishes artistically everything that Joyce's does, while allowing its hero to reclaim his religious faith.[5] To the contemporary reader, however, *Portrait* and *Initiation* seem to have in common only that both protagonists "lose their faith"; in every other way, from the conventionality of Benson's prose to his protagonist's deathbed return to the church, the two works seem to exemplify the gulf between modernism and what preceded it.

By most of the tenets of twentieth-century literary criticism, the unfavorable comparison between *Portrait* and *Initiation* borders on the laughable. But literary criticism that is from one angle laughable can from another be a complex argument with history and philosophy. Catholic reactions to *Portrait* withhold approval of Joyce's experiments because of where they seem to lead, where Joyce himself saw them leading. Perhaps everyone involved would have been surprised to learn that, some thirty years later, Thomas Merton would wryly attribute his conversion in part to reading *Portrait of the Artist*. Also at midcentury, Notre Dame's Frank O'Malley compared Joyce favorably to James T. Farrell, describing Joyce as "inseeing, subtle, incessantly compassionate. His humor for men and their errant ways is cosmical, Dantesque."[6] By the time of Joyce's centenary in 1982, a writer in *America* magazine noted entirely matter-of-factly that "critics well recognize how firmly Joyce's imagination is Catholic, Irish, physical, verbal, musical," and referred to him as a 'Jesuit 'old-boy.'" Going even further, some months later a different writer in the same magazine adduced oral evidence of Joyce's deathbed return to the church and recommended a more appropriate marker for Joyce's grave (supposedly being moved back to Ireland): "The Celtic cross would be an appropriate symbol for his genuine homecoming: back to family, to country, and to his church, none of which he actually ever left."[7]

These reevaluations did not reject the idea that Joyce's Catholicism was relevant to his art. Instead they rejected Joyce's own rejection, so to speak, by the assertion that he had "never left." His art, therefore, by the time of his centenary undoubted as great, could also be reclaimed as Catholic. What had happened in the intervening decades? Did Catholics finally overcome a kind of parochial cultural lag that prevented them from judging twentieth-century art on its own terms? Finally liberated from clerical admonition and ecclesiastical stricture, were they now able to roam freely through the century's excellences?

For some, this interpretation of the change carried great explanatory weight. There was considerable embarrassment by midcentury among some Catholics whose primary professional identity was as literary professionals or academics. The application of principles outside the aesthetic to the definition and evaluation of literature was a transgression against academic propriety; Catholic critics who insisted on bringing in moral and theological criteria were a little like immigrant mothers and fathers and aunts and uncles who did not yet understand that this is not how things are done in America. But the existence of this embarrassment does not discount the persistence of the criteria among other, demonstrably modern, people. Joyce gets reclaimed not just *by* Catholics, but *as* Catholic. His modernism gets redefined not as narcissistic but as "Dantesque."

Joyce's reclamation was not unique. In fact, he probably rode on some other coattails. T. S. Eliot's conversion, for example, allowed Catholic critics to acknowledge that a seriousness of moral and artistic purpose informed *The Waste Land* and "The Hollow Men" no less than *Four Quartets* and "Ash Wednesday," the difference being that the former attempted to account for a world in which divine purpose was missing, while the latter could draw on this resource for meaning and coherence, if not for comfort.[8] And indeed, Eliot's work is one of the centerpieces of the first ten years of *Renascence*, the journal founded at Marquette University in 1958 to foster the scholarly study of the Catholic literary revival. A circle drawn large enough to bring *The Wasteland* into the definition of Catholic literature would almost inevitably encompass *Portrait of the Artist as a Young Man* and even *Finnegans Wake*.

Though not of the generation of high modernists that defined the movement in English, novelist Graham Greene was probably more central to the Catholic reclamation of modernism than any other author. Irrepressibly contrarian, prodigiously talented, he was impossible to dismiss. In the early years of the century, Catholic critics could largely avoid engaging the work of a naturalist such as Frank Norris, or a lapsed Catholic such as James Joyce, by labeling them as outside the fold, beyond the reach of the Church's teaching—their souls to be prayed for, but their work simply to be avoided. Greene, however, after his 1926 conversion and despite his tempestuous relationship both with the wife who occasioned the conversion and with the Church, was self-consciously and contentiously Catholic himself and used Catholic settings seriously in his novels. He depicted sinful people doing scandalous things, but at the same time raised serious theological questions. He therefore had somehow to be incorporated into the network of Catholic literary analysis, and in the process permanently altered the connections that defined the network.

Born in 1904, Greene originally achieved recognition as a writer of what he termed "entertainments"—taut, fast-paced spy thrillers such as *Stamboul Train* or *The Man Within*. Although Greene also called his 1938 *Brighton Rock* an "entertainment," not a novel, it was the first work to bring him to the attention of Catholic reviewers, containing as it did the portrait of Pinkie, an apparently irredeemable hoodlum. At the end of the novel, after Pinkie's death, a priest attempts to comfort Pinkie's pregnant widow (whom Pinkie married only to keep her from testifying against him) by speaking of "the appalling strangeness of the mercy of God." In its depiction of the seediest fringes of society, in its fascination with questions of death and judgment, justice and mercy, and in the proprietary reaction it elicited from Catholic critics, *Brighton Rock* was similar to a number of other Greene novels that followed it.

Set in 1930s Mexico, *The Power and the Glory* (1940) provoked considerable comment in the Catholic press. Its unnamed main character, the "whisky priest," lives a decidedly unsaintly life, but his death is apparently a martyrdom. *America*'s reviewer, Joseph R. N. Maxwell, wrote of *The Power and the Glory* that it "will provoke much thought and give rise to many arguments. It will offend some, and disgust others, and I doubt that it will be entirely accepted by many."[9] Maxwell did acknowledge the novel's force, but his review hesitated to give full approval to a story with so many potentially ambiguous elements.

The hesitations that greeted *The Power and the Glory* were ripples compared to the wave of suspicion that met *The Heart of the Matter* (1948) and *The End of the Affair* (1951). Set in British colonial Africa, *The Heart of the Matter* ends with the suicide of the hapless functionary Scobie, who hopes by his act to stop hurting the people he loves and, above all, God. In *Catholic World* Joseph McSorley wrote, "There is at least a probability that many readers will be encouraged by this book to regard morality as after all a purely subjective matter, unrelated to divinely established standards—not final therefore, not absolute. True, we cannot tell what goes on in the sinner's mind; true, inculpable ignorance annuls guilt. But we know also that . . . it is a pitiful absurdity to tell God we are not going to do what He wants us to do, but we are confident He will understand and excuse. This is the kind of absurdity that invites moral disaster by divorcing mind from will and substituting means for ends."[10] Harold Gardiner, though praising the book as "complex, sincere, deeply felt and deeply moving," warned that Greene had become "slightly ungoverned," evincing too much sympathy, perhaps even admiration, for Scobie.[11]

Catholic reviewers were divided over whether the book suggested that Scobie had been saved or damned, and over whether the answer mattered to the book's quality as art. But virtually all of them addressed the question, in some cases to the exclusion of more-literary issues. Greene's talent, his growing stature in the literary world, and his role as "Catholic novelist" all were more or less presumed, or perhaps subsumed into the discussion of whether his theology was sufficiently orthodox so as not to undercut his art. In fact, it was precisely the combination of Greene's artistic stature and self-identification as Catholic that made the stakes so high for both his supporters and his detractors.

These stakes were clear, and settled decisively, in the debate that followed the 1951 publication of *The End of the Affair*. The most pressing questions in *The Heart of the Matter* had been doctrinal; in *The End of the Affair*, Catholic reviewers and critics were preoccupied with how doctrine and moral teachings interacted with contemporary history and social mores.[12] The affair of the title takes place in London during World War II and ends during the Blitz when the woman involved, Sarah Miles, promises God she will give up her lover, Maurice Bendrix, if he lives through a particularly frightening bombing. Maurice does live, and Sarah keeps her promise, growing closer, somewhat ambivalently, to God, until after her death her intervention seems to be responsible for several miracles. Catholic reviewers did debate whether the miracles were plausible and whether using them as a plot device was potentially blasphemous. But most Catholic critical energy was directed toward launching or countering criticism over whether the novel's depiction of the adulterous love affair was "excessively realistic." As in much of the debate over Greene's work, "realism" was shorthand for overly graphic depiction of sex, the discomfort with which among Catholic critics was likely intensified by their awareness of Greene's own notorious and unapologetic love life.

In the course of this debate, Harold C. Gardiner played a key role. As literary editor of *America*, he had for some years been trying to articulate a set of principles by which Catholic critics could react to contemporary literature and popular culture in ways faithful to the Church's views on art but also sufficiently generous to the culture around them. Gardiner had been spurred into action on this effort in 1942 when his positive review of *A Tree Grows in Brooklyn* had brought a flood of mail critical of the book's mild sexual frankness and apparent casualness about the lapsed Catholicism of the Nolan family. Gardiner identified readers' dismissal of the story for these minor moral difficulties as a symptom of a badly underdeveloped critical sensibility, and in a series of four essays in *America* he articulated a set of "Tenets for Readers and Reviewers." The essays were published in 1944 as a 24-page pamphlet, and revised, extended, and reprinted over the next two decades, at 48 pages long in 1947 and 64 pages in 1953. It became a staple of Catholic libraries, as did Gardiner's 1953 *Norms for the Novel*. *Tenets* prompted novelist Richard Sullivan to write in an effusive personal letter to Gardiner, "Diffidence and lethargy usually keep me from writing letters such as this one; but I can't dodge either the urgent desire or the strong obligation I now feel to tell you immediately how truly good and important your 'Tenets' seem to me, and to express a most sincere personal gratitude to you for writing such a series. The four pieces seem to me to be full of the very virtues they preach—clarity and charity. Those are always brave and difficult virtues, and they take on a special radiance when you bring them to a field where there is, unfortunately, so much muddling and, I'm afraid, some occasional meanness."[13]

Gardiner's initial response to *The End of the Affair* had been reluctantly negative. In his review he suggested the work was "definitely for the perusal of those professionally interested in the study of the novel." In describing the affair, Gardiner maintained, Greene had used phrases "such that the book is by no means to be commended to the attention of all." Three months later, however, Gardiner published a reconsideration, partly in response to the November 1951 review in *Best Sellers* written by Riley Hughes.[14] Hughes had charged that the images of evil and sin in *The End of the Affair* were more compelling than the images of good. In his response to Hughes, Gardiner simultaneously conceded the point and rejected Hughes's conclusion: "The images of evil *are* more vivid than the images of good—but how can that be otherwise, particularly when evil wears the trappings of sensuality?" Gardiner went on to compare Greene's treatment of Sarah after her conversion with St. Augustine's "humble frankness [in depicting] himself after his conversion as still the same passionate man," though now one who could ask of God "what is it that I love when I love you?"[15] It is hard to imagine being welcomed back more thoroughly into the Catholic fold than by being compared to (the postconversion) Augustine.

Reclaiming the Modern

Greene's reclamation as a Catholic writer matters to the history of U.S. Catholic engagement with modernism because critics accomplished it through sympathetically immersing themselves in contemporary history and experience, finding there a renewed locus of meaning as well as a manifest need for a Catholic presence. With regard to *The End of the Affair*, Harold Gardiner argued that accepting the potentially shocking details of Greene's work preserved its "true" realism—Greene's insight into the centrality to life and art of humanity's relationship with God.[16] Gardiner continued explicitly to maintain what his critical forebears had argued earlier in the century: that much contemporary literature and the mainstream secular criticism associated with it were apparently realistic in form and detail, but paradoxically *unreal* in their exclusion of the divine from their depiction of reality. By the late 1940s and increasingly through the 1950s, critics such as Gardiner were much more likely to argue for the freedom of the novelist to use "realistic" techniques as art required.

In the early years of the century, "modernism" and "realism" had been close to mutually exclusive terms. Modernists rejected realist techniques, and to some extent prose entirely, because they saw realism in fiction as reinforcing the bourgeois convention they sought to overturn. But as early as the 1930s, writers and critics of more conventionally "realist" novels were recognizing that their themes and to some extent their technique had more in common with modernism broadly considered than with the generation of "realist" fiction that preceded the Great War. To the extent that Graham Greene can be considered a modernist (and his critics differ on this), his modernism was of this second type. In claiming Greene as Catholic, Catholic critics were also claiming modernism as part of an authentic Catholic expression of the experience of a tragic and devastating century.

The exhausted postwar awareness of the wars' devastation, and of the deepening and apparently permanent threat of nuclear destruction, coincided with the growth to adulthood and middle age of a generation of nonimmigrant Catholics. The thinkers and writers among this generation articulated a notion of "maturity" that made meaning of this coincidence and applied it to their evaluation of art, both high and popular. If, they maintained, the Catholic community in the United States had ever needed moral safeguards and protections comparable to those universally acknowledged to be appropriate to children, that time had now gone. Popular culture had appeared on the American scene at roughly the same time as many of their immigrant grandparents and great-grandparents—their forebears' adaptation to American life was to a significant extent an adaptation to popular culture itself. At the same time that Harold Gardiner was arguing for a more adult approach to sexuality and sexual morality on the part of Catholic readers and critics, the Legion of Decency was battling for a similar maturing on the part of movie audiences.[17] Artists of all sorts, Catholic critics increasingly argued, needed to be able to presume a mature audience for the creation of significant work. Part of their concern stemmed from a growing self-consciousness about the reputation of Catholic criticism in the landscape of American cultural criticism. But emphasizing maturity was not simply a defensive move. It had an explicit, self-conscious Catholic valence. "Maturity" meant living up to a heritage that had been around much longer than the United States. It meant that the Catholic community could and should approach literary and cultural analysis with full confidence that Catholic critical perspectives were adequate tools to deal with contemporary art on its own terms.

America film critic Moira Walsh was not abandoning the Catholic Action project of "Christianizing" culture when she applauded the changes taking place in the early 1960s in the strategies the Legion of Decency used to inform Catholics about movies. She acknowledged that opinions had shifted over time as to whether ignorance of evil was the best protection from it. But "in this age," she argued, "good and evil, truth and falsehood, are so deceptively and inextricably woven together in our affluent, materialistic, post-Christian culture that unwitting corruption is the almost inevitable consequence of ignorance."[18] Thus it was necessary that the Legion judge "films in the rational, humanistic, Christian terms that befit an art form with a right and even a duty to confront the actualities of human existence."[19]

The Legion of Decency's own secretary, Msgr. Thomas Little, took an even more rigorous line: If the kind of approach the Legion had adopted, informed by the values Walsh articulated, presented problems for people used to the older, more directive system, their discomfort was evidence of the old system's "arrogant disregard of conscience and of a properly motivated commitment," and the solution lay in educating and enlightening the average moviegoer: "There is a world of difference between a film that holds up to view a situation that is obviously reprehensible morally and a film that says such a situation is desirable and worthy of emulation. Moviegoers must learn to tell the difference."[20] Similarly, a 1962 editorial in the South Bend–based *Ave Maria* about the changes in the Legion was entitled "Another Sign of Maturity." The piece praised the Legion for extending the possibility of its "special recommendation" to all films in the "A" category— that is, for praising high-quality films even if they fell into the A-II and

A-III categories, suitable in the Legion's recommendation for adolescents and adults, but not for all. (The first A-II film to receive a "special recommendation" was the movie adaption of *The Miracle Worker*.) "American Catholics can be proud," the editorial concludes, "that the Bishops' movie-evaluation group can be depended upon to offer more than a moral judgment—that it had shown itself adept in mature, perceptive criticism of the film art."[21]

This trope of deepening individual responsibility for Catholic presence in American cultural life appears also in a speech given by the Hon. John F. X. McGohey to the forty-first annual convention of the Catholic Press Association in 1951. "We make a good impression when we keep our reporting objective," McGohey exhorts,

> when we show we are well-informed, when we reveal, in the true sense of the words, a progressive and liberal outlook in keeping with the comprehensive and constructive social teaching of the Church. A narrow-minded Catholic is a contradiction in terms. We are not a beleaguered minority trying to fight out of a religious and cultural ghetto! We live in a glorious land of freedom! We should be, in the words of the Divine Founder of our holy religion, "the light of the World," and we are when we make it our one aim to carry His message of truth and hope and love to a world sick unto death of half-truths and falsehoods, of despair and strife and hate.[22]

The language of maturity and responsibility reflects a turn to professional psychology as a supplement or complement to theology. Flannery O'Connor notes in one of her letters to Betty Hester, "I have recently been reading some depth psychologists, mainly Jung, Neumann, and a Dominican, Victor White (God and the Unconscious). All this throws light momentarily on some of the dark places in my brain but only momentarily." And Peter Huff notes of Allen Tate, "Tate increasingly attempted to find a pragmatic answer to his spiritual dilemma in the fusion of classic Catholic devotion with current trends in psychology."[23] Sister Mariella Gable struggled for years personally with nervous breakdowns, hospitalizations, and treatments for psychological suffering, but also drew on the deepening connection between psychology and spirituality in her literary work, depending particularly on Dietrich von Hildebrand's *Liturgy and Personality*, originally published in German in 1934 and appearing in English in 1943. This was and is a paradigm shift with significant implications. It would be a mistake, though, to see it solely as an example of assimilation, that is, to interpret the appearance in Catholic discussions of psychological explanations as further evidence of their awakening to the disenchantment of the world. The "self" that was maturing—whether the major writer, the individual reader-moviegoer, or the collective Catholic population—did not have as its sole goal the unfettered autonomy of liberal individualism. Instead, maturing meant entering more deeply into time and space, history and the cosmos, becoming more connected with humanity and the destiny of the created world rather than independent of it.

For some critics the maturity they discerned and advocated went beyond the institutional and the aesthetic to the historical and cosmic. Not surprisingly, one of the most ambitious frameworks was the work of Walter Ong, who argued that the fragmentation and indeterminacy associated with modernism were part of a necessary evolution in humanity's relationship with knowledge as a whole. "One must not be naïve about the naïveté of earlier man, who was a complicated individual and in his own way quite as profound as we in his perceptions and awarenesses," he cautions. "Yet the fact remains that as late as the age of Erasmus knowledge could be thought of as a kind of totality 'contained' in its entirety in 'the books of the ancients' with a plausibility and lack of reflection which has become impossible today. . . . Only as the human race and/or the human individual becomes older is man able to accept with equanimity and even exhilaration explicit awareness of the fact that all natural knowledge is indefinitely expansible. 'Human kind / Cannot bear very much reality,' T. S. Eliot reminds us, and it can bear less when the individual or the race is young."[24]

By 1959 the race felt rather old, and the writings of American Catholic intellectuals showed it in new ways. Novelist Richard Sullivan had written to his literary agent Henry Volkening in August 1945, "I hope you had a good V-J day, and that you join me in wishing that now these fellows got that atom busted they will devote the rest of this century to putting it back together again."[25] In the decade and a half following V-J day, it became clear that that was not going to happen. Awareness of living in the shadow of nuclear annihilation was accompanied by the need to differentiate Roman Catholicism, especially its American variant, from the totalitarian ideologies that had wracked Europe for most of the century, and of which Catholicism was still more suspect than not among many observers and critics. John McGreevy notes that liberal intellectuals' fear of Catholic power diminished over the course of the 1950s, in part because of their shared anticommunism and the liberals' realization that the Vatican and the Kremlin might be less alike than Paul Blanshard had suggested.[26] McGreevy also credits a decline in Catholic combativeness, which might have been due in its turn to a sense that the events of the century had largely confirmed the theory of history under which Catholics had been operating, in defiance of the secular grand narrative, for more than a century. American intellectuals, moreover, were themselves confronting and attempting to reconcile elements of their own worldview that had become apparently incompatible—as Edward Purcell documented some years ago, it became historically and politically necessary for American intellectuals to espouse democracy as something like an orthodoxy that escaped the strictures of orthodoxy by rooting itself in the methods of scientific naturalism, at precisely the time when entrenched orthodoxy was seen as one of the hallmarks of the Soviet Union's suppression of intellectual and cultural freedoms.[27]

These tidal shifts suggest that one aspect of the American Catholic predicament—wherein they attempted to embrace and defend orthodoxy in a culture defined by the overthrow of tradition and regular episodes of radical reinvention—was becoming less distinctive. As the trajectory of progress became less true, space opened up to rethink the opposition between orthodoxy and iconoclasm that had shaped Catholic intellectual and literary stances for much of the century.

The "opposition" that had helped to define the relationship between Catholicism and modernism had at one pole Catholic adherence to orthodoxy in theology, which they insisted had implications for literature as well. They did so at a time (the early years of the modernist ascendancy) when more clearly than ever the primacy of "art for art's sake" relegated any literature wed to an external framework to the exile of propaganda. Support for maintaining orthodoxy is perhaps the most easily caricatured Counter-Reformation position, and the breaking down and airing out of received beliefs a defining hallmark of intellectual and artistic work in the twentieth century. What could Catholics do but capitulate?

They maintained their distinctive definition of realism as an argument against both sides. That is, they claimed the freedom to explore all of reality, because it was all created and redeemed and sanctified by God. (This is one of the many cultural trends associated with the 1960s that are actually easily discernible in the 1950s.) The limits on what literature could depict that had been debated so vociferously earlier in the century gradually gave way, in the easing of Victorianism in society, surely, but also in response to World War II, when so many people had seen so many things from which in previous generations they had been protected that maintaining Victorian discretion was less and less tenable anyhow. Al and Milly Stephenson, the characters played by Fredric March and Myrna Loy in the 1946 movie *Best Years of Our Lives*, agree that there is little need to worry about what their daughter Peggy (played by Teresa Wright) might see or do during a night on the town, because she had seen so much as a nurse in a hospital during the war that she was much older than they had been at her age. Catholics argued that if other artists were going somewhere, heading into unknown territory, Catholic artists had better be there, too, seeing human experience with Catholic eyes as a counterpoint and counterweight to secular materialism.

In 1897 Condé Pallen had insisted on Dante's organic connection to his age, a connection Pallen believed impossible for contemporary artists if the philosophical assumptions of modernity were to triumph, thereby rendering great art impossible. But the next generation or two of Catholic writers and thinkers eventually found their way around the starkness of this opposition. Not by rejecting the notion of orthodoxy, or the notion that there needed to be some fundamental harmony for a Catholic writer between Catholic belief and the world they imagined and created in their fiction. But to transform modernity, Catholic writers could not simply stand against it; they had to enter into it. And so by 1959 Walter Ong could see and urge the necessity of articulating the Church's place in "cosmic history": "not the adaptation of revelation to the facts, but the integration of the new facts with revelation; not a new understanding of faith and of God in light of the new discoveries, but a new understanding of the new discoveries in the light of faith and in relationship to God."[28] Another crucial perspective here is that of Ong's fellow Jesuit William F. Lynch. In a series of books published from the 1950s throughout the 1960s, Lynch drew together literary learning, an intense interest in how new media were reshaping human experience, and a critical but profoundly sympathetic stance toward postwar culture. Though skilled at fine critical and philosophical distinctions, his thought always tended toward seeking harmony and connection, not separatism or abstraction, because ultimately, as Gerald J. Bednar writes, Lynch was "convinced that our salvation lies in the finite contours of the valley of the human where Christ came to dwell among us."[29]

Even in the glitzy, relentlessly secular context of the New York theater world, Walter Kerr, theater critic for the *New York Herald Tribune*, dared to articulate a reconciliation between these two apparently irreconcilable things. In a series of lectures given at Trinity College in Washington, DC, and published as *Criticism and Censorship*, Kerr argued that art and truth were both best served when those inclined to censor acknowledged the legitimate autonomy of art, and when those inclined to an absolute rejection of censorship acknowledged that art was not good unless it was willing at some level to take human truth into account. "The defender of art and the defender of prudence are actually interested in the same objectives, in slightly different proportions," he concluded hopefully.[30]

In all of these examples, key parameters have shifted—orthodoxy no longer means solely doctrinal fidelity, but a particular imaginative stance consonant with Catholicism as a worldview, in a complicated though not necessarily contentious relationship to doctrinal formulation. Harold Gardiner defended Graham Greene's work by emphasizing Greene's insight that to understand humanity's relationship with God was to plunge into full awareness of modern reality in its ugliness as well as its beauty.[31] And when Frank O'Malley compares James Joyce favorably to James T. Farrell, describing Joyce as "Dantesque,"[32] the circle is complete—Dante has come to represent not Pallen's lost organic integration of Christian belief and society, but an expansive sympathy for human beings in the world as it is.

In his 1960 novel *The Moviegoer*, Walker Percy brought a fresh voice to the scene of Catholic literature in his rootlessly rooted protagonist Binx Bolling, who fights "the grip of everydayness" in order to pursue his "search" for something different from the devout Catholicism of his mother's family or the cheerful atheism of his father's. For what, he has no conventional words, but he takes as his starting point a notion he had jotted down in the middle of a restless night: "It no longer avails to start with creatures and prove God. Yet it is impossible to rule God out." There is no certainty here, but there is deep attentiveness to the world that Binx Bolling sees around him, and courage in exploring that world despite the lack of obvious signposts. "Abraham saw signs of God and believed. Now the only sign is that all the signs in the world make no difference. Is this God's ironic revenge? But I am on to him."[33] Binx Bolling lacks the deeply schooled Jesuit heritage that enables William Lynch and Walter Ong to see evidence of the divine in a disorienting, newly perceived cosmic infinity, nor does he have access to even the more conventional reconciliatory categories Walter Kerr uses to bridge art and prudence. But in the dogged nature of his search, he points to the same truths. Binx Bolling is by the nature of his era cut off from the earlier ages of faith in ways that might seem to confirm all the worst imaginings of those who feared the corrosive effects of modernity. But Percy uses him instead to highlight the perennial receptivity of the human heart to the true grounding of reality, no matter what might intervene. In doing so, he diffuses modernist antipathy for orthodoxy by making the search something new, and calms Catholic anxiety about iconoclasm by leaving ample room to imagine the incarnational reality where Binx could end up.

This reconciliation makes an intellectual resource available, though it does not necessarily effect the transformation it conceives. That is, it offers an intellectually plausible stance that bridges a gap between Catholicism and modernity that had for decades seemed unbridgeable, but it does not in itself demonstrate that anyone used that stance to actually build the bridge. In the emergence of similar reconciliations for the other three oppositions that characterized the Catholic encounter with literary modernism, the connection between idea and action, their institutional manifestations, will be more apparent.

CHAPTER 8

Peculiarly Possessed of the Modern Consciousness

To say that by the 1950s Catholic writers and critics had reconciled an apparently unbridgeable modernist rift between orthodoxy and iconoclasm is to draw on some very old associations. The earliest uses of the verb "to reconcile" in English, in the late fourteenth century, referred to the reconciliation of humanity to God in Christ. The theological etymology reflects the weight of what Catholic critics believed to be at stake. They used theological categories to think through literary problems because literary problems were never only literary. But conversely, the theological ideas they employed could be and were used as *ideas*, as concepts with analytical utility as well as doctrinal authority. This mutually reinforcing mode of analysis helped Catholics involved in literary work address modernism—literary and theological—on their own terms, and helped them effect a reconciliation between apparently irreconcilable oppositions. To be sure, many, many frayed edges remained. But nonetheless, those doing this thinking generated an incomplete, imperfect, enormously fruitful set of conceptual resources—ways of thinking about being in the world—that reveal their belief that the grievances underlying the estrangement were open to genuine healing. The meaning of reconciliation that suggests acquiescence or submission of one party to another is two centuries more recent than the oldest usage. (Even the accounting use of the term preserves some element of mutuality—both sides of the ledger have to be adjusted in order for the figures to come out.) As with orthodoxy and iconoclasm, so also with individual and community, innovation and repetition, openness and closure. By the 1950s, Catholics involved in literary work had found news ways to work within them, too. The result was a multi-layered, multibrowed, frequently cacophonous resituating of Catholicism in the history of modernity.

Central to the cultural work of Catholic literature early in the century, the idea of the Incarnation played a leading role postwar as well. Flannery O'Connor's take is the best known: "One of the awful things about writing when you are a Christian is that for you the ultimate reality is the Incarnation, the present reality is the Incarnation, the whole reality is the Incarnation, and nobody believes in the Incarnation; that is, nobody in your audience."[1] O'Connor's assertion is typical, not idiosyncratic. In support of his point that "to be a Catholic novelist in fact demands a complete understanding of our entire tradition, and by that I mean western tradition from Greek times to the present moment," another Catholic critic wrote, "The Incarnation was not a point in history. It is a living reality which forever conditions all existence, all living."[2] In context, these are not only confessional or doctrinal assertions, but components of an intellectual history that have been overlooked because they have been relegated to the category of piety, and perhaps to the category of not "thinking on one's own." But as well as being a central affirmation of Christian faith, the Incarnation is also an *idea* that an intellectual can take up and ponder and use to think through a particular issue or problem.

As Catholics involved in literary work used the Incarnation and other ideas central to Christian belief and practice to think through the apparent standoff between Catholicism and intellectual and artistic modernity, they developed a set of resources that eventually freed them from the obligation to stand visibly always and only as a counter to modernity. In the process, Catholic literary culture reclaimed both the persistence of Catholicism within modernity and the obligation on the part of Catholics to seek evidence of the Incarnation in the modern world.

As ideas found new expression and renewed purpose, so did the institutions animated by them. For example, as the 1950s progressed, its historians have generally agreed, the "Catholic revival" faded from view. It had been particularly important to American Catholics of the preceding generation because it gave them a sense of connection to and continuity with significant contemporary literary achievement at a time when they were lamenting its lack among their compatriots. The idea of the revival also helped mediate Catholic transition to modernity, giving them a cultural self-conception that could help their version of American innocence to survive an additional generation beyond the Great War, or, alternatively, a distinctive task of "promoting, defending and redeeming."[3] But these accounts depend on a history and a periodization of the revival in which it ends abruptly in the generation after World War II and is only a faintly embarrassing memory by the time of the Council.

But in what sense did the revival actually end? It is true that some organizations declined and disappeared, but others appeared and flourished, and still others took on new tasks and new identities. It is not clear, though, that the extent or self-consciousness of Catholic literary activity appreciably diminished. In fact, the opposite might be the case, that at precisely the cultural moment in which Catholic literary culture took on the greatest influence and prestige, historians of the Catholic revival instead perceived its demise. John McGreevy notes the revived influence of John Henry Newman's theology in the 1940s; it is likely, however, that his prominent inclusion in the works that defined and catalogued the Catholic literary revival helped to preserve a more general awareness of his work so that it was on the horizon when the theological climate became more favorable.[4] It is also difficult to see the diminishment of Catholic literary culture in these observations of Flannery O'Connor in a March 1963 letter to Sally and Robert Fitzgerald: "I haven't seen it in print but somebody told me he thought [Robert] got the Bollingen Prize. I congratulate you. You should have got it if you didn't. I guess you saw that Powers got the National Book Award. I was much cheered at that. I got the O. Henry this year. Walker Percy got the N'tl Book Award last year. Katherine Anne will probably get the Pulitzer Prize. I think you ought to judge the prize by the book but even so these hold up and all these people are Catlicks so this should be some kind of answer to the people who are saying we don't contribute to the arts."[5]

O'Connor's information was perhaps not as reliable as it might have been, but her point is still valid: Robert Fitzgerald received the Bollingen Poetry Translation Prize in 1961 for his translation of the *Odyssey*, but he did not receive the 1963 Bollingen Prize for Poetry. Katherine Anne Porter did not receive the Pulitzer Prize for *Ship of Fools* in 1963 but did receive it in 1966 for her *Collected Stories*. J. F. Powers won the National Book Award in 1963 for *Morte D'Urban*; Walker Percy had won the previous year for *The Moviegoer*. Six of O'Connor's stories were included in the annual O. Henry Award *Prize Stories* anthologies; three ("Greenleaf" [1957], "Everything That Rises Must Converge" [1963], and "Revelation" [1965]) as the first-prize story.

O'Connor's comments were made in the wake of a wave of Catholic self-criticism occasioned by John Tracy Ellis's 1955 excoriation of the state of American Catholic intellectual achievement. Ellis, at the time the best-known historian of U.S. Catholicism, argued at a meeting of the Catholic Commission on Intellectual and Cultural Affairs that Catholics had thus far in their history failed to achieve intellectually at a level commensurate with their numbers, their length of duration in the nation, or their tradition. The talk, later published as an article, galvanized the American Catholic intellectual community, which took to heart many of Ellis's criticisms of the failures of U.S. Catholic culture, including deep-seated anti-intellectualism and a materialistic failure to emphasize education as much as other immigrant groups had. There seems to have been nearly universal agreement that Ellis's criticism was in large measure justified. O'Connor's comments represent not quite a dissenting view, but a concomitant response that pointed toward contemporary signs percolating out of sight as Ellis formulated and launched his critique. Because, though, the realm of the literary, of art and culture, was institutionally becoming so separate from the areas in which Ellis detailed the lack of Catholic intellectual achievement, these signs remained largely unseen even during the period of the most intensive self-scrutiny U.S. Catholic intellectual culture had yet experienced. Literature simply did not figure into Ellis's definition of "intellectual" achievement.

Another observer of the same phenomenon was Harold Gardiner, who in 1962 wrote an article for *America* entitled, "Scholars, Catholic, Who's Got the?" Gardiner had followed his 1940–62 stint as literary editor of *America* with a position at the *Catholic Encyclopedia*.[6] This 1962 *America* piece made the point that there was a, to him, surprising and impressive number of Catholic scholars doing work in a wide variety of areas. While not rejecting the content or the bracing effect of John Tracy Ellis's criticism, Gardiner sketched an optimistic picture of burgeoning intellectual achievement that seemed at least to offer real hope of fulfilling Ellis's dream.

Modernism and Postwar Culture

Even if the end of the Catholic revival might be more apparent than actual, why did it seem to so many to have disappeared from view? Where did it go? Examining this question leads to the site of some of the most significant institutional changes both to literary study and to the culture of U.S. Catholicism in the postwar period, the university. The large-scale entry of Catholics into the university after World War II had at least two significant effects on the intellectual life of 1950s Catholicism and specifically on changing ideas in literary culture. The first resulted from an important shift in the site of theological education. Before the mid-twentieth century, the study of Catholic theology was almost exclusively limited to those preparing for ordination to the priesthood. Catholic literary culture had long been deeply inflected by the theological training of the priests who were prominent as critics, teachers, and reviewers. By the 1950s a significant cohort of laity were studying theology in universities, whose curricula were beginning to expand to include the study of theology per se (as distinct from religious instruction). In addition, a small but influential group of laity were becoming theologically self-educated, as the Catholic revival and Catholic Action promoted awareness of major theological works and trends, along with the responsibility of laypeople to study and be educated in these areas. Sister Mariella Gable had identified "the education of lay people in theology" as one of "six signs of a spiritual awakening in the United States," in a 1948 lecture entitled "This Is the New Pentecost."[7] Lay writers on literature were probably in the 1940s and 1950s more educated theologically than they were before or have been since. They reappropriated the theological tradition as part of their writing about literature.

However, as lay Catholics in larger numbers attended colleges and universities, they were affected by one of the most prominent trends in twentieth-century higher education, specialization. Instead of a cadre of priest-critics, all of whom had some theological training in addition to their literary training, laypeople were more likely to study either theology or literature, but not both, and much of the change in the direction of Catholic literary culture after the 1950s can be attributed to this shift through which literary thinking and theological thinking were informing each other less regularly and less thoroughly.

Another trend that affected U.S. Catholics as they entered in large numbers into university study was a result of the change in literary culture itself. Many of the Catholic critics of the earlier generation exalted literature as part of a genteel vision of life and culture, elitist in its way, but also part of the dream of assimilation, of a population eventually freed enough from earning a living that they could more readily and often contemplate reading, thinking, and all the pleasures of culture. This belles lettres dream, to the extent that it ever actually shaped the university study of literature, was by the 1950s effectively displaced by what Terry Eagleton diagnoses as a by-product of industrialization and the opening of the universities—the mechanical dissection of texts that increasingly characterized New Critical pedagogy as overworked professors dealt with increasing numbers of underprepared students.[8] That is, by defining literary texts as self-contained and interpretation of the "text itself" as the primary work of literary analysis, literary critics and literature teachers could transfer their critical perspective into the classroom on a scale large enough to accommodate the increased demand. In addition, the New Critical focus on close reading and extended interpretation of the text was aptly suited to modernist ideas about the freedom of the text from history and the self-contained, formal nature of the artistic artifact.

At roughly the same time that more lay Catholics were drawing more creatively than ever before on theology as a resource for literary thinking, their entry into, prominence, and growing success within secular literary culture both within and outside the university began to diminish theology's credibility as an intellectual resource. But not before there was an interesting body of reflection available that brought together elements that might otherwise have been thought irrevocably disparate.

The not entirely happy marriage between New Criticism and industrial-scale postwar university pedagogy highlights the persistence of one of the distinctive features of Catholic approaches to literature. More even than earlier secular critical approaches, New Criticism treated literary texts as discrete artifacts, detached from authorial intent and reader reaction, to be approached entirely formally. Although a number of New Critics were Catholic, and New Critical approaches were also adopted critically and pedagogically by Catholic writers and critics, Catholic critics nonetheless retained a commitment to and interest in the connection between art and morality. The state of this commitment varied—for some writers and critics it was integral to their approach; others wrestled with the normative prescriptions of Church authority, seeking to disentangle aesthetic and moral criteria in ways they saw as more consistent with the contemporary context.

Catholic concern with art and morality had the consequence of blurring the boundaries among various kinds of art in ways that some critics found infuriating and others found invigorating. One consequence of this blurring was an inability to keep the literary artifact in the highly limited and refined sphere prepared for it by New Criticism. Instead, for Catholics artworks of any kind were deeply implicated in political and pastoral contexts, in families and parishes and towns and businesses, and any intellectual work on art had in some ultimate way to be made sense of as part of this larger context. The ramifications for modernisms literary and theological are considerable: Catholic attitudes toward literature by the 1950s made it impossible to analyze modernism seriously without applying cosmically theological categories to modernity, as well. Because of the essential connection between art and theology, Catholic critics had to work out a consistent and intellectually credible approach to an issue that other critics could simply dismiss as outmoded or unsophisticated. This was not, even within highly circumscribed boundaries of Catholic literary culture, a calm or uncontested bit of territory. It would be difficult to find anyone outside the Church harder than those within it on mindless or reductive moralism. But that is part of the point: Catholic critics were implicated by the moralism of other Catholics in ways other intellectuals were not. That implication required them to take up intellectual—literary critical—tasks that other critics had abandoned or attempted to discredit. William Lynch wrote in 1959, "There was undoubtedly a generation when we had to defend the autonomy of art and the artefact, to defend its right to be itself over against every other kind of human performance. In certain circles, especially among the absolute 'moralists,' this is still necessary. But I think the more overwhelming necessity of these years is not to defend the autonomy of the artefact and the right it has to its own act of self-possession, its own *prise de conscience*, but to recall to ourselves its high human status and relation to reality."[9]

In deference to contemporary philosophical understandings of value judgments as devoid of intellectual content, New Critics, for example, consciously set aside—"evaded and explicitly exiled"—discussions of the value of literary works.[10] By accepting an alternative epistemology that deemed value judgments not only possible but necessary, Catholic philosophy prescribed a very different stance toward literature. The centrality of philosophy to Catholic intellectual work—and its increasingly central place in Catholic higher education and therefore in the training of scholars in many disciplines (especially those who were clerics and religious)—meant that evaluation had a philosophical rationale and imperative absent in mainstream critical work.[11] Therefore Catholic critics were unable, as other critics did, to "exile evaluation," and, especially, to see a work of art as hermetically sealed off from its contexts.

While her boldness might not be readily apparent, Sister T. A. Doyle, OSB, was staking out contested critical ground when she wrote in the 1955 *Benedictine Review* about going "Beyond the New Criticism": "A consideration of the ontological and the epistemological phases of a literary object will give criticism a new dimension and will strengthen the Aristotelian concept of technique as the soul of the work rather than a mechanical device; it will raise 'close reading,' 'rhetorical' and 'structural' analyses beyond the descriptive level of science and make possible literary response and evaluation which need not degenerate into 'impure' criticism."[12] The reference is to an influential essay by critic Robert Penn Warren, for whom "impure" criticism was that which brought to bear on the literary text anything outside what was required for its interpretation. New Critics certainly found room for theological and religious ideas within the scope of their notion of interpretation, but the Catholic insistence on locating the literary artifact in a temporal and communal context within which evaluation was inescapable was a textbook example of how to make criticism "impure."

The resources developed over the course of the preceding decades in trying to maintain this intellectual balancing act stood many Catholic critics in good stead as critical discussion of the relationship between art and morality shifted markedly in the Cold War context of the 1950s. Intellectuals who had long articulated and defended the notion of art for art's sake, of the autonomy of art and the artist, found themselves in a new and peculiar bind. Early in the century, defending the autonomy of the artist—and specifically, of the modernist artist—presumed a critique of bourgeois convention, the moral pieties and societal strictures of Victorian life. Within the context of the Cold War, artistic autonomy still seemed worth defending, especially in contrast to the artist's role in Soviet propaganda. This defense became, however, instead of a critique of American life an exemplar of its strengths and superiority in contrast with Soviet restrictiveness. It would be an exaggeration to say that Cold War intellectuals abandoned all critique of American life, but preserving and defending liberal democratic values became enough of a shared goal that the context for discussions of issues of art and morality was distinctly changed.[13]

One aspect of this change was the simultaneously shifting politics of modernism as an artistic movement. The politics of modernism had always been complex. It was both defiantly apolitical and deeply politicized. Early in the twentieth century, modernist artists claimed to speak from a place outside social and formal convention. In the United States after the Great War, modernism was initially a symbol of European decadence but was drawn into the oppositional dynamic by which capitalist democracy defined itself against "totalitarianism," that amalgam of the political poles of communism and fascism.[14] In this reconceptualization of modernism, the artist, instead of being a decadent European, becomes the free voice speaking freely in a free society, a symbol of the absence of the repression and political control of art that characterized Soviet communism and Nazi Germany.

From this angle, modernism seems to have been enlisted on the liberal side of the great postwar divide, but the picture is made much more complex if we look at the politics of modernism's most famous practitioners. T. S. Eliot's 1927 conversion, to, as he described it in the preface of *For Lancelot Andrewes*, "classicist in literature, royalist in politics, and anglo-catholic in religion," left the movement without the creator of perhaps its most famous document, *The Waste Land*. Ezra Pound's descent into fascism and madness could be read differently from different directions—it either discredited modernism or reconfirmed the burden of taking on the weight of history and politics, but he still was not by the 1950s any kind of political role model for a context in which there was little room for ambiguity and complexity.

The complexity—perhaps the incoherence—of modernism's political valence reflects its fate by the 1950s in the path of the century's various cultural storm fronts. In part it had simply suffered the apparently inevitable "vicissitudes of the avant-garde"—William Gass's term for the impossibility of any artistic movement's long remaining out in front culturally. The more a movement defines itself by its distance from the mainstream, the more its transgressive stance is challenged by being taken up into the art world's machinery of exhibition and criticism, especially by critical approbation. When, by the 1950s, modernist writers and artists were available in paperback at the neighborhood drugstore and in inexpensive prints to decorate suburban living rooms, their power to shock had been defused.[15]

Aiding in this defanging of the modernist tiger was its institutionalization as part of the literary establishment. Instead of posing a challenge to the very definition of literature, as modernism had done for the belles-lettres generation between the wars, modernist authors now became fodder for critical reputations and a well-worn path to academic respectability. Increasingly important to the curricula of English departments in the rapidly growing postwar universities, modernist texts, instead of cultivating in their young readers the uncreated conscience of the race, became a means of access to the bourgeois credentials they had been created to flout.

Perhaps even more ignominiously, modernism was also by the 1950s thoroughly commodified. Not only were paperback books and cubist prints the set-dressing of middle-class life, but a modernist aesthetic had permeated advertising and design to such an extent that it could be sent up in the production numbers of the 1957 movie *Funny Face*.[16] The mock advertisements that promote the "Think Pink!" campaign invented by editor and style titan Maggie Prescott both parody and celebrate the pervasiveness of modernist design. The movie's look is reinforced by its themes. By the time photographer Fred Astaire rescues naive bookstore-clerk-turned-fashion-model Audrey Hepburn from the clutches of her deceptive Beat seducer, it is clear that love and truth lie not with the enervated modernism of artistic poseurs but with the transparently commodified modernism of the fashion industry. A similar attitude had been evident three years earlier in

Choreography, the Danny Kaye parody of Martha Graham in 1954's *White Christmas*.[17] The number's lyrics lament that "choreography" is taking over "the theatah," but undercut themselves by featuring Vera Ellen tap-dancing circles around the Graham-style corps backing Kaye. Modernism's pretensions had long been fair game for popular culture, but by the 1950s popular culture's association with popular will and the freedom of the free market gave it the moral upper hand in the Cold War cultural arena.

A significant component of modernism's self-definition decades earlier had been the ability to stand outside bourgeois culture and reject its inauthenticity. The rise of mass culture seemed to make this role even more necessary: the endless replicability of an artwork, ready accessibility to the masses, the inevitable degradation of taste and artistic vision necessary to make art palatable to the masses and to satisfy commercial rather than aesthetic motives—all these things coalesced into an aesthetic other against which modernists asserted their authenticity, energy, and individuality.[18] But once consumer culture had demonstrated it could commodify even modernism's most experimental and unconventional impulses, was there anything left? Was it possible any longer for art to function critically, to hold up the flaws and hypocrisies of bourgeois culture to the light, when bourgeois culture had become an international symbol not of complacency and comfort but of the moral superiority of democracy?

By the postwar period, such anxieties over mass culture were familiar and pervasive, but certain elements of the Cold War context rendered them newly urgent. The structures of meaning in a mass society, it was feared, could be so easily centralized and manipulated (whether by the state or by increasingly powerful corporations) that the agency necessary for democratic citizenship was constantly imperiled. This anxiety, however, brought two distinguishing aspects of modernity into stark conflict. On the one hand, the manufactured, commercial nature of mass culture risked obliterating individual creativity, taste, and art's potential for disruption and innovation. At its most dangerous it could pacify and anesthetize the masses to an extent communist propaganda could only aspire to. On the other hand, the very capacities exemplified by mass culture—systematized efficient production, extensive distribution, the riotous proliferation of images and stories, worldwide profit and imaginative influence—were also evidence of what the unleashing of human capabilities in a democratic capitalist system permitted, which a communist society would have squelched. Little wonder that the debate over mass culture ranged so widely and so vociferously throughout the postwar years. It was the site at which art was most clearly susceptible to being co-opted by commerce and thus deprived of its capacity to keep democracy true to its ideals.[19] But if thriving commerce was itself one of the key components of a flourishing democracy, as proponents of the free market steadfastly maintained, then what?

Anxiety over mass culture and the accompanying concern over its corrosive effect on modernism's power in their turn reflected a larger set of apprehensions about materialism and American life. Postwar prosperity was simultaneously a sign of the superiority of American democratic capitalism and a potentially harmful drug. The triumph of industrial capitalism produced a standard of living that both confirmed its righteousness and evoked nostalgia for the virtues it rendered unnecessary. The producerist character traits of industry, thrift, independence, and stoic endurance seemed on the verge of giving way to a passive conformity that benefited from affluence while surrendering the struggle to achieve it anew in each generation. From popular fiction to sociology, from motion pictures to elite cultural analysis, the union of democracy with consumer capitalism produced both patriotic celebration and systemic anxiety. This deep cultural ambivalence stemmed from a growing realization that it was not impossible—in fact, it was increasingly likely—that the engulfing nature of the market could ultimately undermine the resources necessary to sustain democratic individualism, and the logic of Cold War polarization was pushing inexorably in only one direction. Increasingly throughout the postwar period, the market co-opted the language of freedom, and by the 1950s there remained no widely operative notion of American democracy that was not attached to the "free" market.

Individual and Community

Seen from one angle, U.S. Catholics were quite thoroughly of this postwar American mainstream. Evidence is plentiful of their attempts to bring a Catholic perspective to bear on the great questions of the age, attempts that occasionally came close to enlisting Catholic theology, art, and culture into the militaristic nationalism of the arms race. For example, a play for grade-schoolers entitled "Our Atom Bomb, the Rosary," appeared in the *Catholic School Journal* in 1948. Written by Sister M. Pierre of Mt. Mercy Junior College and Academy in Cedar Rapids, Iowa, the play opens with a "Reader" saying: "For months there has been much discussion in international circles as to who will control the atom bomb. But there is another type of atom bomb which will insure peace for a war-weary world. Let me tell you about this atom bomb—the rosary."[20] The play goes on to link the rosary not so much with nuclear war as with the historical associations of Fatima, Lepanto, and the Albigensians—with, that is, the triumph, political as well as theological, of true belief over heresy in the long view of Western history.

From the time of the drastic curtailing of immigration in the early 1920s, much of the energy of the American Catholic community was focused on assimilation and upward mobility. By the 1950s Catholics were well on their way to achieving economic parity in U.S. society, surely a consummation long devoutly wished for by their immigrant forebears. But while the achievement of the immigrant dream might have salved the heartache and the thousand natural shocks before the postwar generation could inherit them, it had effects on the survival and identity of a distinctive Catholic worldview that its proponents did not anticipate. By the 1950s there was an explicit and widely articulated tension between, on the one hand, the undeniably positive benefit of moving from poverty and struggle to prosperity and, on the other, the continuing sense that materialism could stifle and corrode spiritual and communal life. This anxiety seemed to deepen and extend simultaneously with an increasing (and more widely noted and acknowledged) outward confidence in democracy and the beneficence of religious liberty.[21]

On the whole, Catholics in the postwar United States identified increasingly against the totalitarian regimes of Europe and with the democratic liberalism of the United States. Many of them retained, nonetheless, a persistent skepticism about the connection between American political ideals and the free market. It would be inaccurate to characterize this as a majority view—so many postwar Catholics were still striving to achieve middle-class status that critiquing it seemed self-defeating or self-indulgent, a luxury available only to saints strong enough to live without it or to those solidly ensconced enough to be in little danger of losing it.

But if it was never the view of the majority, a significant number of Catholics involved in political and cultural analysis nonetheless attempted to describe a dissonance, an unease with the easy equation of freedom with free-market capitalism. In public political discussion, at some point in the twentieth century, the autonomous individual of liberal political philosophy had become conflated with the consumer, and the defense of individual liberty became inextricable from defending the indefinite expansion of consumer choice.[22] Even while participating in many ways in this shift, Catholics who engaged in explicit and self-conscious analysis of the postwar situation remained distinctive in their recognition of the inescapably communal dimension of economic relationships. This recognition permanently complicated the relationship with postwar democratic liberalism. Even after the rapprochement was under way, Catholics maintained a critique of American individualism that sustained its democratic bona fides by speaking the language of democracy, but protected a space for the critique of individualism by aligning itself with wider cultural critiques of conformity and materialism that had, at their base, an inescapably communal ethos and theology.

This balancing act exemplifies the terms on which Catholics declined the opposition between individual and community that had helped conceptually structure modernism. Catholics were indeed bound by communal obligations and hierarchical authority; however, by the 1950s they were more explicitly refusing to accept that this obligation defined them as premodern or antiquated. It is in this context that they also reimagined the responsibility of the individual in terms of a "maturity" that could accommodate cultural ideals of autonomy while retaining a commitment to a normative, communal morality.

Early in the century, at the high noon of Catholic encounters with modernism, individualism had been one of the most excoriated and rejected tropes, one of the things that was most explicitly rejected about modernist sensibility. As with so much else, Joyce's "uncreated conscience of the race" was an ur-moment, in which the exhilaration of modernist freedom from history became the thing that severed the protagonist/author from the Christian community. Catholic criticism participated in this opposition (often with histrionic language about the lack of self-control on the part of modernists that is indistinguishable from bourgeois disdain for the rejection of social and sexual convention), but early in the process they articulated a middle ground within which participation in community and tradition, and submission to lawful authority, were the things that made the individual self possible, kept it intact, and enabled it to flourish.

This process was not without conflict or division. Immigrant desires for assimilation, the call for obedience to church authority, the apparently unvarying conformity of suburban life—all these strands in twentieth-century U.S. Catholic culture were experienced by writers and critics from Theodore Dreiser to Harry Sylvester as crippling limitations on individuality, in contrast with which the opportunity for self-definition and reinvention afforded in the kaleidoscopic landscape of American freedom and prosperity beckoned irresistibly. A significant number of writers and critics left the Church under the pressure of this opposition. Given its apparent starkness, this is not surprising. It does, though, then raise a question directly related to the issue of the individual's relationship to community: On what terms did those who stayed reconcile the contradiction?

The reconciliation of this opposition was facilitated by the grim postwar recognition that modernity had for at least the better part of a century not been progressing inevitably in the direction of human liberation and freedom. If Catholics increasingly accepted the moral legitimacy, even necessity, of religious liberty and of other components of democratic polity, their compatriots faced the possibility, in the light of Hiroshima and Nagasaki (and Dresden and Cologne), that human technology and ingenuity suffered from an innate amorality that had brought the human species perilously close to destruction. N. Elizabeth Monroe noted in a 1953 article, "Man has been forced through suffering to grow and extend himself, to deepen his whole nature, to take his part in breaking down the walls that separate man from man, to cooperate with the whole redemptive process."[23] Philip J. Scharper of Fordham's English Department noted in *America* in 1952 that "literature since the Renaissance represents a defection from grace, but it has also taught us more about ourselves, and has given us techniques through which these new insights into our nature could be expressed."[24] Catholics' eventual embrace of certain aspects of modernity, even modernism, was tempered by their belief in a growing awareness even among secular liberals of the ways in which modernity constricted human freedom, and of how the long history of reflection on human nature and its limitations embodied in the major religious traditions could provide resources to help preserve it.

Innovation and Repetition

This mutual recognition happened at the level of elite intellectual analysis and criticism, but it also occurred where writers and critics engaged mass culture. Here the communal dimensions, from a Catholic perspective, of both aesthetics and economics came to the fore and created a distinctive configuration on the landscape. Because for Catholics the communal dimension of art always included economic relationships, Catholics were aware of literature and popular culture not isolated as artistic objects but embedded in a context as commodities to be sold. As a result they were vocally critical of the amorality of the sales impulse and righteously suspicious of the commercial exploitation of the imagination at which mass culture excelled. Catholic commentators criticized the dominance of the profit motive in the creation of popular art, warning against "purveyors of filth" who were unconcerned whether they corrupted their audiences as long as they had a healthy bottom line. Catholic critics expressed unanimous contempt for the excuse of producers of material they judged morally harmful that the producers were "just giving the people what they want." This criticism was too often, shamefully, tied up with anticommunism and anti-Semitism—the fear that communists, most often portrayed as atheistic Jews, were infiltrating U.S. society and aiming for domination by corrupting America's youth. Such conspiracy theories were not the fundamental philosophical basis for Catholic concern about the effect of mass art, but they suggest how Cold War politics could reinforce and fuel old prejudices.

Because of the conceptual connection forged between literature and popular culture by the Index of Forbidden Books and the Legion of Decency (which the controversies over the NODL kept in the public eye throughout the 1950s), Catholic literary critics and teachers of literature probably wrote and thought more about mass media and popular culture than most other intellectuals. It is difficult to find someone who did only one or the other. Catholics were certainly, from the advent of mass culture onward, like many of their compatriot intellectuals critical of its lowest-common-denominator effect on artistic taste. Many Catholics involved in literary work in the generation after the Great War saw Catholic access to the genteel tradition as the goal of their work and were as disconcerted as other Victorian-Edwardian Americans by the modernists' rejection of convention and deliberate scorn for the pretty or tidy.[25] But by the 1950s, after several decades of an emerging critical discussion and extensive nationwide organizational development, the Catholics most critical of popular culture, most engaged in criticism of it, were also the ones with the most expansive visions of the possibilities it presented for the widening of human horizons.

From popular art's earliest beginnings, Catholics had celebrated its democratic possibilities. Affordable reproduction of visual art gave low-wage workers access to realms of culture that the members of the upper classes had had free entry to during their grand tours (and viewed as an explicitly Catholic heritage), but that immigrants—in many cases from those same countries that made up the Grand Tour—could not see by any other means. Inexpensive paperbound books might facilitate the proliferation of the dime novel, but they also put Dante and Shakespeare in pocket-money range. Not all celebrations of popular culture relied on its making high culture accessible and inexpensive, however—there was strong affirmative Catholic support for popular culture on its own terms from its earliest years, rooted in the legitimacy of the need for leisure and entertainment, a conviction that intensified along with Catholicism's identification with the industrial working class.

As Catholic writers and critics continued to reject the notion that their distinctively configured perspective was sectarian, their language and rationale shifted away from the Thomistic categories of natural law. By the 1950s, when they insisted on the necessity of intellectuals conceiving themselves as part of and accountable to the people as a whole, they were more likely to justify their stance not only theologically or pastorally but also as part of the obligation of intellectuals in a democracy. This responsibility included but was not limited to thinking about popular culture in a way that would bolster America's cultural and spiritual superiority to the Soviet Union.

The anxiety of secular intellectuals about the effect on the free democratic individual of the repetitive mass production that characterized popular culture took a distinct form for Catholic intellectuals. Because of the Catholic aesthetic imperative to serve all classes—to address as much what ordinary people read and watched as what critics and scholars analyzed and esteemed—criticisms of repetition could not simply dismiss the capacities or taste of popular culture's devotees. Modernist and New Critical disdain for the idea that mass production could result in anything worthy of the term "art" had to be tempered by the radical continuity presumed by official Catholic teaching and quotidian Catholic practice. This continuity aided in reconciling the opposition between innovation and repetition, and it did so at least in part at a site that might seem unlikely: the liturgy.

Repetition characterizes popular culture, both in the mass production of the artistic object and in the development of genres (mysteries, romance, science fiction, westerns) that seek to satisfy the desire of consumers for a predictable, repeatable experience. These features of popular culture had long been seen in elite analysis as key contributors to the narcotizing effect of mass culture. Artistic innovation that depended on fresh seeing, constantly encountering the world anew, was consequently prized as characteristic of real art and literature. Within a wider secular cultural framework, repetition was seen, almost irresistibly, as mechanical, and therefore as not only inartistic but also as deadening and inhuman. In a 1950s television interview for the series *Writers of Today*, Walter Kerr interviewed poet W. H. Auden. In the course of the interview Kerr asked what explained "the relative estrangement of the poet in our society." Auden replied that, for people living in this particular technological age, poetry was a kind of ritual and "it's also rhythmical, it has repetition." He went on to say, "I think repetition in people's minds now is so associated with the dullest part of life, routine, punching a time clock and so on, that they can't see that anything that repeats as poetry does, it to them it is a little antipathetic."

Kerr followed up by asking whether mechanization depersonalized matters so that the poet's function was no longer so personal. Auden replied by saying, "It may be the other way round—the difficulty for a poet living in a technological age is that in fact he can only write about personal matters. In the past so much poetry was written about public events, and now it is almost impossible to do. The question interests me and worries me very much . . . that in order to write about or celebrate a hero or heroine, their greatness, is that they must combine virtue, excellence of some kind with power. Now in a technological age, power is taken over by a machine, and however excellent a person may be the power isn't theirs, it's in the machine."[26] While Catholics and other Christians certainly saw and acknowledged and were on patrol against such danger, repetition was a less univocal notion for them, because (appropriately understood) it also characterized the central act of Catholic worship, the Mass and the sacraments. Auden could therefore both make and lament others' inability to make the distinction between repetition as mechanization and repetition as ritual.

Conceived liturgically, innovation does not reject repetition but depends on it. Repeated encounter makes fresh understanding possible. Few Catholic writers, even quite self-conscious ones, spell out this connection. Flannery O'Connor's 1955 conviction that she can say almost nothing about the Eucharist outside a story is a variation two decades on of Richard Sullivan's 1933 caution to himself as he outlines an ambitious series of one-act plays for Catholic schools, "Christmas, Passion Play, Easter Play, Ascension Play, Pentecost Play. Perhaps also a cycle including the holy days: All Saints, Immaculate Conception, Assumption; the various saint-days.—A hand book of drama for the liturgical year. And nothing soppy about it."[27] William F. Lynch further illustrates this complexity when he includes ritual in a chapter on the "theological imagination" in *Christ and Apollo*: "By every instinct in them men desperately need to think and move together, ritually," a truth, he argues, that leads to freedom, not to the conformity that contemporary society seems to fear. He then refers to the "sense of freedom" available in "the higher reserve of the divine liturgy," a sense that he describes as "having escaped from society." He is chagrined by this, but, he says, he will let it stand "as a symbol that the language of the solipsist, of the romantic hero, has taken over in these highest matters, so that I as a Catholic am trapped into the use of them when I am talking of my most social, my most ritual, my freest moment."[28] Lynch poses and dismisses the danger of conformity, then also pulls back from the opposite danger of exaggerated individualism. Though he, like O'Connor, retreats from his attempt to capture something he decides he is incapable of capturing, both of them point toward a cosmic horizon with literary implications. Liturgy is a source not of mindlessness but of access to something that unites or transcends apparent opposites: the free individual is also deeply social, the familiar and traditional are always new and newly created.

If repetition were not inherently stultifying but could create the conditions for new awareness and greater connection, then Catholic critics and scholars could not relinquish popular culture to the realm of the commercial; the more extensive their reflection, the likelier they were to highlight its high destiny and its possibilities to participate in the work not just of entertainment but of great art in the largest sense of the human tradition. Their ability to link the time-bound and the timeless offered a way of thinking about the literary that went beyond modernist and New Critical strictures and back into history and culture at a moment when both the Catholic intellectual world and the secular literary academy could find renewed resources there.

Openness and Closure

As a way of finding itself on the intellectual landscape of the twentieth-century United States, Catholic writing about literature retold the entire intellectual history of modernity, this time with Catholics as constitutive participants, not solely as antagonists or villains. This concern with history and with the historicity of Catholic thinking about literature may seem counterintuitive, given the strength (and to some extent the accuracy) of the stereotype of the pre–Vatican II Church being convinced of its own timelessness. But the assertion of timelessness provided a canvas on which it became possible to map territory at first seemingly unfamiliar, but within which it eventually became necessary to be at home. By evaluating all kinds of literary production—and indeed all kinds of art—as equally contingent in light of a reality they affirmed as eternal, Catholic writers and critics produced by the 1950s a body of criticism distinctively responsive to contemporary experience.

This body of criticism displayed the same range of address and subtlety as had characterized Catholic literary culture several decades earlier. At its most unsubtle it was still a moralistic club with which to pound the familiar pests of sex and lawlessness. In other variations, however, it resulted in a conceptual framework peculiarly suited to reconcile the views of knowledge and the cosmos that had helped structure the modernist opposition of openness and closure.

Openness and closure were both formal and substantive; they had to do both with a work's formal structure and with the story it told or the ideas it embodied. As David Robey said of Umberto Eco's notion of "the open work": "Through its lack of conventional sense and order, it represents by analogy the feeling of senselessness, disorder, 'discontinuity' that the modern world generates in all of us." In this world, the role of art is clear: "Thus, although open works are not the only kind of art to be produced in our time, they are the only kind that is appropriate to it; the conventional sense and order of traditional art reflect an experience of the world wholly different from ours, and we deceive ourselves if we try to make this sense and order our own."[29] This is one means by which to resolve the opposition between openness and closure—define as "inappropriate" any work that does not observe the distinction.

The substantive component of openness and closure was articulated by Nathan Scott in his essay "The Name and Nature of Our Period-Style," in which he drew on sociologist Karl Mannheim's 1954 *Diagnosis of Our Time* to argue that because of the "evaporation of those primordial images which objectify a people's faith and provide the moral imagination with its basic premises," he says, "nothing is any longer revealed as having decisive importance, and men are ruled . . . by a kind of kaleidoscopic concept of life which, in giving equal significance to everything does, in effect, attribute no radical significance to anything. In such an age, the individual is condemned to the awful prison of his own individuality. . . . This, then, is the intractable and unpromising reality which the modern writer has been up against."[30]

Kaleidoscopic and unpromising, senselessness, disorder, and discontinuity—this diagnosis of "the" modern condition seems even well after midcentury to define Catholicism out of the landscape, leaving conceptual room only for opposition. But one of the ideas integral to Catholic thinking and writing about literature—the idea of the Incarnation—functioned in perhaps surprising ways to remap this apparently unwelcoming territory. Taken seriously, the idea of the Incarnation meant that a Catholic analysis could never deem the world—modern or otherwise—to be "disenchanted" in the most foundational sense of that defining term.[31] Once the potential intellectual credibility of creation, Incarnation, and redemption is granted, making sense of the occasional vision or healing does not present much of a stumbling block.

By the 1950s, Catholic writers and critics had been thinking through modernism from a literary standpoint, using fundamentally theological tools, for half a century. These theological tools are infamous for being "closed"—neoscholasticism for its dessication of Thomas's legacy, moral theology for cultivating repression and shame, Catholic intellectual culture generally for a sense of certitude and finality that refused to acknowledge or address new questions or a plurality of answers. There is some justification for this reputation, but if it were the totality of Catholic intellectual culture, there would little possibility of understanding where the Second Vatican Council, or the wave of theological and intellectual change that followed it, came from, except from outside the boundaries of U. S. Catholicism—either from European Catholic circles or from trends within U.S. intellectual culture.

To an extent largely underappreciated, U.S. Catholic literary culture found ways to inhabit the openness characteristic of modernism and modernity, while maintaining an intellectual continuity with the very strands of Catholic intellectual culture most notorious for their closure. Catholic writers and critics used the idea of the Incarnation, and all of the various ideas that followed from it as a theological premise, to rethink not only the history of intellectual modernity but the history of the century in which they were living. As they did this, they saw two things in particular—their solidarity with the people bereft by disenchantment and left without resources in the face of the century's events, and a cosmic horizon that joined Tridentine timelessness to the incomprehensible timescale of evolution and cosmic history.

Early in the century the assertion of God's absence—the bleak naturalism of Dreiser or Frank Norris, for example—provoked in most Catholic critics a defensive response, an impulse to shield Catholic tradition and teaching, to shield even God himself, from such assertion, as though they were vulnerable to naturalism's assault. The events of the ensuing half century drenched in tragedy any sense that the world had been somehow reinvented or recreated. By the 1950s the most formative voices—Eliot, Pound, Auden—of literary modernism, for better or for worse, had relocated themselves within Christianity's narrative.

By the 1950s, holding the central intellectual claims of Christianity up to the light produced a different effect—whatever the Enlightenment had illuminated that disconnected it from Christian commitments to reason took on a different appearance in the light of the flash at Hiroshima. So Flannery O'Connor saw Jesus in the backwoods prophet and Walker Percy saw something he could not even quite name yet in the movies, and Moira Walsh at about the same time said Catholics had to learn to judge movies for themselves. They were laypeople, they had appropriated a theological tool kit, and they were crafting a way to talk about things that guarded old sanctities but made it possible to see the Incarnation in the world *they* lived in. To the extent that modernism was about freedom from history, the anguish of the individual coming to terms with the utter incapacity of old things to help them live in the world, it was almost impossible to assimilate within a

Catholic intellectual framework. But by the 1950s this anguish was such a common experience that the response to it was less likely to be alienation than solidarity.

Besides this renewed sense of a common lot (predicament, in Walker Percy's word) with their compatriots, American Catholics who wrote and thought about literature brought their theological ideas to bear on the contemporary situation in an outward direction, as well. They did so, crucially, in a way that incorporated the literary per se into their overall narrative. Walter Ong matter-of-factly put literature's bread-and-butter tasks in the context of a cosmic sense of space and an evolutionary scale of time: "Literature and literary forms are a part of the mysterious pattern of cosmic evolution planned by Almighty God and must be evaluated with some appreciation of this pattern."[32] In company with a number of their European counterparts, most influentially Pierre Teilhard de Chardin, U.S. Catholic critics, by widening their interpretive framework out to this scale could appear to be on the cutting edge of science and *sub specie aeternitatis* at the same time. The scientific revolution, rather than being the turn that initiated the demystifying of the world, instead extends human horizons and consciousness so far that wonder increases instead of evaporating. "Openness" and its literary analogues, instead of requiring as a first principle the rejection of the notion that art, as creative activity by created beings, needed to reflect in some meaningful way the mind of the Creator, becomes a reaffirmation of the infinitely open order God built into the world. Condé Pallen ("God made the world in measure, weight and number, and in measure, weight and number it will endure") could not have asked for more elegant a reconciliation.

Epilogue
The Abrogation of the Index

There may seem to be a great distance between the abstractions of modernist oppositions—iconoclasm and orthodoxy, individual and community, innovation and repetition, openness and closure—and the ecclesial bureaucracy of the *Index Librorum Prohibitorum*. But the same remapping of the territory of artistic modernism and other components of intellectual modernity that enabled Catholic writers and critics to reconcile what had seemed antagonistic polarities reconfigured this quintessentially Counter-Reformation institution as well.

The Index and the system of thought it stood for continued to loom large in the public image of American Catholicism past the twentieth century's midpoint. (In his key 1960 campaign speech to the Houston ministers' association, John F. Kennedy included censorship in his list of issues on which as president he would not be influenced by the Vatican.) But it would be difficult to exaggerate the fervor and ferment of the years between 1959 and 1965, and beyond into the 1970s, within U.S. Catholicism. The 1959 election to the papacy of the aged John XXIII, famously intended by his brother cardinals to be a seat-warmer for a few years until more likely contenders could emerge, brought about the most unintended consequences seen within the walls of the Vatican for centuries. Shortly after his election he called an ecumenical council, which came to be known as Vatican II. Convening in 1962 and closing three years later, in the pontificate of Paul VI

(John XXIII died on June 3, 1963), the Council channeled and accelerated the most widespread rethinking of key theological and ecclesiological issues since the early modern era.

In the years leading up to the Council, the Index and the system of censorship it represented had continued to reflect the complexity of relationships among actors in Catholic print, literary, and intellectual culture. Whereas public discussion tended to pit "the Vatican" against whatever author was under suspicion, we see the density and delicacy of relationships in the case of Graham Greene, when *The Power and the Glory* was referred for investigation—not on first publication, but when it was being translated into German for a Swiss publisher. The work was never officially condemned (though Greene was reprimanded by his bishop and asked to aim at literature's nobler purposes in the future), but the noncondemnation involved the French and German publishers, the English archbishop of Westminster, the secretary of the Congregation of the Holy Office, the Vatican pro-Secretary of State for ordinary affairs (not coincidentally, Giovanni Battista Montini, the future Paul VI), and at least three highly varied consultor's reports.[1]

The consultors' reports varied in their assessment of the worth of what Greene was trying to do, but they had in common a sense that the world was watching, that the audience for the decision was not just the Catholic faithful but those for whom a judgment on Greene reflected the Vatican's very capacity to cope with contemporary art's engagement with the world. His most sympathetic consultor, Msgr. Giuseppe De Luca, put the situation bluntly: "In the case of Graham Greene, his harsh and acerbic art touches the hearts of the least receptive and reminds them, however gloomy they be, of the awe-inspiring presence of God and the poisonous bite of sin. He addresses those who are most distant and hostile—those whom we will never reach."[2] Greene himself was uncharacteristically restrained in his manner in his public statements and also, apparently, in his dealings with Vatican personnel (it likely helped to have a future pope on his side). Similarly, Flannery O'Connor, who described her own intended audience as "the people who think God is dead," as late as 1957–58 was asking Father James McCown for permission to read Gide and Sartre as part of a reading group organized by a local Episcopal priest.[3]

One way of telling the story of twentieth-century U.S. Catholic intellectual history would be to demonstrate the extent to which condemned ideas were within a very few decades thoroughly vindicated and wholeheartedly embraced. Some of these examples, such as the so-called "raid" on the French Dominicans, eventually reached the level of Rome (of Vatican condemnation); others remained at the lower level of "silencing" by religious superiors or local bishops.[4] Although in hindsight the consistent pattern of this timeline may seem to lend itself to an irenic reading (patience is a virtue), the situation seemed urgent to a number of its central constituents. To a 1960 session of the Society of Catholic College Teachers of Sacred Doctrine entitled "The Problem of Prohibited Books and the American Catholic Intellectual," Father Gerard Sloyan (b. 1919) excoriated the Index: "This much is clear," he said, "students in Catholic colleges are being taught at this moment by half-educated faculty members in every discipline but the pure sciences. We must face the bitter truth that every man-jack of us in this room was irreparably maimed in his education in its early stages."[5]

In the spring of 1962 (the Vatican Council's first session was scheduled for October), *Critic* magazine sponsored a forum in which "six well-qualified American Catholics" were asked to respond to the question "What is your hope for possible action by the coming Ecumenical Council on the Index of Forbidden Books?"[6] The answers ranged from a desire for the strongest possible restatement of the Church's right and obligation to forbid the reading of bad books, from the longtime staunch antimodernist (and opponent of much of the liberalizing spirit of the Council) Msgr. Joseph C. Fenton, to pragmatic hopes for streamlined procedures, especially in obtaining permission to read forbidden books, to a strong proposal for radical modernization from Chicago judge Roger J. Kiley (though he still acknowledged the Church's responsibility to ensure that correct doctrine was taught).

None of the six commentators asked for or predicted what happened just four years later. The Council, which closed in 1965, did not take up the issue of censorship and the Index. (Harold Gardiner began his contribution to the *Critic* symposium by acknowledging that "it is by no means certain that the Council will do anything. . . . It must be admitted in all realism that the problems posed by the Index are relatively minor when compared with the other problems the Council will be called upon to face.") Instead, in the year following the Council's close, the Congregation for the Doctrine of the Faith (CDF), successor to the Holy Office, quietly "abrogated" the Index's authority. In its issue of June 25, 1966, *The Tablet* reprinted a *Notificatio* from the CDF that had appeared the previous week in *L'Osservatore Romano*. It read in part: "The Sacred Congregation for the Doctrine of the Faith, having consulted the Holy Father, hereby announces that the Index retains its moral force, insofar as it informs the conscience of the faithful that they should be aware of those writings that can endanger faith and good morals, as the natural law itself demands, but that it no longer has the force of ecclesiastical law with the sanctions attached to it. Hence the Church puts its trust in the mature conscience of the faithful, particularly Catholic writers and publishers and those concerned with the education of the young."[7] An article accompanying the announcement of the Index's abolition in *L'Osservatore Romano* stated: "Today to want to keep track of the output of the world's presses in order to judge and evaluate individual works, and to draw up an exact catalogue of those that are harmful or dangerous for faith and morals, would be a very difficult undertaking, and that too in view of the altered psychological climate, both individual and social."[8]

This was a highly nuanced finale ("abrogation," not "abolition"), in which all of the goods that the Index was established to protect remained central but were protected now not primarily by ecclesiastical structures but by the "mature conscience of the faithful," in which the waning of the need for the Index was acknowledged, but the advisability or effectiveness of the Index at any other point in its history was not addressed. It is doubtful that most ordinary Catholics ("Change is in the air," Judge Kiley began his *Critic* call for the Index's modernization) appreciated the fine balance this decision achieved. By the early 1960s they were probably more familiar with experiences like that of a Notre Dame undergraduate in the 1950s, who recalled the same books that were in a locked cage in the library being available for sale on open shelves in the bookstore.[9] The Index had long functioned in the American Catholic imagination in ways disconnected from its canonically precise particulars.

In this, of course, it was not unlike a number of other key elements of Roman Catholic belief and practice. In the final chapters of Evelyn Waugh's novel *Brideshead Revisited*, the Flyte family are discussing whether the dying Lord Marchmain should receive the last rites. Charles Ryder, still at this point in the novel the obstinate agnostic, opposes what he regards as superstition. He justifies his opposition with the argument that even those who want Lord Marchmain to receive the last rites cannot explain why. Speaking to Julia, Charles Ryder says: " 'There were four of you,' I said. 'Cara didn't know the first thing it was about, and may or may not have believed it; you knew a bit and didn't believe a word; Cordelia knew about as much and believed it madly; only poor Bridey knew and believed, and I thought he made a pretty poor show when it came to explaining. And people go round saying "At least Catholics know what they believe" ' " (330).

With his characteristic genius for witty and uncharitable overstatement, Waugh got a good bit right about the Index in particular and Catholic literary culture in general. Some people barely knew the Index existed; others knew all the details of its functioning. Some accepted its authority without question and insisted in retrospect on its necessity; others thought it absurd at the time and harmful in hindsight. What the end of the novel makes clear, and what Waugh also got right, is that correctness in teaching takes on its meaning and importance in the context of the sacraments. Lord Marchmain's deathbed sign of the cross is high drama, and Waugh himself eventually backed away in embarrassment from its unabashed, grand emotion, but it captures vividly the interdependence between word and sign, between believer and community, between the present and the past, that made Catholic literary culture so distinctive and so integral to the intellectual and cultural history of U.S. Catholicism in the twentieth century.

NOTES

Introduction

1. James Joyce, *A Portrait of the Artist as a Young Man* (New York: Viking Press, 1964), 253.

2. Review of James Joyce, *A Portrait of the Artist as a Young Man*, *Catholic World*, June 1917, 395–97.

3. The quotation is from Woolf's 1924 essay "Mr. Bennett and Mrs. Brown." For context, see Peter Stansky, *On or About December 1910: Early Bloomsbury and Its Intimate World* (Cambridge, MA: Harvard University Press, 1996).

4. John McGreevy, *Catholicism and American Freedom: A History* (New York: Norton, 2003); Peter D'Agostino, *Rome in America: Transnational Catholic Ideology from Risorgimento to Fascism* (Chapel Hill: University of North Carolina Press, 2004).

5. Jay P. Dolan, *The American Catholic Experience: A History from Colonial Times to the Present* (Garden City, NY: Doubleday, 1985), 156. According to James Hennesey, 85 percent of U.S. Catholics in 1920 were estimated to be descendants of people who had immigrated since 1820 (*American Catholics: A History of the Roman Catholic Community in the United States* [New York: Oxford University Press, 1981], 220). See Jay Dolan's more recent summary of this period in *In Search of an American Catholicism: A History of Religion and Culture in Tension* (New York: Oxford University Press, 2002), 71–126.

6. Charles R. Morris, *American Catholic: The Saints and Sinners Who Built America's Most Powerful Church* (New York: Random House, 1997), 113. The number of Catholics in the United States quadrupled between 1860 and 1900. The growth had started more than a century earlier—there was a 900 percent increase in the U.S. Catholic population between 1830 and 1860 (Dolan, *The American Catholic Experience,* 356); Sydney Ahlstrom notes an increase in the U.S. Catholic population from 7 million in 1880 to 12.5 million in 1895 (*A Religious History of the American People* [New Haven, CT: Yale University Press, 1972], 827).

7. David J. O'Brien, *Public Catholicism,* 2nd ed. (Maryknoll, NY: Orbis Books, 1996); Philip Gleason, *Keeping the Faith: American Catholicism Past and Present* (Notre Dame, IN: University of Notre Dame Press, 1987); and Gleason, *Contending with Modernity: Catholic Higher Education in the Twentieth Century* (New York: Oxford University Press, 1995).

8. Una M. Cadegan, " 'Running the Ancient Ark by Steam': Catholic Publishing," in *Print in Motion: The Expansion of Publishing and Reading in the United States, 1880–1940,* ed. Carl F. Kaestle and Janice A. Radway, vol. 4 of *A History of the Book in America* (Chapel Hill: University of North Carolina Press, 2009), 392–408.

9. Clifford Geertz, *The Interpretation of Cultures: Selected Essays* (New York: Basic Books, 1973), 250, 5; Murray G. Murphey, *Philosophical Foundations of Historical Knowledge* (Albany: State University of New York Press, 1994), 269–72.

10. Henry H. Glassie, *Material Culture* (Bloomington: Indiana University Press, 1999), 25.

11. Jane P. Tompkins, *Sensational Designs: The Cultural Work of American Fiction, 1790–1860* (New York: Oxford University Press, 1985), 200.

12. "Editorial Announcement," *America*, April 17, 1909, 5–6.

13. Leon Hutton, "Catholicity and Civility: John Francis Noll and the Origins of *Our Sunday Visitor*," *U.S. Catholic Historian* 15 (Summer 1997): 11.

14. "The traditional anti-Catholic philosophy of history is evidenced," a 1923 account of the *Catholic Encyclopedia*'s beginnings asserted, quoting a 1902 *Messenger* review of "Appleton's University Cyclopædia and Atlas," "in the dogmatic pronouncement by a well-known university professor, in the article on 'Teutons,' that in the Middle Ages 'it was the emperor against the Pope': in the transition period 'it was German Protestantism against Roman Catholicism: and to-day it is Teutonic science against the Syllabus and the Vatican. The Teutonic spirit has given to modern civilization its freedom of thought and conscience.'" Paul H. Linehan, "The Catholic Encyclopedia," in *Catholics in the Liberal Professions*, vol. 4 of *Catholic Builders of the Nation: A Symposium on the Catholic Contribution to the Civilization of the United States* (Boston: Continental Press, 1923), 204–18, at 204–5.

15. "The Making of the Catholic Encyclopedia (1917)," New Advent Catholic Encyclopedia, http://www.newadvent.org/cathen/00001a.htm.

16. Thomas F. O'Connor, "American Catholic Reading Circles, 1886–1909," *Libraries and Culture* 26, no. 2 (Spring 1991), 334–47.

17. F. M. Edselas, "Institute for Woman's Professions," *Catholic World*, June 1893, 373–80, at 379. See Ursulines of New York [Mother Seraphine Leonard], *Immortelles of Catholic Columbian Literature: Compiled from the Work of American Catholic Women Writers* (Chicago: D. H. McBride, 1896), 180–81; and Paula M. Kane, *Separatism and Subculture: Boston Catholicism, 1900–1920* (Chapel Hill: University of North Carolina Press, 1994), 352n169.

18. A Sister of St. Joseph, *Ideal Catholic Reader*, vol. 4 (New York: Macmillan, 1916; 14th printing 1924); note that it includes an Imprimatur though published by a secular publisher. Also see Colleen McDannell, *Material Christianity: Religion and Popular Culture in America* (New Haven: Yale University Press, 1995), 59–61, on the popularity of printed images of Murillo's painting.

19. The story is illuminating and is told fully in Sr. Mary Charles Bryce, *The Influence of the Catechism of the Third Plenary Council of Baltimore on Widely Used Elementary Religion Text Books from Its Composition in 1885 to Its 1941 Revision* (Washington, DC: Catholic University of America, 1970).

20. See Cadegan, "'Running the Ancient Ark.'"

21. Hutton, "Catholicity and Civility."

22. Una M. Cadegan, "A Very Full and Happy Life: Kathleen Thompson Norris and Popular Novels for Women," *Records of the American Catholic Historical Society of Philadelphia* 107 (Fall–Winter 1996): 19–38.

23. Tompkins, *Sensational Designs*, 200.

24. Kevin Starr, *The Dream Endures: California Enters the 1940s* (New York: Oxford University Press, 1997), 38.

25. Letter from Brother Leo to Francis X. Talbot (n.d., but likely early 1928), box 43, folder 39, *America* magazine papers, Georgetown University archives.

26. Thomas Walsh, "Our Catholic Poetry," in *Catholic Builders of the Nation*, 4:182–83.

27. William M. Halsey, *The Survival of American Innocence: Catholicism in an Era of Disillusionment, 1920–1940* (Notre Dame, IN: University of Notre Dame Press, 1980).

28. John Henry Newman, *The Idea of a University* (New Haven, CT: Yale University Press, 1996), 161; Daniel A. Lord, SJ, *I Can Read Anything: All Right, Then Read This* (St. Louis: Queen's Work Press, 1930).

29. Daniel A. Lord, SJ, *Played by Ear: The Autobiography of Daniel A. Lord, S.J.* (Chicago: Loyola University Press, 1956), 254. See also Arnold J. Sparr, *To Promote, Defend, and Redeem: The Catholic Literary Revival and the Cultural Transformation of American Catholicism, 1920–1960* (New York: Greenwood Press, 1990).

30. Paul T. Dix, "Flame into Youth," *St. Anthony Messenger,* November 1939, 6. "His next," the profile continues, "'The Democracy Follies,' will take up the problems of government and the governed, and the role of the Church in the democratic form of social organization. 'The democratic form of government is impossible unless based upon the teachings of Christ,' Father Lord says. 'In Catholicism, democracy has its only reason for existence.'"

31. Bakewell Morrison, SJ, introduction to Lord, *Played by Ear*, viii.

32. "Youth and Today's Literature," *Catholic Action* 18 (January 1936): 18–19.

33. Sr. M. Agatha, OSU, "Suggesting Catholic Books as Xmas Gifts a Practical Form of Catholic Action," *Catholic Library World,* December 15, 1931, 25.

34. Rev. Peter M. H. Wynhoven, *Swim—or Sink* (Marrero, LA: Hope Haven Press, 1939), 107–8.

35. Calvert Alexander, *The Catholic Literary Revival: Three Phases in Its Development from 1845 to the Present* (Milwaukee: Bruce, 1935).

36. Burton Confrey, *Readings for Catholic Action* (Manchester, NH: Magnificat Press, 1937); and Confrey, *The Moral Mission of Literature and Other Essays* (Manchester, NH: Magnificat Press, 1939). Confrey also published *Secularism in American Education: Its History* (Washington, DC: Catholic Education Press, 1931), *Social Studies: A Textbook in Social Science for Catholic High Schools* (New York: Benziger Brothers, 1934), and *A Catholic Philosophy of Literature* (New York: Exposition Press, 1966).

37. "Catholic Action in Action," *Catholic Library World,* January 15, 1932, 30.

38. Stephen J. Brown, SJ, and Thomas McDermott, *A Survey of Catholic Literature* (Milwaukee: Bruce, 1949), 160.

39. Brother David Martin, CSC, ed., *Catholic Library Practice* (Portland, OR: University of Portland Press, 1947), 96.

40. Stephen J. M. J. Brown, SJ, *An Introduction to Catholic Booklore* (London: Burns, Oates and Washbourne, 1933), vi.

41. See Charles Taylor, *A Secular Age* (Cambridge, MA: Belknap Press of Harvard University Press, 2007), 54–61, on "secular time" and "higher time."

42. Thomas J. Shahan, "The Study of Church History," *Catholic Historical Review* 8, no. 3 (October 1922): 303–32; 316.

43. Blanche Mary Kelly, "The Catholic Theory of Arts and Letters," in *Catholic Builders of the Nation: A Symposium on the Catholic Contribution to the Civilization of the United States,* ed. C. E. McGuire (Boston: Continental Press, 1923), 103–16, at 106, 115.

1. U.S. Catholic Literary Aesthetics

1. Condé B. Pallen [1858–1929], "Free Verse," *America,* April 1921, 578–79. Layman Condé Benoist Pallen (1858–1929) was born in St. Louis and served for a number of years as editor of its *Church Progress* and *Catholic World* before becoming managing editor of the *Catholic Encyclopedia* from 1907 to 1913. Not coincidentally, Pallen was also a vocal and ardent literary critic, convinced that contemporary literature was on a trajectory toward destruction from which only Catholicism could save it.

2. Pallen's work contradicts Paul Giles's assertion that self-consciously Catholic literary critics "elide philosophical assumptions into literary judgments without knowing it. Their competing philosophies are seen not as competing philosophies but as absolute truths, with their opinions on literature emerging as a byproduct of these deeply-held but unstated beliefs" (Giles, *American Catholic Arts and Fictions: Culture, Ideology, Aesthetics* [New York: Cambridge University Press, 1992], 204). Whatever the contemporary assessment of Pallen's philosophy, it is impossible to argue that he did not know he had one.

3. Philip Gleason, *Contending with Modernity: Catholic Higher Education in the Twentieth Century* (New York: Oxford University Press, 1995), 114–15.

4. Malcolm Cowley, *After the Genteel Tradition: American Writers since 1910* (Gloucester, MA: P. Smith, 1959 [1937]).

5. Gerald Graff, *Professing Literature: An Institutional History* (Chicago: University of Chicago Press, 1987); David R. Shumway, *Creating American Civilization: A Genealogy of American Literature as an Academic Discipline* (Minneapolis: University of Minnesota Press, 1994).

6. Eric Cheyfitz (quoting Leo Marx), "Matthiessen's American Renaissance: Circumscribing the Revolution," *American Quarterly* 41 (June 1989): 341–61, at 350.

7. Giles, *American Catholic Arts and Fictions.*

8. Brother Leo (Francis Meehan), *Religion and the Study of Literature* (New York: Schwartz, Kirwin and Fauss, 1923), 10.

9. Daniel J. O'Neill, *A Book about Books* (Providence: Oxford Press, 1936), 22; Stephen J. M. J. Brown, SJ, *Libraries and Literature from a Catholic Standpoint* (Dublin: Browne and Nolan, 1937), 101; Burton Confrey, *The Moral Mission of Literature and Other Essays* (Manchester, NH: Magnificat Press, 1939), 13.

10. On the "Gallery," see Arnold Sparr, *To Promote, Defend, and Redeem: The Catholic Literary Revival and the Cultural Transformation of American Catholicism, 1920–1960* (New York: Greenwood Press, 1990); on Tate, see Peter A. Huff, *Allen Tate and the Catholic Revival: Trace of the Fugitive Gods* (New York: Paulist Press, 1996), 88–89.

11. Theodore Maynard, "The Catholicism of Dickens," *Thought* 5 (June 1930): 87–105.

12. Brother Leo, *Religion and the Study of Literature*, 25, 32, 97.

13. Review of *The Great Gatsby* by F. Scott Fitzgerald, *America*, May 30, 1925, 166.

14. Blanche Mary Kelly, *The Well of English* (New York: Harper and Brothers, 1936), xiii.

15. O'Neill, *A Book about Books*, 64.

16. Course lecture notes, "On the Place of Literature among the Arts," n.d., box 10, folder 9, John L. Bonn, SJ, papers, Boston College Archives. See also Richard Sullivan, Assorted Lecture and Class Notes [ca. 1942–59], box 11, folder 3, Richard Sullivan: Manuscripts (hereafter cited as CSUL)/University of Notre Dame Archives (hereafter cited as UNDA).

17. "One of the awful things about writing when you are a Christian is that for you the ultimate reality is the Incarnation, the present reality is the Incarnation, the whole reality is the Incarnation, and nobody believes in the Incarnation; that is, nobody in your audience. My audience are the people who think God is dead. At least these are the people I am conscious of writing for." Flannery O'Connor to A. [Betty Hester], August 2, 1955, *Collected Works* (New York: Library of America, 1988), 943. See also Confrey, *Moral Mission of Literature*: "Those readers who lack a Catholic sense must be content with speculative criticism; but for us, when Divinity spoke the first word in Genesis, complemented in the Gospel of Saint John, the Catholicity of literature began" (10).

18. Harold C. Gardiner, SJ, introduction to Mary Kiely, *Traffic Lights, or Safe Crossways into Modern Children's Literature* (New York: Pro Parvulis Book Club, 1941), ix.

19. In C. E. McGuire, ed., *Catholic Builders of the Nation: A Symposium on the Catholic Contribution to the Civilization of the United States* (Boston: Continental Press, 1923, 4:168.

20. Also see Condé B. Pallen, *The Philosophy of Literature* (St. Louis: B. Herder, 1897); Stephen J. Brown, SJ, and Thomas McDermott, *A Survey of Catholic Literature* (Milwaukee, WI: Bruce, 1945).

21. Gerald A. McCool, *From Unity to Pluralism: The Internal Evolution of Thomism* (New York: Fordham University Press, 1989).

22. Jeanette Murphy Lynn, comp., *An Alternative Classification for Catholic Books: A Scheme for Catholic Theology, Canon Law and Church History, to Be Used with the Dewey Decimal, Classification Décimale, or Library of Congress Classifications* (Milwaukee, WI: Bruce; Chicago: American Library Association, 1937), ix.

23. Handwritten note, "The Problem of Reality," n.d., box 10, folder 9, John L. Bonn, SJ, papers, Boston College Archives.

24. Box 11, folder 1, Miscellaneous Lecture Notes [ca. 1940], CSUL/UNDA.

25. Philip H. Vitale, ed., *Catholic Literary Opinion in the Twentieth Century* (Chicago: Auxiliary University Press, 1958), ix.

26. Brother Leo, *Religion and the Study of Literature*, 25.

27. And few Catholic critics did, in fact, attempt to defend it; e.g., Art Kuhl, in "Mostly of *The Grapes of Wrath*" (*Catholic World*, November 1939, 160–65), calls it "so much hokum." Katherine Bregy acknowledged Catholic criticisms of Steinbeck's

realism but still saw *The Grapes of Wrath* as a great novel; "[as] great as was Hugo's tragic *Les Miserables*, not with vision but with gripping realism and the unfailing gift of compassion." Keep in mind that *Les Miserables* was on the Index (Bregy, "Of John Steinbeck," *America*, August 19, 1944, 496–97).

28. John Desmond Sheridan, "Indecency in Literature," *Catholic Mind*, May 22, 1935, 190–93, at 191. Originally published in Dublin *Standard* in 1934.

29. Ibid., 190.

30. Brother Leo, *Religion and the Study of Literature*, 32.

31. Confrey, *Moral Mission of Literature*, 38.

32. John Bonn, SJ, Boston College Archives, box 10, folder 9, "Lecture on Literature (Philosophical)."

33. James J. Daly, SJ, "Catholic Action among the Cultured," in *A Call to Catholic Action: A Series of Conferences on the Principles Which Should Guide Catholics in the Social-Economic Crisis of To-Day* (New York: Joseph F. Wagner, 1935), 2: 137–45.

34. Sr. M. Catherine (Ursuline), review of Percy Boynton, *American Literature* (Ginn, 1923), *Catholic Educational Review* 13 (1923): 317.

35. "The Intention of the Novel," box 11, folder 4, Lecture Notes [1942–59], CSUL/UNDA.

36. Brother Leo, *Religion and the Study of Literature*, 25, 32, 97.

37. Michael McLaughlin, review of *Black Boy* by Richard Wright, *Catholic World*, April 1945, 85–86.

38. See Umberto Eco, *The Aesthetics of Thomas Aquinas* (1956; Cambridge, MA: Harvard University Press, 1988), chap. 4, "The Formal Criteria of Beauty," for an analysis of the original context in Aquinas and of how this passage was appropriated by the scholastic tradition.

39. *Nam ad pulchritudinem tria requiruntur. Primo quidem, integritas sive perfectio: quae enim diminuta sunt, hoc ipso turpia sunt. Et debita proportio sive consonantia. Et iterum claritas: unde quae habent colorem nitidum, pulchra esse dicuntur.*

40. Anthony Yorke, "Be Ye Cultured," *Catholic World*, November 1897, 188–93.

41. Brother Leo, *Religion and the Study of Literature*, 45–49.

42. O'Neill, *A Book about Books*, 50–51. In the 1946 edition, O'Neill adds examples of novels with the "soul-inspiring" theme (*The Song of Bernadette*) and the "degenerate" theme (*Forever Amber*).

43. Pallen, *The Philosophy of Literature*, 90.

44. Agnes Repplier, "Picturesqueness and Piety," *Catholic World*, March 1911, 730–38, at 730–31.

45. Valentine Long, OFM, *Not on Bread Alone* (St. Bonaventure, NY: Franciscana Press, 1935), 231–32.

46. *Summa theologiae*, pt. 1, question 39, art. 8.

47. Long, *Not on Bread Alone*, 133, 130.

48. Herbert O'Halloran Walker, *The Power and Apostolate of Catholic Literature* (St. Louis: The Queen's Work Press, 1938).

49. Calvert Alexander, SJ, *The Catholic Literary Revival: Three Phases in Its Development from 1845 to the Present* (Milwaukee: Bruce, 1935), 11.

50. Rev. Thomas J. Hagerty, "The Ethics of Realism," *Catholic World*, December 1899, 352–57, at 354.

51. Pallen, *The Philosophy of Literature*, 69.

52. Maurice F. Egan, "A Chat about New Books," *Catholic World*, February 1887, 701–13, at 704. For more on Egan, see Paul R. Messbarger, *Fiction with a Parochial Purpose: Social Uses of American Catholic Literature, 1884–1900* (Boston: Boston University Press, 1971).

53. Stansky, *On or About December 1910*, chap. 8, "The Exhibition," 188–236. Similarly, in New York City the 1913 International Exhibition of Modern Art, better known as the Armory Show, introduced cubism and other forms of post-impressionist painting and sculpture to a larger American audience than ever before, resulting in a raucous and public clash between tastes for the old and for the new. One of the most notorious paintings in the exhibition, Marcel Duchamp's *Nude Descending a Staircase*, was fantastically popular with the crowds who attended the exhibition, sold sight unseen to a well-known collector, drew tremendous critical acclaim—and was famously likened by a critic for the *New York Times* to "an explosion in a shingle factory" (JoAnne Mancini, " 'One Term Is as Fatuous as Another': Responses to the Armory Show Reconsidered," *American Quarterly* 51 [December 1999]: 833–70).

54. Stansky, *On or About December 1910*, 241.

55. Virginia Woolf, "Mr. Bennett and Mrs. Brown," in *The Captain's Death Bed and Other Essays* (London: Hogarth Press, 1950), 109.

56. Arnold Bennett, *Books and Persons: Being Comments on a Past Epoch, 1908–1911* (London: Chatto and Windus, 1917).

57. "With Our Readers," *Catholic World*, September 1917, 863.

58. Francis X. Talbot, ed., *Fiction by Its Makers* (New York: America Press, 1928), 84.

59. N. Elizabeth Monroe, *The Novel and Society: A Critical Study of the Modern Novel* (Chapel Hill: University of North Carolina Press, 1941), 258, 28.

60. CSUL 11/4, UNDA.

61. Francis X. Talbot, SJ, "Novelists and Critics, Both Catholic," *America*, November 2, 1929, 91–93. See also Theodore Maynard, "Religion and Culture," in *A Call to Catholic Action*, 2:146–52: "Catholics, unfortunately, are sometimes a little shy about endorsing her without qualification—mainly, it must be supposed, because of her forthright treatment of sexual sin. We might remember, however, that Cardinal Newman told us that we should not expect a sinless literature of sinful humanity. Never for an instant does Sigrid Undset attempt to exculpate the sin which she depicts" (151).

62. William Dean Howells, "A Number of Interesting New Novels," *North American Review* 200 (1914), 912; quoted in Henry F. May, *The End of American Innocence: A Study of the First Years of Our Own Time, 1912–1917* (1959; New York: Columbia University Press, 1992), 17.

63. Arnold Sparr, *To Promote, Defend, and Redeem: The Catholic Literary Revival and the Cultural Transformation of American Catholicism, 1920–1960* (New York: Greenwood Press, 1990), 87.

64. Kathleen Norris, "Religion and Popular Fiction," in *Fiction by Its Makers*, ed. Francis X. Talbot, SJ (New York: America Press, 1928), 27, 29.

65. Kathleen Norris, *Red Silence* (Garden City, NY: Doubleday, Doran and Co., 1929), 316–17.

66. Katherine Burton, "Woman to Woman," *The Sign*, November 21, 1941, 235. On Burton, see the entry by Rebecca L. Kroeger in *Catholic Women Writers: A Bio-Bibliographical Sourcebook*, ed. Mary R. Reichardt (Westport, CT: Greenwood Press, 2001), 18–23.

67. Letter from Richard Sullivan to Buck Moon, June 22, 1946, CSUL/UNDA.

68. Letter from Richard Sullivan to Henry Volkening, February 16, 1948, CSUL/UNDA.

69. Philip C. Moore, CSC, to John Tully, n.d. (probably September/October 1942), carbon in CSUL 4/3, UNDA. *Books on Trial* also published something of a rebuttal by Leo L. Ward, CSC, head of Notre Dame's English department and Sullivan's mentor and friend. In their introduction to Ward's letter, they acknowledged that "the use of the term 'peep-holing' was unfortunate, since it apparently was taken to mean more than was intended" (*Books on Trial* 1, no. 4 [1942]: 16). See also Edward Fischer, "How Realistic Can a Catholic Writer Be?," *Catholic Library World*, December 21, 1949, 73–74.

70. Rochelle Gurstein, *The Repeal of Reticence* (New York: Hill and Wang, 1996).

71. See, for example, Compton Mackenzie, "The Trend of the Novel," in Talbot, *Fiction by Its Makers*, 74.

72. Joseph R. N. Maxwell, "Slums, Cynicism and Starvation," review of *Christ in Concrete* by Pietro di Donato, *America*, September 1939, 501.

73. Letter from Katherine Bregy to Francis X. Talbot, SJ, January 8, 1928, box 43, folder 39, America magazine archives, Catholic Book Club material—Editor's correspondence, 1928 (1928–49), Georgetown University.

2. Modernisms Literary and Theological

1. Thomas E. Woods, *The Church Confronts Modernity: Catholic Intellectuals and the Progressive Era* (New York: Columbia University Press, 2004).

2. Quoted in Robert A. Slayton, *Empire Statesman: The Rise and Redemption of Al Smith* (New York: Free Press, 2001), 316.

3. "Foreign Periodicals," *Catholic World*, December 1910, 411.

4. Peter Gay, *Modernism: The Lure of Heresy from Baudelaire to Beckett and Beyond* (New York: Norton, 2008); Stephen Schloesser, *Jazz Age Catholicism: Mystic Modernism in Postwar Paris, 1919–1933* (Toronto: University of Toronto Press, 2005).

5. R. Scott Appleby, *"Church and Age Unite!": The Modernist Impulse in American Catholicism* (Notre Dame, IN: University of Notre Dame Press, 1992), 1–10.

6. Pius X, *Pascendi dominici gregis*, par. 3.

7. Appleby, *"Church and Age Unite!,"* 230–34.

8. William L. Portier, "Americanism and Inculturation, 1899–1999" (paper presented at the Religious Studies Department Colloquium, University of Dayton, September 8, 1999), 3. Published in *Communio* 27 (Spring 2000): 139–60.

9. Ibid.; Gerald P. Fogarty, *The Vatican and the Americanist Crisis: Denis J. O'Connell, American Agent in Rome, 1885–1903* (Rome: Universitá gregoriana, 1974); Thomas Timothy McAvoy, *The Great Crisis in American Catholic History, 1895–1900* (Chicago: H. Regnery, 1957); Robert D. Cross, *The Emergence of Liberal Catholicism in America* (Cambridge, MA: Harvard University Press, 1958). Also see two theme

issues of the *U.S. Catholic Historian*: 11, no. 3 (Summer 1993), entitled "The Americanist Controversy: Recent Historical and Theological Perspectives"; and 17, no. 1 (Winter 1999), "Americanism and Americanization: Essays in Honor of Philip Gleason."

10. Appleby, *"Church and Age Unite!,"* 1–12.

11. Pius X, *Pascendi dominici gregis*, par. 45. See also John Inglis, *Spheres of Philosophical Inquiry and the Historiography of Medieval Philosophy* (Leiden: Brill, 1998).

12. See Woods, *The Church Confronts Modernity*; Edward A. Purcell, *The Crisis of Democratic Theory: Scientific Naturalism and the Problem of Value* (Lexington: University Press of Kentucky, 1973).

13. Gerald Graff, *Professing Literature: An Institutional History* (Chicago: University of Chicago Press, 1987).

14. "Foreign Periodicals," *Catholic World*, December 1910, 411.

15. William J. Kerrigan, "Index Bugaboo," *Catholic Digest*, November 12, 1947, 63–64.

16. See Paul Misner, "Catholic Anti-Modernism: The Ecclesial Setting," in *Catholicism Contending with Modernity: Roman Catholic Modernism and Anti-Modernism in Historical Context*, ed. Darrell Jodock (Cambridge: Cambridge University Press, 2000), 56–87.

17. See Sandra Yocum Mize, "The Common-Sense Argument for Papal Infallibility," *Theological Studies* 57 (June 1996): 242–63; Mize, "Defending Roman Loyalties and Republican Values: The 1848 Italian Revolution in American Catholic Apologetics," *Church History* 60 (December 1991), 480–92. Also see Peter R. D'Agostino, *Rome in America: Transnational Catholic Ideology from the Risorgimento to Fascism* (Chapel Hill, NC: University of North Carolina Press, 2004).

18. Purcell, *Crisis of Democratic Theory*.

19. E. Boyd-Barrett, SJ, articles in *America*: "Studies in Practical Psychology," December 13, 1924, 197–99; "Human Reactions and Adjustments," December 27, 1924, 245–47; "Neurotic Elements in Character," January 3, 1925, 269–71; "Normal and Abnormal Impulses," January 17, 1925, 317–19; "Wanderlust," January 31, 1925, 365–66; "Cleptomania," February 7, 1925, 390–92.

20. Leslie Woodcock Tentler, *Catholics and Contraception: An American History* (Ithaca, NY: Cornell University Press, 2004).

21. D'Agostino, *Rome in America*.

22. The classic source on this attitude is Philip Gleason, "American Catholics and the Mythic Middle Ages," in *Keeping the Faith: American Catholicism Past and Present* (Notre Dame, IN: University of Notre Dame Press, 1987), 11–34. For evidence that medieval nostalgia, as a component of antimodernism, was a characteristic of others besides Catholics, see T. J. Jackson Lears, *No Place of Grace: Antimodernism and the Transformation of American Culture, 1880–1920* (Chicago: University of Chicago Press, 1981), chap. 4, "The Morning of Belief: Medieval Mentalities in a Modern World."

23. Misner, "Catholic Anti-Modernism," 73.

24. Francis L. Broderick, *Right Reverend New Dealer, John A. Ryan* (New York: Macmillan, 1963); Benjamin K. Hunnicutt, "Monsignor John A. Ryan and the Shorter Hours of Labor: A Forgotten Vision of 'Genuine' Progress," *Catholic Historical Review* 69, no. 3 (July 1983): 384–402.

25. James M. Gillis, *False Prophets* (New York: Macmillan, 1925), 20–44, quoted in Francis Beauchesne Thornton, ed., *Return to Tradition: A Directive Anthology* (Milwaukee, WI: Bruce, 1948).

26. Robert Morse Crunden, *American Salons: Encounters with European Modernism, 1885–1917* (New York: Oxford University Press, 1993), xi. Also see Susan Hegeman, *Patterns for America: Modernism and the Concept of Culture* (Princeton: Princeton University Press, 1999); Michael North, *Reading 1922: A Return to the Scene of the Modern* (New York: Oxford University Press, 1999); Schloesser, *Jazz Age Catholicism.*

27. Philip Gleason, "American Catholics and Liberalism, 1789–1960," in *Catholicism and Liberalism: Contributions to American Public Philosophy*, ed. R. Bruce Douglass and David Hollenbach (Cambridge: Cambridge University Press, 1994), 45–75, at 58.

28. Ann Douglas, *Terrible Honesty: Mongrel Manhattan in the 1920s* (New York: Farrar, Straus and Giroux, 1995), 203.

29. Several recent historians of modernism make clear how central it still is to the self-definition of much "postmodern" analysis.

30. John Murray Cuddihy, *No Offense: Civil Religion and Protestant Taste* (New York: Seabury Press, 1978), 29.

31. John T. McGreevy, "Thinking on One's Own: Catholicism in the American Intellectual Imagination, 1928–1960," *Journal of American History* 84, no. 1 (June 1997): 98.

32. North, *Reading 1922*, 3.

3. Declining Oppositions

1. Arthur E. Holt, review of George N. Shuster, *The Catholic Spirit in America*, and Winfred Ernest Garrison, *Catholicism and the American Mind*, *American Journal of Sociology* 34, no. 4 (January 1929): 715–18.

2. Michael North, *Reading 1922: A Return to the Scene of the Modern* (New York: Oxford University Press, 1999): 3.

3. Paul Giles, *American Catholic Arts and Fictions: Culture, Ideology, Aesthetics* (New York: Cambridge, 1992). Though Giles declines to do so, his analysis can be usefully extended to also include Catholic theories of literature. Although some such writing is what Giles calls "didactic," and therefore perhaps unhelpful from the standpoint of literary criticism (that is, for deciding what pieces of writing are aesthetically more satisfying than others), the cultural historian approaches it with questions about the "aspects of social reality" it defines (to use Jane Tompkins's term). If we ask these questions, then all literature and writing about literature is potential evidence—Hopkins poems, missionary magazine editorials, juridical applications of canon law, and so on.

4. Catherine Beach Ely, "Mean Minds in Modern Print," *America*, October 14, 1922, 610–12, at 611.

5. Maurice Francis Egan, "Five Novels by Americans," *America*, February 26, 1921, 458. The five novels were Edith Wharton, *Age of Innocence*; Zona Gale, *Miss Lulu Bett*; Sinclair Lewis, *Main Street*; Gertrude Atherton, *The Sisters-in-Law*; and Floyd Dell, *Moon-Calf.*

6. Francis Beauchesne Thornton, *Return to Tradition: A Directive Anthology* (Milwaukee: Bruce Publishing Company, 1948), 281; E. I. Watkin, *The Catholic Centre* (New York: Sheed and Ward, 1939), 12.

7. Eric Cheyfitz, "What Work Is There for Us to Do? American Literary Studies or Americas Cultural Studies?," *American Literature* 67, no. 4 (December 1995): 843–53.

8. Barbara Herrnstein Smith, *Contingencies of Value: Alternative Perspectives for Critical Theory* (Cambridge, MA: Harvard University Press, 1988), 18.

9. Jane Tompkins, *Sensational Designs: The Cultural Work of American Fiction, 1790–1860* (New York: Oxford University Press, 1985); and Nina Baym, "Melodramas of Beset Manhood: How Theories of American Fiction Exclude Women Authors," *American Quarterly* 33 (Summer 1981): 123–39.

10. Sharon O'Brien, "Becoming Noncanonical: The Case against Willa Cather," in *Reading in America: Literature and Social History*, ed. Cathy N. Davidson (Baltimore: Johns Hopkins University Press, 1989), 240–58, at 247. See also Sharon O'Brien, *Willa Cather: The Emerging Voice* (New York: Oxford University Press, 1987).

11. C. McC. [Camile McCole], "New Books" (review of *Shadows on the Rock* by Willa Cather), *Catholic World*, September 1931, 752–53.

12. Harry Lorin Binsse, review of *Sapphira and the Slave Girl* by Willa Cather, *Commonweal*, January 11, 1941, 306–7; Francis X. Connolly, "The American Novel through Fifty Years—IV. Willa Cather," *America*, April 21, 1951, 70–73.

13. Blanche Mary Kelly, *The Well of English* (New York: Harper and Bros., 1936), 323–23.

14. Ralph Waldo Emerson, *Nature: Addresses and Lectures* (1876; repr., Boston: Houghton Mifflin, 1903), 3. Jaroslav Pelikan invokes this passage in *The Vindication of Tradition* (New Haven, CT: Yale University Press, 1984), 65.

15. Condé B. Pallen, *The Philosophy of Literature* (St. Louis: B. Herder, 1897), 183–84.

16. Stephen J. M. Brown, *Libraries and Literature from a Catholic Standpoint* (Dublin: Browne and Nolan, 1937).

17. Daniel Lord, SJ, "Training Youth for Authorship," in *Catholics and Scholarship: A Symposium on the Development of Scholars*, ed. John A. O'Brien (Huntington, IN: Our Sunday Visitor, 1938), 236–51, at 240.

18. Grenville Vernon, "Modernism *in Extremis*," *Commonweal*, May 14, 1930, 53.

19. Lawrence F. Hanley, "Cultural Work and Class Politics: Re-reading and Remaking *Proletarian Literature in the United States*," *Modern Fiction Studies* 38, no. 3 (Autumn 1992): 715–32. See also David R. Shumway, *Creating American Civilization: A Genealogy of American Literature as an Academic Discipline* (Minneapolis: University of Minnesota Press, 1994), chap. 8, "Left Criticism and the New York Intellectuals."

20. Quoted in Hanley, "Cultural Work and Class Politics," 729.

21. "Proletarianitis and Christianity," *Commonweal*, January 22, 1937, 343–44.

22. H. O'H. Walker, SJ, *The Power and Apostolate of Catholic Literature* (St. Louis: Queen's Work Press, 1938), 28.

23. See David E. Whisnant, *All That Is Native and Fine: The Politics of Culture in an American Region* (Chapel Hill: University of North Carolina Press, 1983); and Ann

Douglas, *Terrible Honesty: Mongrel Manhattan in the 1920s* (New York: Farrar, Straus and Giroux, 1995).

24. Jackson Lears discusses this point as it relates to modern art in *Fables of Abundance: A Cultural History of Advertising in America* (New York: Basic Books, 1994).

25. Benjamin Musser, "The Newness of New Poetry," *America*, March 21, 1931, 579–81.

26. Evelyn Waugh, *Brideshead Revisited* (Boston: Little, Brown, 1945), 351; T. S. Eliot, "East Coker," *Four Quartets* (1943; New York: Harcourt Brace Jovanovich, 1971), 28–29.

27. Flannery O'Connor, letter to A. [Betty Hester], December 16, 1955, in *Collected Works* (New York: Library of America, 1988), 977.

28. Henry Glassie, "Meaningful Things and Appropriate Myths: The Artifact's Place in American Studies," in *Material Life in America, 1600–1860*, ed. Robert Blair St. George (Boston: Northeastern University Press, 1988), 62–92, at 67.

29. John Bunker, "The Justification of 'Vers Libre,'" *America*, October 27, 1917, 65–66.

30. Brown, *Libraries and Literature*, 171.

31. Lord, "Training Youth for Authorship," 246.

32. Kelly, *The Well of English*, 345.

33. William F. Lynch, *Christ and Apollo: The Dimensions of the Literary Imagination* (New York: New American Library, 1960), 179.

34. This point applies to some forms of cultural production better than others; for instance, motion pictures for most of the first seventy years of their existence had to be available to everyone in their potential audience, but other sorts of things—radio programs, genre fiction, pulp magazines—targeted segments of the mass audience from their earliest years.

35. Lawrence W. Levine, *Highbrow/Lowbrow: The Emergence of Cultural Hierarchy in America* (Cambridge, MA: Harvard University Press, 1988).

36. Joan Shelley Rubin, *The Making of Middlebrow Culture* (Chapel Hill: University of North Carolina Press, 1992).

37. See Smith, *Contingencies of Value*, chap. 2, "The Exile of Evaluation."

38. See Judith Fetterley, *The Resisting Reader: A Feminist Approach to American Fiction* (Bloomington: Indiana University Press, 1978); Paul Lauter, ed., *Reconstructing American Literature: Courses, Syllabi, Issues* (Old Westbury, NY: Feminist Press, 1983).

39. James T. Fisher, "Catholicism as American Popular Culture" (paper presented at the Commonweal Colloquium, "American Catholics in the Public Square," January 26–28, 2001), http://www.catholicsinpublicsquare.org/papers/winter2001com monweal/fisher/fisher1.htm.

4. The History and Function of Catholic Censorship, as Told to the Twentieth Century

1. John T. McGreevy, "Thinking on One's Own: Catholicism in the American Intellectual Imagination, 1928–1960," *Journal of American History* 84, no. 1 (June 1997): 97–131, 99. The Schlesinger quote is from Arthur M. Schlesinger Jr., *The Vital Center: The Politics of Freedom* (Boston: Houghton Mifflin, 1949), 245. Mc-

Greevy's article was incorporated in large part into chap. 6 of McGreevy's 2003 book, *Catholicism and American Freedom: A History*.

2. I am using the terms "Counter-Reformation," "Catholic Reformation," and "early modern Catholicism" advisedly in what follows. That is, while I am aware of and generally in agreement with contemporary historiographical arguments for a revised terminology that favors "Catholic Reformation" and "early modern Catholicism," I retain "Counter-Reformation" in some places here to refer to views of the sixteenth and seventeenth centuries being created and reacted to by Catholic historians and literary critics in the early and mid twentieth century, because it was the "Counter-Reformation" to which, in their minds, they were responding. See John W. O'Malley, *Trent and All That: Renaming Catholicism in the Early Modern Era* (Cambridge, MA: Harvard University Press, 2000).

3. See James Turner, *Language, Religion, Knowledge: Past and Present* (Notre Dame, IN: University of Notre Dame Press, 2003); Christopher Jencks and David Riesman, *The Academic Revolution* (Garden City, NY: Doubleday, 1968); Laurence R. Veysey, *The Emergence of the American University* (Chicago: University of Chicago Press, 1965); John R. Thelin, *A History of American Higher Education* (Baltimore: Johns Hopkins University Press, 2004).

4. Peter Godman, *The Saint as Censor: Robert Bellarmine between Inquisition and Index* (Leiden: Brill, 2000).

5. Edward Peters, *Inquisition* (New York: Free Press, 1988), 231.

6. Ibid., 287–93.

7. "We have seen that the Ages of Faith, to which romantic dreamers regretfully look back, were ages of force and fraud, where evil seemed to reign almost unchecked, justifying the current opinion, so constantly reappearing, that the reign of Anti-christ had already begun. Imperfect as are human institutions to-day, a comparison with the past shows how marvellous [*sic*] has been the improvement, and the fact that this gain has been made almost wholly within the last two centuries, and that it is advancing with accelerated momentum, affords to the sociologist the most cheering encouragement" (Henry Charles Lea, *History of the Inquisition of the Middle Ages*, vol. 3 [1887; New York: S. A. Russell, 1955], 649).

8. It should be noted that Lea's work is on the medieval and Spanish Inquisitions, not the post-Reformation Roman Inquisition that generated the Index, but it might also be argued that as imaginative constructs, "Inquisitions" are largely indistinguishable.

9. William V. Hudon, "Religion and Society in Early Modern Italy: Old Questions, New Insights," *American Historical Review* 101, no. 3 (1996): 783–804; O'Malley, *Trent and All That*.

10. Hudon, "Religion and Society," 802.

11. P. W. Browne, "The Roman Index: The Church's Process of Condemning a Book," *The Sign*, May 1934, 629–30.

12. See Joseph Maria Pernicone, *The Ecclesiastical Prohibition of Books* (Washington, DC: Catholic University of America, 1932), 18; and Redmond Burke, *What Is the Index?* (Milwaukee: Bruce, 1952). Burke also notes, "These works were valued at 'fifty thousand pieces of silver'" (5).

13. John W. Miller, *The Origins of the Bible: Rethinking Canon History* (New York: Paulist Press, 1994).

14. Marilyn Rye, "Index Librorum Prohibitorum," *Journal of the Rutgers University Libraries* 43, no. 2 (December 1981): 66–79.

15. *Catholic Encyclopedia* (1913), "Censorship of Books."

16. *Catholic Encyclopedia* (1913), "Pope St. Gelasius I." Redmond Burke is at pains to emphasize that Gelasius's "index" was much more than a list of proscribed works; it also included recommended works—especially of the Church fathers (6). The frequent citation of Gelasius's index is additional evidence that Catholic historians felt a need for the Index to provide a pre-Reformation history for censorship of books.

17. Pernicone, *Ecclesiastical Prohibition of Books*, 41, cites Hilgers in indicating that it was enforced only at Cologne, for unknown reasons.

18. Rye, "Index Librorum Prohibitorum," 68, citing Steinberg, *Five Hundred Years of Printing*.

19. Pernicone, *Ecclesiastical Prohibition of Books*, 42; *Catholic Encyclopedia*, "Censorship." See also John M. Todd, *Luther: A Life* (New York: Crossroad, 1982), 188–92.

20. *Catholic Encyclopedia* (1913), "Martin Luther."

21. Elizabeth L. Eisenstein, *The Printing Press as an Agent of Change: Communications and Cultural Transformations in Early-Modern Europe* (Cambridge: Cambridge University Press, 1979), 2:695.

22. Frederick J. McGinness, "Gregory XIII (1572–85): Father of the Nations," in *The Great Popes through History: An Encyclopedia*, ed. Frank J. Coppa (Westport, CT: Greenwood Press, 2002), 344–45.

23. Pernicone, *Ecclesiastical Prohibition of Books*, 46.

24. Eisenstein, *The Printing Press*, 2:639.

25. Ibid., 2:652.

26. Paul F. Grendler, *The Roman Inquisition and the Venetian Press, 1540–1605* (Princeton: Princeton University Press, 1977).

27. Paul F. Grendler, "The Roman Inquisition and the Venetian Press, 1540–1605," *Journal of Modern History* 47 (March 1975): 48–65, at 58.

28. Michael A. Mullett, *The Catholic Reformation* (London: Routledge, 1999), chap. 7, "The Catholic Reformation and the Arts," 196–214; and the following articles in Coppa, *Great Popes through History*: Sergio Pagano (ed. William Hudon), "Pius V (1566–72)," 333–42; McGinness, "Gregory XIII," 343–55; and William V. Hudon, "Paul V (1605–21)," 373–80.

29. J. L. Heilbron, *The Sun in the Church: Cathedrals as Solar Observatories* (Cambridge, MA: Harvard University Press, 1999).

30. Reneé Haynes, *Philosopher-King: The Humanist Pope Benedict XIV* (London: Weidenfeld and Nicolson, 1970); David Hammerbeck, "Voltaire's *Mahomet*: The Persistence of Cultural Memory and Pre-Modern Orientalism," *Agora: Online Graduate Humanities Journal* 2, no. 2 (April 20, 2003), http://www.humanities.ualberta.ca/agora/; Hanns Gross, *Rome in the Age of Enlightenment: The Post-Tridentine Syndrome and the Ancien Regime* (Cambridge: Cambridge University Press, 1990); Paula Findlen, "Science as a Career in Enlightenment Italy: The Strategies of Laura Bassi," *Isis* 84, no. 3 (September 1993): 441–69.

31. Haynes, *Philosopher-King*, 188.

32. Hudon, "Religion and Society," 785.

33. Quoted in Eisenstein, *The Printing Press*, 2:671.

34. See Darrell Jodock, ed., *Catholicism Contending with Modernity: Roman Catholic Modernism and Anti-Modernism in Historical Context* (Cambridge: Cambridge University Press, 2000).

35. David W. Noble, *Death of a Nation: American Culture and the End of Exceptionalism* (Minneapolis: University of Minnesota Press, 2002); James C. Turner, *The Liberal Education of Charles Eliot Norton* (Baltimore: Johns Hopkins University Press, 1999).

36. Hilgers, "Censorship of Books," *Catholic Encyclopedia*; Michael J. Walsh, "Church Censorship in the 19th Century: The Index of Leo XIII," in *Censorship and the Control of Print: In England and France, 1600–1910*, ed. Robin Myers and Michael Harris (Winchester, UK: St Paul's Bibliographies, 1992).

37. "The Prohibition and Censorship of Books," in *The Great Encyclical Letters of Pope Leo XIII* (New York: Benziger Brothers, 1903), 407–21.

38. Not everyone agreed that each diocese achieved this objective: Bakewell Morrison, July 18, 1943, "More Questions and Answers": "I judge that it may be printed. My multitudinous remarks are not to be taken as adverse criticisms of the manuscript. But it is known to me that the diocesan censors are most captious, most unpleasant, and most dilatory" (Midwest Jesuit Archives, Daniel Lord Papers; folder: Censors—Fr. Lord—1941–45).

39. Pernicone, *Ecclesiastical Prohibition of Books*, 57.

40. "Chronicle," *Catholic Historical Review* 10, no. 1 (April 1924): 103–4.

41. H. Joseph Schneider, "The Catholic Index of Forbidden Books," *Catholic Library World*, February 1931, 29–30.

5. Censorship in the Land of "Thinking on One's Own"

1. Boston College Archives, John Bonn, SJ, papers, box 11, folder 10: "Lecture 21: The Moral Effect of Literature."

2. Joseph Hilgers, *Der Index der Verbotenen Bucher* (Freiburg im Breisgau: Herder, 1904).

3. "The Index: A Study Outline," *Journal of Religious Instruction* 9 (February 1939): 768–73. The other suggested units were "The Right and Duty of the Church to Legislate on the Publication and Use of Books Touching on Questions of Faith and Morals," "The History of *The Roman Index of Forbidden Books*," "How a Book Is Examined before It Is Placed on the Index," "Classes of Books Forbidden by the General Index Laws," and "The Obligations of Catholics toward the Index."

4. Paul R. Coyle, "The Code of Canon Law," *The Priest*, August 1958, 685–87.

5. W. Conway, "Notes and Queries: Prohibition of Books and of Films Based on Prohibited Books," *Irish Ecclesiastical Record* (S series) 70 (March 1948): 253–55.

6. William J. Kerrigan, "Index Bugaboo," *Catholic Digest*, November 1947, 63–64.

7. Ibid., 64.

8. In the case of both philosophers and novelists, some had only one work on the Index; some were condemned *opera omnes* (all works) or *omnes fabulae amatoriae* (literally, all love stories—the Latin neologism for "novel").

9. Eleanore K. Stockum, interview with author, 1995.

10. Francis Sales Betten, *The Roman Index of Forbidden Books Briefly Explained* (Chicago: Loyola University Press, 1925), 19.

11. Luis G. Alonso Getino, *Del gran número de los que se salvan y de la mitigación de las penas eternas* (Madrid: Editorial FEDA, 1934) [Decr. S. Off. 19 febr. 1936].

12. J. LaFarge, "Being Placed upon the Index," *America*, July 18, 1936, 347.

13. Midwest Jesuit Archives, Daniel A. Lord, SJ, papers; folder: Censors—Fr. Lord—1941–45.

14. Edward A. Purcell Jr., *The Crisis of Democratic Theory: Scientific Naturalism and the Problem of Value* (Lexington, KY: University Press of Kentucky, 1973).

15. Will Durant, *Transition: A Sentimental Story of One Mind and One Era* (New York: Simon and Schuster, 1927), 56, 62–63.

16. Daniel A. Lord, *I Can Read Anything: All Right, Then Read This* (St. Louis: The Queen's Work Press, 1930), 27–28.

17. Daniel A. Lord, *Played by Ear* (Chicago: Loyola University Press, 1956), 101–4.

18. Joseph Maria Pernicone, *The Ecclesiastical Prohibition of Books* (Washington, DC: Catholic University of America, 1932), 6.

19. Redmond Burke, *What Is the Index?* (Milwaukee: Bruce, 1952), 16.

20. It is not clear whether the dioceses in question did not appoint censors or did not report the names to the *Catholic Directory*; Redmond Burke notes that "their names usually appear in the *Official Catholic Directory*" (16), but doesn't say where that mandate comes from.

21. Midwest Jesuit Archives, Daniel A. Lord, SJ, papers; folder: Censors—Fr. Lord—1941–45.

22. Leroy Eid, interview with author, 1997.

23. Letter from L. J. Kelly to Tierney, January 22, 1925, box 43, folder 23, *America* Magazine archives, Georgetown University.

24. Reports from Joseph Husslein, SJ, Peter M. Dunne, SJ, and Francis X. Talbot, SJ, box 43, folder 23, *America* Magazine archives, Georgetown University.

25. E. Boyd-Barrett, SJ, "Normal and Abnormal Impulses," *America*, January 17, 1925, 317–19, 318.

26. "Wanderlust," *America*, January 31, 1925, 365–66; "Cleptomania," *America*, February 7, 1925, 390–92.

27. Censor's report from Bakewell Morrison on Lord's pamphlet "Preparation for Holy Communion," December 21, 1948; Midwest Jesuit Archives, Daniel Lord Papers; folder: Censors—Fr. Lord—1941–45.

28. Midwest Jesuit Archives, Daniel Lord Papers; folder: Censors—Fr. Lord—1941–45.

29. In a 1954 censor's report, Morrison wrote [capitalization *sic*], "IS THERE NOT ROOM*AND*NEED FOR TELLING THAT, THOUGH FORCED, THE FORCER EXPECTS THEM TO STUDY, TO LEARN, TO SEE FOR THEMSELVES WHY THEY ARE SO ORDERED? Ought you not tell the 'psychology' of doing-what-is-good-for-me-because-I-must and learning to enjoy and appreciate so that I can fully obey the command, and reasonably obey it, not slavishly?"

30. See R. Scott Appleby, *"Church and Age Unite!": The Modernist Impulse in American Catholicism* (Notre Dame, IN: University of Notre Dame Press, 1992): 230–34.

31. Leo Latz to Monsignor R. C. Maguire, October 22, 1932, Archives of the Archdiocese of Chicago. Leslie Tentler notes that by 1950 Latz's book had sold over four hundred thousand copies (*Catholics and Contraception: An American History* [Ithaca, NY: Cornell University Press, 2004], 175; see also 106–22). The vaguer formula "with ecclesiastical approval" (or "with ecclesiastical approbation") seems to have no basis in canon law. Redmond Burke notes, "This incomplete formula is not in strict accord with the prescriptions of the *Code*."

32. Redmond A. Burke, *What Is the Index?* (Milwaukee: Bruce, 1952), 17. See also Ellen Skerrett, *Born in Chicago: A History of Chicago's Jesuit University* (Chicago: Loyola Press, 2008), 158–59.

33. Michael Williams, "Views and Reviews," *Commonweal*, September 23, 1938, 555–56.

34. Letter Mivart to Steinhuber, August 29, 1899, Archives of the Congregation for the Doctrine of the Faith, Index, Protocolli 133, fol. 297.

35. See, for example, James J. Walsh, *Education of the Founding Fathers of the Republic: Scholasticism in the Colonial Colleges; A Neglected Chapter in the History of American Education* (New York: Fordham University Press, 1935).

36. Edward Mahoney, "The Index of Forbidden Books," *Catholic Library World*, January 1946, 99–108.

6. Art and Freedom in the Era of "The Church of Your Choice"

1. "Many Ideas of Censorship: Republican Club Hears Broad Discussion of Free Expression," *New York Times*, February 25, 1917, http://query.nytimes.com/mem/archive-free/pdf?res=F20E1EFF395F1B7A93C7AB1789D85F438185F9.

2. James T. Fisher, "Catholicism as American Popular Culture," in *American Catholics, American Culture: Tradition and Resistance*, ed. Margaret O'Brien Steinfels (Lanham, MD: Rowman and Littlefield, 2004). See also Anthony Burke Smith, *The Look of Catholics: Portrayals in Popular Culture from the Great Depression to the Cold War* (Lawrence: University Press of Kansas, 2010).

3. Frank Walsh, *Sin and Censorship: The Catholic Church and the Motion Picture Industry* (New Haven, CT: Yale University Press, 1996), 261–68.

4. Box 11, folder 10, papers of Rev. John L. Bonn, SJ, Boston College Archives.

5. For a fuller account of these issues, see Una M. Cadegan, "Guardians of Democracy or Cultural Storm Troopers? American Catholics and the Control of Popular Media, 1934–1966," *Catholic Historical Review* 87 (April 2001): 252–82.

6. Francis G. Couvares, "Hollywood, Main Street, and the Church: Trying to Censor the Movies before the Production Code," *American Quarterly* 44, no. 4 (December 1992): 584–616.

7. This story has been told fully elsewhere, particularly in Walsh, *Sin and Censorship*. Also see Gregory D. Black, *The Catholic Crusade against the Movies, 1940–1975* (Cambridge: Cambridge University Press, 1998); Black, *Hollywood Censored: Morality Codes, Catholics, and the Movies* (Cambridge: Cambridge University Press, 1994); James M. Skinner, *The Cross and the Cinema: The Legion of Decency and the National Catholic Office for Motion Pictures, 1933–1970* (Westport, CT: Praeger, 1993).

8. Walsh, *Sin and Censorship*, 101–2.

9. "The Campaign against Bad Films," *America*, April 28, 1934, 51.

10. See Thomas Doherty, *Hollywood's Censor: Joseph I. Breen and the Production Code Administration* (New York: Columbia University Press, 2007).

11. Walsh, *Sin and Censorship*, 159.

12. Thomas Doherty, *Pre-Code Hollywood: Sex, Immorality, and Insurrection in American Cinema, 1930–1934* (New York: Columbia University Press, 1999), 345.

13. R. Laurence Moore, *Selling God: American Religion in the Marketplace of Culture* (New York: Oxford University Press, 1994), 229.

14. Walsh, *Sin and Censorship*, 99–100.

15. Pius XI, *Vigilanti cura*, June 29, 1936, http://www.vatican.va/holy_father /pius_xi/encyclicals/documents/ hf_p-xi_enc_29061936_vigilanti-cura_en.html.

16. Daniel A. Lord, *Played by Ear: The Autobiography of Daniel A. Lord, S.J.* (Chicago: Loyola University Press, 1956), 303.

17. Walsh, *Sin and Censorship*, 151.

18. See John Tebbel and Mary Ellen Zuckerman, *The Magazine in America: 1741–1990* (New York: Oxford University Press, 1991), 342. Also, on the origins of the pulps, see Frank Luther Mott, *A History of American Magazines* (Cambridge: Harvard University Press, 1939–68), vols. 4 and 5; and Theodore Peterson, *Magazines in the Twentieth Century* (Urbana: University of Illinois Press, 1964). An interesting compilation of typical pulp fare (including a number of the kinds of illustrations to which the NODL objected) is Tony Goodstone, ed., *The Pulps: Fifty Years of American Popular Culture* (New York: Chelsea House, 1970).

19. See NODL correspondence, John Francis Noll Manuscripts (hereafter cited as CNOL), 3/4 and 3/5, University of Notre Dame Archives (hereafter cited as UNDA), passim. In the NODL's earliest days, Noll often included the code in his letters; as the organization became more formalized he apparently included a printed copy of it with his letters. The early five-point code was later expanded when the NODL extended beyond pulp magazines to comic books and paperbound books. See Harold C. Gardiner, *Catholic Viewpoint on Censorship* (Garden City, NY: Hanover House, 1958), 112–38, 163–200.

20. CNOL 4/32 (NODL Indianapolis), UNDA.

21. CNOL 4/32 (NODL Indianapolis), UNDA. *Peek* was one of the numerous new photographic magazines attempting in the late 1930s to capitalize on the success of *Life* and *Look* (Peterson, *Magazines*, 354).

22. Thomas F. O'Connor, "The National Organization for Decent Literature: A Phase in American Catholic Censorship," *Library Quarterly* 65, no. 4 (October 1995): 386–414.

23. See letter from William Smith to Jesse Murrell, July 2, 1948 (CNOL 3/15, UNDA). See also O'Connor, "National Organization for Decent Literature."

24. See Kenneth C. Davis, *Two-Bit Culture: The Paperbacking of America* (Boston: Houghton Mifflin, 1984); Frank L. Schick, *The Paperbound Book in America: The History of Paperbacks and Their European Background* (New York: R. R. Bowker, 1958). See also Jan Radway's discussion of changes in the paperback publishing industry in *Reading the Romance: Women, Patriarchy and Popular Literature* (Chapel Hill: University of North Carolina Press, 1984), chap. 1, "The Institutional Matrix."

25. Otis Ferguson, "The Legion Rides Again," *New Republic*, December 22, 1941, 861.

26. *Mutual Film Corporation v. Industrial Commission of Ohio*, No. 456, Supreme Court of the United States, 236 U.S. 230; 35 S. Ct. 387; 59 L. Ed. 552; 1915 U.S. Lexis 1755.

27. Letter from Noll to Raymond R. Cameron, April 14, 1941 (UNDA, CNOL 3/9).

28. University of Notre Dame Archives, *The Frank C. Walker Papers* (finding aid to the Walker collection), 1992, iii–v.

29. See Cadegan, "Guardians of Democracy"; O'Connor, "National Organization for Decent Literature."

30. Drew Pearson, "Effective Censorship," *Washington Post*, March 25, 1943, 12.

31. Letter from Noll to John J. Glennon, December 19, 1941 (UNDA, CNOL 3/10).

32. A detailed description of the controversy appears in Walsh, *Sin and Censorship*, 250–55.

33. Ibid., 254.

34. Ibid., 262–66.

35. Rochelle Gurstein, *The Repeal of Reticence: A History of America's Cultural and Legal Struggles over Free Speech, Obscenity, Sexual Liberation, and Modern Art* (New York: Farrar, Straus and Giroux, 1996).

36. The "Statement" is reprinted in Harold C. Gardiner, *Catholic Viewpoint on Censorship*, 173–78.

37. John Fischer, "The Harm Good People Do (Editor's Easy Chair)," *Harper's*, October 1956, 14–20; John Courtney Murray, "The Bad Arguments Intelligent Men Make," *America*, November 3, 1956, 120–23.

38. O'Connor, "National Organization for Decent Literature," 393, 408–10.

39. "Reverend Harold C. Gardiner, S.J.," in *The Book of Catholic Authors (Sixth Series): Informal Self-Portraits of Famous Modern Catholic Writers*, ed. Walter Romig (Grosse Pointe, MI: W. Romig and Co., 1966), 191.

40. In Gardiner, *Catholic Viewpoint on Censorship*, 172.

41. John Courtney Murray, *We Hold These Truths: Catholic Reflections on the American Proposition* (New York: Sheed and Ward, 1960), 167.

42. Ibid., 171.

43. Ibid., 158,174.

44. William F. Lynch, *The Image Industries* (New York: Sheed and Ward, 1959), 147.

45. One of the many virtues of Robert A. Orsi's *Thank You, St. Jude: Women's Devotion to the Patron Saint of Hopeless Causes* (New Haven, CT: Yale University Press, 1996) is the way in which Orsi integrates intergenerational issues into his analysis.

46. Will Herberg, *Protestant–Catholic–Jew: An Essay in Religious Sociology* (Chicago: University of Chicago Press, 1955), 160–61.

47. "What Would You Like to Know about the Church?," *Catholic Digest*, August 1957, 118.

48. Herberg, *Protestant–Catholic–Jew*, 77.

49. John Murray Cuddihy, *No Offense: Civil Religion and Protestant Taste* (New York: Seabury, 1978).

7. Reclaiming the Modernists, Reclaiming the Modern

1. See Una M. Cadegan, "'Blessings on Your Old Head, Kid': The Friendship of Richard Sullivan and Harry Sylvester," *U.S. Catholic Historian* 15, no. 3 (Summer 1997): 39–56.

2. Una M. Cadegan, "How Realistic Can a Catholic Writer Be? Richard Sullivan and American Catholic Literature," *Religion and American Culture* 6, no. 1 (Winter 1996): 35–61.

3. James Turner, *The Liberal Education of Charles Eliot Norton* (Baltimore: Johns Hopkins University Press, 1999).

4. Walter J. Ong, SJ, *American Catholic Crossroads: Religious-Secular Encounters in the Modern World* (New York: Macmillan, 1959), ix.

5. Review of *A Portrait of the Artist as a Young Man* by James Joyce, *Catholic World*, June 1917, 395–97.

6. In Harold C. Gardiner, ed., *Fifty Years of the American Novel: A Christian Appraisal* (New York: Scribner's, 1951), 250.

7. Thomas Merton, *The Seven Storey Mountain* (New York: New American Library, 1948), 208–9; Joseph J. Feeney, "James Joyce: A Lyric 100," *America*, March 6, 1982, 173; Marcella M. Holloway, "James Joyce on His Deathbed," *America*, June 19, 1982, 477–79. See also Herbert Marshall McLuhan, "Joyce, Aquinas and the Poetic Process," *Renascence* 4, (1951): 3–11; Edward Morin, "Joyce as Thomist," *Renascence* 9 (1956): 127–31.

8. See, for example, John B. Vickery, "T. S. Eliot's Poetry: The Quest and the Way," *Renascence* 10 (1957): 3–10, 31, 59–67. Eliot's *The Love Song of J. Alfred Prufrock* is the final poem in Maurice B. McNamee, SJ, *Reading for Understanding* (New York: Holt, Rinehart and Winston, 1950), a college literature textbook prepared by the chair of the Department of English of St. Louis University.

9. Joseph R. N. Maxwell, "Provocative of Thought, Offense, Even Disgust," review of *The Power and the Glory* by Graham Greene, *America*, April 6, 1940, 722.

10. Joseph McSorley, review of *The Heart of the Matter* by Graham Greene, *Catholic World*, September 1948, 564–65.

11. Harold C. Gardiner, "'Heart of the Matter": Greene's Greatest?," review of *The Heart of the Matter* by Graham Greene, *America*, July 17, 1948, 350–51.

12. A 1963 work intended to emphasize the role of books, reading, and study in the sister formation movement included in the literature category all of Greene's Catholic novels except *The End of the Affair* (Sr. Mary Fabian Harmer, comp., *Books for Religious Sisters: A General Bibliography* [Washington, DC: Catholic University of America Press, 1963]).

13. Letter from Richard Sullivan to Harold C. Gardiner, SJ, January 27, 1944, Richard Sullivan: Manuscripts (hereafter cited as CSUL) 1/6, University of Notre Dame Archives (hereafter cited as UNDA).

14. Riley Hughes, review of Graham Greene's *The End of the Affair*, in *Best Sellers*, November 15, 1951, 154–55. See also "Riley Hughes," in *The Book of Catholic Authors (Fifth Series): Informal Self-Portraits of Famous Modern Catholic Writers*, ed. Walter Romig (Grosse Pointe, MI: W. Romig and Co., [1957], 144–49, though this cheery self-portrait does not convey the persistent conflict between Hughes and

many other people involved in Catholic literary work, who saw Hughes as too censorious, particularly in his involvement with the periodical *Books on Trial.*

15. Harold C. Gardiner, "Mr. Greene Does It Again," review of *The End of the Affair* by Graham Greene, *America*, October 27, 1951, 100–101; Gardiner, "Second Thoughts on Greene's Latest," *America,* December 15, 1951, 312–13. Both reviews are included in Harold C. Gardiner, *Norms for the Novel* (Garden City, NY: Hanover House, 1960), 9–18.

16. From "Reverend Harold C. Gardiner, S.J.," in *The Book of Catholic Authors (Sixth Series)*, ed. Walter Romig (Detroit: W. Romig and Company, 1942–): "A truly Catholic attitude is what is of the essence—not only with regard to literature, but with regard to all the multitudinous facets of contemporary life—an attitude that really faces reality and endeavors to leaven that reality with the spirit of Christ and His Church" (191).

17. Gardiner still held to the unchanging nature of the moral law, though: as one of several commenters in *Time* magazine's April 12, 1948, article on the recently released Kinsey Report on human sexuality, Gardiner quipped, "If a 'Dr. Binsey' made a scientific survey to prove that 99 out of 100 boys steal, . . . parents would not demand a change in the larceny laws. Demanding a change in laws regarding sex on the basis of Kinsey's findings is just as senseless" ("Behavior, after Kinsey," *Time,* April 12, 1948, 79–80).

18. Moira Walsh, "Right Conscience about Films: II," *America*, May 16, 1964, 685–86.

19. Ibid., 658.

20. Msgr. Thomas F. Little, "The Modern Legion and Its Modern Outlook," *America*, December 11, 1965, 744–45.

21. "Another Sign of Maturity," *Ave Maria*, June 2, 1962, 17.

22. John F. X. McGohey, "The Catholic Press and the Catholic Layman," in *The Catholic Mind through Fifty Years, 1903–1953*, ed. Benjamin L. Masse (New York: America Press, 1953), 261–62.

23. Letter to A., September 15, 1955, *Collected Works*, Library of America, 955; Peter A. Huff, *Allen Tate and the Catholic Revival: Trace of the Fugitive Gods* (New York: Paulist Press, 1996), 108.

24. Ong, *American Catholic Crossroads*, 127.

25. Richard Sullivan to Henry Volkening, August 30, 1945, CSUL/UNDA.

26. John T. McGreevy, *Catholicism and American Freedom: A History* (New York: Norton, 2003), 208–13. He gives as three reasons the views of Catholic leaders on racial segregation, anticommunism, and the shifting of the posture of U.S. Catholicism to a less combative stance.

27. Edward A. Purcell Jr., *The Crisis of Democratic Theory: Scientific Naturalism and the Problem of Value* (Lexington: University Press of Kentucky, 1973).

28. Ong, *American Catholic Crossroads*, 10.

29. Gerald J. Bednar, John F. Kane, and David S. Toolan, "'Into the Valley of the Human': The Contribution of William F. Lynch, S.J., to American Catholic Intellectual Life," in *American Catholic Traditions: Resources for Renewal*, ed. Sandra Yocum Mize and William Portier (Marynoll, NY: Orbis Books, 1996), 130–51.

30. Walter Kerr, *Criticism and Censorship* (Milwaukee, WI: Bruce, 1954), 85.

31. See Gardiner, *Norms for the Novel*, 9–18.

32. In Harold C. Gardiner, ed., *Fifty Years of the American Novel: A Christian Appraisal* (New York: Scribner's, 1951), 250.

33. Walker Percy, *The Moviegoer* (1960; New York: Ivy Books, 1990), 128–29.

8. Peculiarly Possessed of the Modern Consciousness

1. Flannery O'Connor, letter to A., August 2, 1955, *Collected Works* (New York: Library of America, 1988), 943.

2. Francis Beauchesne Thornton, *How to Improve Your Personality by Reading* (Milwaukee: Bruce, 1949), 64. The Incarnation is also the idea that drives William Lynch's search for "contraries" that are not opposites but depend on each other for their existence and coherence. See Lynch, *Christ and Apollo: The Dimensions of the Literary Imagination* (New York: New American Library, 1960).

3. William M. Halsey, *The Survival of American Innocence: American Catholicism in an Era of Disillusionment, 1920–1940* (Notre Dame, IN: University of Notre Dame Press, 1980); Arnold Sparr, *To Promote, Defend, and Redeem: The Catholic Literary Revival and the Cultural Transformation of American Catholicism, 1920–1960* (New York: Greenwood Press, 1990).

4. John T. McGreevy, *Catholicism and American Freedom: A History* (New York: W. W. Norton, 2003), 195–96. Newman anchors the beginning of the Catholic literary revival in England in the influential chronology in Calvert Alexander's *The Catholic Literary Revival: Three Phases in Its Development from 1845 to the Present* (Milwaukee: Bruce, 1935).

5. Flannery O'Connor, *The Habit of Being: Letters of Flannery O'Connor*, ed. Sally Fitzgerald (New York: Farrar, Straus and Giroux, 1979), 511.

6. Harold C. Gardiner, "Scholars, Catholic, Who's Got the?," *America*, October 16, 1965, 442–43.

7. Mariella Gable, OSB, and Nancy Hynes, OSB, eds., *The Literature of Spiritual Values and Catholic Fiction* (Lanham, MD: University Press of America, 1996), xxvii. See Leslie Woodcock Tentler, *Catholics and Contraception: An American History* (Ithaca, NY: Cornell University Press, 2004), chap. 5, "'It Isn't Easy to Be a Catholic': Rhythm, Education for Marriage, Lay Voices, 1941–1962," for insight on the effect, in a very different area, of the increasing theological sophistication of a small group of highly motivated laity.

8. Terry Eagleton, *Literary Theory: An Introduction* (Minneapolis: University of Minnesota Press, 1996); Gerald Graff, *Professing Literature: An Institutional History* (Chicago: University of Chicago Press, 1987); David R. Shumway, *Creating American Civilization: A Genealogy of American Literature as an Academic Discipline* (Minneapolis: University of Minnesota Press, 1994).

9. William F. Lynch, *The Image Industries* (New York: Sheed and Ward, 1959), 141.

10. Barbara Herrnstein Smith, *Contingencies of Value: Alternative Perspectives for Critical Theory* (Cambridge, MA: Harvard University Press, 1988), 17; Edward A. Purcell Jr., *The Crisis of Democratic Theory: Scientific Naturalism and the Problem of Value* (Lexington: University Press of Kentucky, 1973).

11. See, for example, Philip Gleason, *Contending with Modernity: Catholic Higher Education in the Twentieth Century* (New York: Oxford University Press, 1995), 251.

12. Sr. T. A. Doyle, OSB, "Beyond the New Criticism," *Benedictine Review* 10 (July 1955): 29–32, 32.

13. In *Left Intellectuals and Popular Culture in Twentieth-Century America* (Chapel Hill: University of North Carolina Press, 1996), Paul R. Gorman writes of the role of mass-culture critique in the self-definition of liberal intellectuals that it "encouraged the intellectuals' paternalism and hastened the formation of what might be called a 'democratic clerisy,' an intelligentsia that justified its superior standing by devotion to protecting democracy."

14. Purcell, *Crisis of Democratic Theory*.

15. William H. Gass, "Vicissitudes of the Avant-Garde," in *Finding a Form: Essays* (New York: Knopf, 1996), 199–212.

16. See Jackson Lears, *Fables of Abundance: A Cultural History of Advertising in America* (New York: Basic Books, 1994); Susan Sellers, "How Long Has This Been Going On?: *Harper's Bazaar, Funny Face* and the Construction of the Modernist Woman," *Visible Language* 29, no. 1 (Winter 1995): 13–34.

17. "The theatre, the theatre / What's happened to the theatre? / Chaps who did taps / They're not tapping anymore, they're doing choreography / Chicks who did kicks / They're not kicking anymore, they're doing choreography / Heps who did steps / That would stop the show in days that used to be / Through the air they keep flying / Like a duck who is dying / Instead of dance it's choreography."

18. Susan Hegeman, *Patterns for America: Modernism and the Concept of Culture* (Princeton: Princeton University Press, 1999).

19. See Steven Watts, "Walt Disney: Art and Politics in the American Century," *Journal of American History* 82, no. 1 (1995): 84–110; Warren I. Susman, *Culture as History: The Transformation of American Society in the Twentieth Century* (New York: Pantheon, 1984).

20. Sister M. Pierre, "Our Atom Bomb, the Rosary," *Catholic School Journal* 48 (May 1948): 165–66.

21. See Eugene McCarraher, *Christian Critics: Religion and the Impasse in Modern Social Thought* (Ithaca, NY: Cornell University Press, 2000).

22. See Janice A. Radway, *A Feeling for Books: The Book-of-the-Month Club, Literary Taste, and Middle-Class Desire* (Chapel Hill: University of North Carolina Press, 1997). Also, T. J. Jackson Lears, "From Salvation to Self-Realization: Advertising and the Therapeutic Roots of Consumer Culture, 1880–1930," in *The Culture of Consumption: Critical Essays in American History, 1880–1980*, ed. Richard Wightman Fox and T. J. Jackson Lears (New York: Pantheon, 1983), 1–38.

23. N. Elizabeth Monroe, "The New Man in Fiction," *Renascence* 6 (1953): 9–17, at 9.

24. Philip J. Scharper, "Providence and Modern Literature," *America*, August 2, 1952, 440–42, at 441.

25. Rochelle Gurstein, *The Repeal of Reticence: A History of America's Cultural and Legal Struggles over Free Speech, Obscenity, Sexual Liberation, and Modern Art* (New York: Hill and Wang, 1996).

26. "Writers of Today," video recording, with W. H. Auden, poet and critic, and Walter Kerr, drama critic, New York Herald Tribune; produced by the Educational Television and Radio Center in cooperation with the American Book Publishers Council; filmed by Dynamic Films, Inc.; directed by Lee R. Bobker (New York: First Run/Icarus Films, 1990), my transcription/paraphrase.

27. *The Habit of Being*, 125; Sullivan, "Record of Work Begun and Ideas for Stories," 1932–33, CSUL 1/1, UNDA.

28. Lynch, *Christ and Apollo*, 180–81.

29. Umberto Eco, *The Open Work*, trans. Anna Concogni (Cambridge, MA: Harvard University Press, 1989), xiii–xiv.

30. Nathan A. Scott Jr., "The Name and Nature of Our Period-Style," in *The Broken Center: Studies in the Theological Horizon of Modern Literature* (New Haven, CT: Yale University Press, 1966), 124–25.

31. A recent body of interesting historical scholarship aims at countering the claim that the world ever was actually "disenchanted," scholarship that documents the persistence of belief in the supernatural, in miracles, and in magic, and of devotional practices and "religious enthusiasm" that evince this belief. This scholarship, however, focuses tightly on the role that Church authorities played in controlling access to the supernatural, "legitimizing orthodoxy," "defending the church's thaumaturgic monopoly." Andrew Keitt, "Religious Enthusiasm, the Spanish Inquisition and the Disenchantment of the World," *Journal of the History of Ideas* 65, no. 2 (April 2004): 231–50. Left largely unexplored is the question of theology's role in the history of ideas, and the extent to which reasoned engagement with theological claims shapes the intellectual history of Catholicism distinctively in a wide variety of fields.

32. Walter J. Ong, *American Catholic Crossroads: Religious-Secular Encounters in the Modern World* (New York: Macmillan, 1959), 111.

Epilogue

1. Peter Godman, "Graham Greene's Vatican Dossier," *Atlantic Monthly*, July/August 2001, 84–88.

2. Cited in ibid., 86. The consultor who presumed as Greene's audience the people the church was least likely to reach was most generous to his work and harshest on the literary capacities of many Catholics, including the clergy ("unlettered bondslaves to puerile literature in bad taste").

3. Letters, December 29, 1957, and January 12, 1958.

4. Timothy O'Meara, "'Raid on the Dominicans': The Repression of 1954," *America*, February 5, 1994, 8–16.

5. Gerard S. Sloyan, "The Problem of Prohibited Books and the American Catholic Intellectual," *Proceedings of the Annual Meeting, Society of Catholic College Teachers of Sacred Doctrine* 6 (1960), 83–95, at 87.

6. "Cross Section: The Index of Forbidden Books," *Critic* 20 (April–May 1962): 54–59. The participants were Harold C. Gardiner, SJ; Robert Giroux; Redmond A. Burke, CSV; Roger J. Kiley; Msgr. Joseph C. Fenton; and Francis X. Canfield.

7. "Index Officially Abolished," *The Tablet*, June 18, 1966, 711.

8. "More about the Index," *The Tablet*, June 25, 1966, 739–40, at 740.

9. Francis Henninger, personal communication.

Index

Abelard, 91
abstraction, 24, 53
Acolyte, 139
Acta Apostolicae Sedes, 109
Acton, Lord, 109
Acts of the Apostles, 28, 90, 122, 146
Addams, Jane, 125
aestheticism as movement, 34
After the Genteel Tradition (Trilling), 68
Ahlstrom, Sydney, 197n6
Albany Evangelist, 140
Alexander, Calvert, 37
Alexander VI, Pope, 92
America, 7, 13, 20–21, 23, 25, 41, 44–45,
    56, 66, 76–77, 110, 115–16, 130–31,
    145, 160–62, 164, 174, 184
American Catholic Arts and Fictions (Giles), 66
American Catholic Crossroads (Ong), 156–57
American Civil Liberties Union (ACLU),
    142
American Ecclesiastical Review, 106
Americanism, 50–51, 55, 83
American Journal of Sociology, 64–65
American literary culture, 21–22, 24,
    67–68, 83, 175–78, 186, 188
American Renaissance, 22
anti-Catholicism, 4, 198n14
anticommunism, 11, 12, 67, 166, 185,
    217n26
anti-Semitism, 185
Appleby, Scott, 50, 54
Appleton's Cyclopedia, 9, 198n14
Aquinas, Thomas, 28–36, 52, 106, 125,
    186, 189
Aristotle, 28, 29, 177
Arius, 91, 122
Armory Show (1913), 58, 203n53
Arnold, Matthew, 8, 9, 29
art, 75, 83, 147, 149, 152, 155–56, 168–69,
    177–78, 185
art for art's sake, 34–35, 167
Arvin, Newton, 69

"Ash Wednesday" (Eliot), 74, 159
assimilation, 4, 8, 148, 150, 151, 163–65,
    175, 182–83, 185
Astaire, Fred, 179
Atlantic Monthly, 43–44, 153–54
Auden, W. H., 186–87, 190
Augustine, St., 162
autonomy of art, 168–69, 177–78
Ave Maria, 107, 164–65

Bacon, Francis, 108
Baltimore Catechism, 10
Balzac, Honoré de, 108
Barlow, Rev. John, 123–24
Barrett, E. Boyd, 56, 115–16
beauty, 29, 31, 34–36
Bednar, Gerald J., 168
Bellarmine, Robert, 120
Belloc, Hilaire, 15, 40, 64
Bells of St. Mary's, The, 140
Benedictine Review, 177
Benedict XIV, Pope, 95, 96–97, 99, 100, 103
Bennett, Arnold, 39–40
Benson, Robert Hugh, 158
Bentham, Jeremy, 108
Berengarius of Tours, 91
Bergman, Ingrid, 140, 150
Bernanos, Georges, 15
Best Sellers, 162
Best Years of Our Lives, 167–68
Betten, Francis, 105, 110
Bible, 26–28, 49, 90, 122, 107, 146
Black Boy (Wright), 33
blank verse, 78
Blanshard, Paul, 166
Blockade, 131
Bloy, Leon, 15
Bok, Edward, 12
Bonn, John L., 27, 28, 32, 105, 126
Book-of-the-Month Club, 13, 46
Books on Trial, 44, 217n14
Boston American, 123

Boston College, 27, 32, 126
boycott, 130, 142, 144, 145, 151
Breen, Joseph, 131, 134, 141
Bregy, Katherine, 46, 201–2n27
Brideshead Revisited (Waugh), 195–96
Brighton Rock (Greene), 160
Brown, Stephen J. M., 16, 23, 71, 80
Browne, P. W., 89
Brownson, Orestes, 66
Bruno, Giordano, 95
Bunker, John, 80
Burke, Kenneth, 73
Burke, Redmond A., 105, 209n12, 210n16, 212n20, 213n31
Burton, Katherine, 43

canon law, 3, 85, 86, 88, 100–107, 109, 113, 117, 145–46
Cantos (Pound), 58
capitalism, 52, 56, 58, 72, 124, 137, 151, 180–82
Capra, Frank, 150
Cather, Willa, 68–69
Catholic Action, 14–16, 23, 24, 36, 82, 139, 143, 164, 175
Catholic Action, 15
Catholic bibliography, 16
Catholic Book Club, 46
Catholic Builders of the Nation, 17–18
Catholic Church, 4, 6, 16–17, 25, 45, 47–48, 50–52, 53–55, 71, 81, 77, 83, 88, 92, 94, 98, 100–107, 109, 113, 117, 125–29, 145–52, 156–57, 186, 187–88, 190, 197nn5–6
Catholic Commission on Intellectual and Cultural Affairs, 174
Catholic Digest, 54, 107, 150
Catholic Directory, 113, 212n20
Catholic Encyclopedia, 6, 8–10, 20, 91, 93, 95, 105–06, 174, 198n14, 200n1
Catholic Historical Review, 16–17, 103
Catholic Library Association, 16, 124
Catholic Library World, 15, 103, 121
Catholic literary aesthetics: and account-ability, 24, 81–84, 86; activist role of, in service of nonaesthetic ends, 23–25, 73–74; Alexander's history of, 37; beauty as literary criterion, 29, 31, 34–36; contours of, 26–36; and Dante's *Divine Comedy,* 28, 71, 80, 168; definition and evaluation of works of art within, 25–36; Gardiner on, 145–46, 161–62; goodness as moral criterion in, 29–32; and

iconoclasm/orthodoxy, 62, 69–74, 167–70; and individual/community, 22, 23, 57, 61, 62, 65–70, 181–84; and innovation/repetition, 62, 74–77, 184–88; during interwar period, 21–26; liturgy's impact on, 77, 186, 187; and mission of literature, 23, 27, 71–72, 126; and openness/closure, 62, 78–81, 188–91; and realism during interwar period, 21, 38–46, 48; and rise of liberalism, 36–37; scriptural framework of, 26–28; Thomistic framework of, 28–36; and timelessness, 25, 45, 51–52, 188, 190; truth as doctrinal criterion in, 29, 31–34; and unified communal identity, 22–23, 47–48; and unity of goodness, truth, and beauty, 29, 31–32, 36; versus professionalization and nationalization of American literary culture, 21–22
Catholic literary culture in Europe, 15, 67
Catholic literary culture in U.S.: activist role of, in transforming culture, 13–16, 23–25; and Catholic bibliography, 16; and "Catholic revival," 37, 172–75; collaboration between hierarchy and laity in, 10–11, 22; content of literary aesthetics in early decades of twentieth century, 20–46; and definition of culture, 5–6; as distinctively Catholic, American, and modern, 7–9; and divisions among Catholics, 22–23; Ellis's criticisms of, 174; and guarding against socialist threat, 11–13; and immigrants, 9, 22, 46, 125, 128, 152, 163–64, 182, 185, 197n5; and Incarnation, 27, 33, 36, 79, 123, 172, 189–91; infrastructure for, 5; internal and external focus of, 9–11, 22; during interwar period, 21–26; and literature as intellectual history, 154–57; and New Criticism, 175–78, 186, 188; overview of, in 1920s-1960s, 4–19; in postwar period of 1950s and 1960s, 174–81; and presumption of maturity and responsibility in audiences following World War II, 163–70; and print materials needed for Catholic practice and formation, 10, 14; and problems of Catholic writers, 153–54, 183; and professionalization and nationalization of American literary culture, 21–22; and realism during interwar period, 21, 38–46, 48; and reclaiming of modernist writers in 1950s, 157–63; reconciliation

between modernism and, during 1950s-1960s, 153–72; and unified communal identity, 22–23, 47–48

Catholic Literary Revival, The (Alexander), 37

Catholic Messenger, 107

Catholic Press Association, 15, 165

Catholics and Contraception (Latz), 213n31

Catholic School Journal, 181–82

Catholic Spirit in Modern English Literature, The (Shuster), 64–65

Catholic University of America, 103, 105

Catholic Viewpoint on Censorship, The (Gardiner), 105, 143

Catholic War Veterans, 140

Catholic World, 1–2, 11, 20, 33–34, 39–40, 48, 58, 69, 77, 158, 160–61, 200n1

Cathrein, Victor, 8

censorship: ACLU on, 142; in apostolic times, 28, 90, 122, 146; and autonomy of art, 168–69; before invention of movable type, 90–91; and boycott strategy, 130, 142, 144, 145, 151; canon law on, 85, 86, 88, 100–107, 109, 113, 117; and Catholic scholars, 105, 108–12; and censor from each diocese, 101, 113; and condemnation of heresy, 91, 122; definition of, 120, 123; enforcement of, 95–96; explanation of and rationale for, in twentieth century, 86–87, 89, 100, 104–8, 111–12, 120–24, 127; and expurgation, 33; and First Amendment, 120–21, 129, 133, 137, 140; Gardiner on, 105, 143, 145–47, 164, 194; during Great War, 121; histories of, 28, 89–99, 100, 122, 124, 145–46; and humility of Catholic scholars, 110–11; implementation of, during twentieth century, 112–22; and Inquisition, 87, 89, 93–94, 96; by Jesuits, 56; of Joyce's *Ulysses,* 2, 30; Kennedy on, 192; of Martin Luther, 92–93; in mid-fifteenth through mid-eighteenth centuries, 90, 92–96; in modern period, 90, 96–99; of movies, 126, 127, 129–35, 137, 139–43, 146, 150, 156, 164, 185; Murray on, 143–47; opposition to and criticism of, 136–39, 142, 144, 145, 150–51; and presumption of maturity and responsibility in audiences following World War II, 163–65; prior censorship versus prohibition after publication, 95, 100–101, 146; for protection of truth, 90, 91, 110–11, 114, 120–23; and Protestant

Reformation, 92–93, 122; of pulp magazines, 134–38, 142; by Soviet Union, 122, 137, 151, 167, 178; twentieth-century regulation of reading and publication, 99–103; U.S. Post Office censorship of obscene materials, 121

Chautauqua, 8

Chesterton, G. K., 15, 24, 40

Chicago Theological Seminary, 65

Choreography, 180

Christ and Apollo (Lynch), 187

Christ in Concrete (di Donato), 44–45

Church Progress, 20, 200n1

Civiltà Cattolica, 48

classicism, 37

Claudel, Paul, 15

closure. *See* openness/closure

Code of Canon Law. *See* canon law

Cold War, 121, 122, 151, 166, 178, 180–82, 185, 186

Collected Stories (Porter), 173

Collegio Romano, 96

Columbian Exposition's World Parliament of Religions, 9

comic books, 5, 25, 31, 124, 126, 136, 137–38, 149, 214n19

commodification, 156, 179–81, 184–85

Commonweal, 64, 73, 77, 119

community. *See* individual/community

Confrey, Burton, 16, 23, 199n36, 201n17

Congregation for the Doctrine of the Faith (CDF), 194–95

Congregation for the Propagation of the Faith, 25

conservatism, 37, 51

contraception, 30, 43, 56, 118–19, 213n31

Conway, J. D., 150

Cooper, James Fenimore, 22

Copernicus, Nicolaus, 93, 96

Council of Trent, 91, 93–94, 96

Counter-Reformation, 86, 88, 89, 94, 113, 127, 167, 209n2

Crane, Stephen, 39

creation by God, 26–27, 33, 35–36, 73, 123, 191

Critic, 194, 195

Crosby, Bing, 150

cubism, 20, 79, 179

Cuddihy, John Murray, 60, 151

cultural work, 6, 25

culture, 5–6, 83, 147, 149, 149, 152, 155–56, 185

Dallinger, Frederick W., 124
Daly, James J., 32
Dante Alighieri, 28, 71, 80, 168, 169, 185
Darrow, Clarence, 47
Days Without End (O'Neill), 72
Death Comes for the Archbishop (Cather),
    68–69
decadence, 31, 34–35, 178
Declaration on Religious Freedom
    (Second Vatican Council), 57
De Goncourt, Jules, 39
Delaney, John J., 143, 145
De Luca, Msgr. Giuseppe, 193
democracy, 56, 61, 137, 146–51, 167,
    178–83, 199n30
DePaul University, 29
De Profundis (Wilde), 31
De Revolutionibus (Copernicus), 96
Descartes, René, 108
Dewey, John, 61
Diagnosis of Our Time (Mannheim), 189
Dickens, Charles, 24, 42, 78
Diderot, Denis, 108
Di Donato, Pietro, 44–45
dime novels, 30, 128
Divine Comedy (Dante), 28, 71, 80, 168
divorce, 30, 31, 56, 102, 153
Doherty, Tom, 131
Dolan, Jay, 4
Dolce Vita, La, 141
Dougherty, Dennis, 130
Douglas, Ann, 60
Doyle, Sister T. A., 177–78
Dreiser, Theodore, 39, 66, 183, 190
Duchamp, Marcel, 203n53
Dumas, Alexandre *père* and *fils,* 108
Dunne, Peter M., 115
Durant, Will, 111–12

Eagleton, Terry, 175
Ecclesiastical Prohibition of Books (Pernicone),
    90, 105, 111–12
Eco, Umberto, 188–89, 202n38
Edselas, F. M., 9
Egan, Maurice Francis, 39, 67
Eisenstaedt, Alfred, 150
Eisenstein, Elizabeth, 93, 98
Eliot, George, 21
Eliot, T. S., 24, 58–59, 64, 67, 74, 77–78,
    80, 159, 166, 178–79, 190
Ellis, John Tracy, 174
Ely, Catherine Beach, 66
Emerson, Ralph Waldo, 22, 70

End of the Affair, The (Greene), 160, 161–62,
    163, 216n12
Engels, Friedrich, 36
England, 49, 87, 99
Enlightenment, 3, 56, 87, 98, 148, 154,
    190
Episcopal Committee for Motion Pictures
    (ECOMP), 130, 143
epistemology, 56
Erasmus, 94, 166
Esprit des Lois, L' (Montesquieu), 97
Esquire, 138–39
"Everything That Rises Must Converge"
    (O'Connor), 173
evolution, 56, 58
excommunication, 92, 94
expurgation, 33
Exsurge, Domine (Leo X), 92–93

Farrell, James T., 66, 158, 169
Faulkner, William, 59–60
Fenton, Msgr. Joseph C., 194
Ferguson, Otis, 137
Fiction by Its Makers (Norris), 42
Fifth Lateran Council (1512), 92
First Amendment, 120–21, 129, 133,
    137, 140
Fischer, John, 142, 144
Fisher, James T., 83–84, 125
Fitzgerald, F. Scott, 25, 66, 83
Fitzgerald, Sally and Robert, 173
Fitzgerald, Rev. William J., 114
Flaubert, Gustave, 108
folk art, 75
Ford, John, 150
Fordham University, 184
foreign films, 140–41
Forever Amber, 107–8, 202n42
For Lancelot Andrewes (Eliot), 178–79
Four Quartets (Eliot), 74, 159
France, 15, 38, 49, 51, 75, 98
France, Anatole, 108
Freemasonry, 102
free verse, 20–21, 53, 80
Freudian psychoanalysis, 56
Funny Face, 179
futurism, 20

Gable, Sister Mariella, 165, 175
Galileo Galilei, 96
Galsworthy, John, 39
"Gambler, the Nun and the Radio, The"
    (Hemingway), 150

Gardiner, Rev. Harold C., 27, 105, 143–47, 161–64, 169, 174, 194, 217nn16–17
Gass, William, 179
Geertz, Clifford, 5
Gelasius I, Pope, 91, 210n16
genre fiction, 138, 149, 186, 208n34
Germany, 49, 87, 98, 99, 137, 178
Getino, Luis G. Alonso, 110, 119
Gide, André, 193
Giles, Paul, 66, 200n2, 206n3
Gillis, James M., 58
Glassie, Henry, 6, 78
Gleason, Philip, 21
gnosticism, 24
God, 26–27, 29, 33–36, 58, 73, 123, 171, 191
Going My Way, 140
Golden Girl (Sylvester), 153
Gone with the Wind, 126, 127
goodness, 29–32
Goodyear, William, 8
Gorman, Paul R., 219n13
Graham, Martha, 180
Grapes of Wrath, The (Steinbeck), 30, 201–2n27
Great Depression, 130, 133, 148
Great Gatsby, The (Fitzgerald), 25, 66
Great War, 3, 13, 53, 58–59, 78, 80, 121
Greene, Graham, 157, 159–63, 169, 193, 216n12, 220n2
"Greenleaf" (O'Connor), 173
Gregorianum, 96
Gregory XIII, Pope, 94, 96
Grendler, Paul, 96
Griffith, D. W., 125
Gurstein, Rochelle, 44

Hagerty, Thomas J., 38
Halsey, William, 13
Hanley, Lawrence F., 73
Hardy, Thomas, 21
Harper's Magazine, 142, 143, 144
Hawthorne, Nathaniel, 22, 44
Hays, Will, 129
Heart of the Matter, The (Greene), 160–61
Hegel, G. W. F., 63
Hemingway, Ernest, 150
Hennesey, James, 197n5
Hepburn, Audrey, 150, 179
Herberg, Will, 149
heresy, 91, 122
Hester, Betty, 165
Hicks, Granville, 69

high art versus popular art, 83, 147, 149, 152, 155–56, 185
higher education, 5, 12–13, 22–23, 87, 96–97, 109, 155, 174–76, 179
Hildebrand, Dietrich von, 165
Hilgers, Joseph, 95, 105–6, 210n17
historical-critical biblical study, 26
History of the Vatican Council (Acton), 109
Hitler, Adolf, 137
Hobbes, Thomas, 108
"Hollow Men, The" (Eliot), 59, 74, 159
Holmes, Oliver Wendell, 22, 52
Holt, Arthur E., 65
Holy Name Society, 140
Homiletic and Pastoral Review, 106, 109
Hopkins, Gerard Manley, 15
Howells, William Dean, 38–39, 42, 43
Huckleberry Finn (Twain), 65–66
Hudon, William, 89
Huff, Peter, 165
Hughes, Riley, 162, 216–17n14
Hugo, Victor, 108, 202n27
Hume, David, 108
humility of Catholic scholars, 110–11
Hunter College, 64
Hus, Jan, 91
Husslein, Joseph, 115

I Can Read Anything: All Right! Then Read This (Lord), 90, 111
iconoclasm/orthodoxy, 62, 69–74, 167–70
Ideal Catholic Reader (Sister of St. Joseph), 9, 198n18
idealism, 28
Image Industries, The (Lynch), 147
immigration, 4, 9, 22, 46, 83, 125, 128, 148, 152, 163–64, 182, 185, 197n5
imprimatur, 118–19, 198n18
Incarnation, 27, 33, 36, 79, 123, 172, 189–91
Index der Verbotenen Bucher, Der (Hilgers), 106
Index of Forbidden Books: authors included in, 38, 97, 108–9, 211n8; awareness of, by literary academics, 156; and Catholic scholars and university students, 105, 108–12, 194; classes of prohibited books in, 101–2, 107; and connection between literature and popular culture, 185; and Council of Trent, 91, 93–94; and Counter-Reformation, 86, 88, 89, 94, 127; demise of, in 1966, 19, 86, 88, 192–96; enforcement of, 95–96; establishment of (1564), 86, 93–94; explanation of and

Index of Forbidden Books (*continued*)
    rationale for, in twentieth century, 86–87,
    89, 100, 104–8, 111–12, 120–24, 127;
    on general rules about forbidden books,
    94, 99–100; histories of, 89–99, 100;
    and Inquisition, 87, 89, 96; link between
    morality of popular culture and, 126–27;
    in mid-sixteenth through mid-eighteenth
    centuries, 90, 93–96; in modern period,
    90, 96–99; precedents of, 91–92;
    revisions and reforms of, 95, 96–103,
    105–6; "Roman" Index of Forbidden
    Books, 94; rules for procedures and
    functioning of, 102–3, 109, 112–22; and
    theological modernism, 54; Tridentine
    Index, 94–95; and twentieth-century
    regulation of reading and publication,
    99–103; valid reason for reading
    prohibited books, 105, 109–10
individual/community, 22, 23, 57, 61, 62,
    65–70, 181–84
industrialization, 57–58, 75, 175–76
Initiation (Benson), 158
Innocent III, Pope, 93
Innocent VIII, Pope, 92
innovation/repetition, 62, 74–77, 184–88
Inquisition, 25, 87, 89, 93–94, 96,
    209nn7–8
intellectual freedom, 87, 124
Inter multiplices (Innocent VIII), 92
International Exhibition of Modern Art
    (1913), 58, 203n53
International Federation of Catholic
    Alumnae (IFCA), 132–34
Inter sollicitudines (Leo X), 92
Introduction to Catholic Booklore (Brown), 16
Irving, Washington, 22
Italy, 3, 49, 87, 93, 99

jazz, 79
Jesuits, 7, 14, 36–37, 56–57, 116–17,
    143–47
Jesus Christ, 27, 33–34, 36, 79, 123,
    156–57, 171–72, 189–91
John, Gospel of, 27
John XXIII, Pope, 192–93
Jolson, Al, 125
Journal of Religious Instruction, 106
"Journey of the Magi" (Eliot), 74
Joyce, James, 1–2, 30, 39, 48, 58, 61, 64,
    65, 67, 70, 78, 126, 157–59, 169, 183
Julius II, Pope, 92
Jung, Carl, 165

Kant, Immanuel, 108
Kaye, Danny, 180
Kelly, Blanche Mary, 17–18, 26, 70, 80
Kennedy, John F., 192
Kepler, Johannes, 95
Kerr, Walter, 168–69, 186–87
Kerrigan, William, 107–8
Kiley, Roger J., 194, 195
Kinsey Report, 217n17
Kristin Lavransdatter (Undset), 15, 41–42,
    203n61

Ladies Home Journal, 12
La Sapienza (University of Rome), 96–97
Lateran Council, Fifth (1512), 92
Latz, Leo, 118–19, 213n31
Lea, Henry Charles, 87, 209nn7–8
legal realism, 52
Legion of Decency, 126, 127, 129–37,
    139–43, 146, 150–51, 164–65, 185
Leo, Brother, 12–13, 23–24, 27, 29–31,
    33, 34
Leo X, Pope, 92–93
Leo XIII, Pope, 11, 58, 88, 98–102, 106
Les Jeunes, 13
liberalism: 3, 11, 36–37, 49–50, 61, 87, 146,
    166, 178–79
*Libraries and Literature from a Catholic
    Standpoint* (Brown), 80
Life, 150
Lincoln, Abraham, 121
Lippmann, Walter, 61
literary awards, 15, 41, 173
Literary Guild, 46
literature: Catholic view of, mission of, 23,
    27, 71–72, 126, 175, 185; definition of
    American literature, 67–68; as intellec-
    tual history, 154–57; and New Criticism,
    24, 83, 175–78, 186, 188; Ong on, 191;
    and problems of Catholic writers, 153–54
Little, Msgr. Thomas, 164
Little Ships (Norris), 42
liturgy, 77, 186, 187
Liturgy and Personality (Hildebrand), 165
Locke, John, 108
Long, Valentine, 27, 36
Longfellow, Henry Wadsworth, 22, 78
Lord, Daniel A., 13–14, 23, 72, 80, 90,
    111, 113–14, 116–18, 133–34, 199n30
"Love Song of J. Alfred Prufrock, The"
    (Eliot), 58, 74
Lowell, James Russell, 22
Loy, Myrna, 167

Luther, Martin, 92–93, 122
Lynch, William F., 82, 147, 168, 169, 177, 187, 218n2

Mackenzie, Compton, 41
Mahomet (Voltaire), 97
Mahoney, Edward, 121
Mahoney, E. W., 136
Maiden Voyage (Norris), 68
Mancini, JoAnne, 203n53
Mannheim, Karl, 189
Man Within, The (Greene), 160
March, Fredric, 167
Maritain, Jacques, 15
Marquette University, 159
Marx, Karl, 36
materialism, 28, 52, 56, 67, 179–81
Matthiessen, F. O., 22
Mauriac, Francois, 15
Maxwell, Joseph R. N., 44–45, 160
Maynard, Theodore, 24, 203n61
McCarthy, Mary, 77, 187
McClafferty, Edward T., 140
McCown, Father James, 193
McDermott, Thomas, 16
McFarland, Grenville S., 123–24
McGohey, Hon. John F. X., 165
McGoldrick, Rita, 134
McGreevy, John T., 61, 85, 166–67, 173, 217n26
McLaughlin, Rev. Michael, 33
McMahon, Father Joseph H., 124
McSorley, Joseph, 160
Meehan, Francis. *See* Leo, Brother
Melville, Herman, 22, 66
Merton, Thomas, 158
Michelangelo, 96
"middlebrow" culture, 83
Mill, John Stuart, 108
Minister's Charge, The (Howells), 39
Miracle case, 140–41, 142, 151
Miracle Worker, The, 165
Miserables, Les (Hugo), 202n27
Misner, Paul, 58
Mivart, George, 119
Moby Dick (Melville), 66
modernism, 2, 6, 17–18, 19, 22, 23, 25, 38–40, 45–49, 51, 53–63, 65–84, 86, 98, 124, 153–72, 174–191
modernity, 6, 10, 16, 21, 24, 29, 30–31, 38–46, 48–49, 55–57, 61–63, 80–81, 121, 146–52,
Monroe, Elizabeth, 41, 184

Montesquieu, Charles-Louis de Secondat, Baron de La Brède et de, 97
"Moon Is Blue, The," 126
Moore, Philip C., 44
Moore, R. Laurence, 132
Moral Mission of Literature and Other Essays, The (Confrey), 16
Morelli, Henry, 123–24
Morrison, Bakewell, 111, 117, 118, 211n38, 212n29
Morte D'Urban (Powers), 173
Mother (Norris), 12, 42
Motion Picture Herald, 129, 133
Motion Picture Producers and Distributors of America, 129
Motion Picture Producers of America (MPPA), 141
Motion Picture Production Code (MPPC), 129, 133–34
Moviegoer, The (Percy), 169, 173
movies, 78–79, 125–43, 146, 149, 150, 156, 164, 185, 208n34
"Mr. Bennett and Mrs. Brown" (Woolf), 39–40
Mundelein, Cardinal George, 133
Murphey, Murray, 5
Murray, John Courtney, 57, 142–47
Musser, Benjamin, 76
My Antonia (Cather), 68

National Catholic Office for Motion Pictures (NCOMP), 141–42
National Catholic War Council, 3
National Catholic Welfare Conference, 14–15, 136
National Council of Catholic Men, 136
nationalization of American literary culture, 21–22
National Office for Decent Literature, 142–43
National Organization for Decent Literature (NODL), 127, 129, 134–39, 142–46, 150–51, 156, 185, 214n19
naturalism, 38–39, 56, 126, 159, 190
natural law, 29, 31, 33, 52, 102, 105, 106, 107, 117, 120, 139, 186
Nature (Emerson), 70
neoscholasticism, 28–36, 52, 56, 59, 189
Nestorians, 91
Netherlands, 99
Neumann, Erich, 165
New Age, 40
New Criticism, 24, 83, 175–78, 186, 188

Newman, John Henry, 15, 173, 203n61, 218n4

New Republic, 137

newspapers, 5, 124

New York Armory Show (1913), 58, 203n53

New York Herald Tribune, 168

New York Times, 123–24

New York Times Book Review, 105, 143

Noll, Bishop John F., 7, 134–35, 138–39, 143–44, 214n19

Norms for the Novel (Gardiner), 145–46, 162

Norris, Charles, 42, 68

Norris, Frank, 39, 42, 68, 190

Norris, Kathleen Thompson, 12, 42–44, 45, 68

North American Review, 42

Not on Bread Alone (Long), 27

Noyes, Alfred, 119

nuclear weapons, 19, 163, 166, 181–82, 184

Nude Descending a Staircase (Duchamp), 203n53

Oberlin College, 66

O'Brien, Sharon, 68–69

obscenity, 2, 30, 102, 107–08, 121

Osservatore Romano, L', 194–95

O'Connor, Flannery, 27, 77, 165, 172–74, 187, 190, 193, 201n17

O'Connor, John G., 135

Odyssey, 173

Officiorum ac munerum (Leo XIII), 99–100

O'Malley, Frank, 158, 169

O'Neill, Daniel J., 23, 34–35, 202n42

O'Neill, Eugene, 72, 83

Ong, Walter J., 156–57, 166, 168, 169, 191

openness/closure, 62, 78–81, 188–91

O! Pioneers (Cather), 68

Origen, 91

Orsi, Robert A., 215n45

orthodoxy. *See* iconoclasm/orthodoxy

"Our Atom Bomb, the Rosary" (Sister M. Pierre), 181–82

Our Sunday Visitor, 7, 11, 107

Outline of History (Wells), 24

Pallen, Condé Benoist, 20–21, 27, 35, 38, 70–71, 74, 157, 168, 169, 191, 200n1, 200n2

paperback novels, 126, 136, 137–38, 179, 185, 214n19

Pascal, Blaise, 109

Pascendi dominici gregis (Pius X), 48, 49–50, 52, 53–54, 71, 83, 100, 113

Passion Flower (Norris), 68

Pater, Walter, 34

Path to Rome, The (Belloc), 64

Paul, St., 90, 100

Paul III, Pope, 93

Paul IV, Pope, 94

Paul V, Pope, 96

Paul VI, Pope, 192–93

Paulist Fathers, 1, 58

Pearson, Drew, 139

Peek, 136, 214n21

Pelagius, 91

Percy, Walker, 169, 173, 190, 191

Pernicone, Joseph M., 28, 90, 105, 111–12

Personal Romances Monthly Magazine, 135

philosophy, 52, 56, 106, 155, 177

Pierre, Sister M., 181–82

Pius V, Pope, 93, 96

Pius IX, Pope, 3, 98

Pius X, Pope, 49–50, 83

Pius XI, Pope, 14, 133

Pius XII, Pope, 117

Played by Ear (Lord), 111

poetry: Auden on, 186–87; blank verse, 78; free verse, 20–21, 53, 80; by Les Jeunes, 13

popular art versus high art, 83, 147, 149, 152, 155–56, 185

popular culture, 30, 75–79, 83–84, 124–29, 134–38, 142, 146–52, 156, 163–64, 179–81, 184–86, 208n34

Porter, Katherine Anne, 173

Portrait of the Artist as a Young Man, A (Joyce), 1–2, 48, 58, 70, 158

Post Office, U.S., 121, 138–39

Pound, Ezra, 58, 61, 65, 78, 179, 190

Power and Apostolate of Catholic Literature, The (Walker), 36

Power and the Glory, The (Greene), 160, 193

Powers, J. F., 173

Prendergast, Marian, 113–14

printing press, 91, 92, 93, 125

Prodigal Son parable, 27

Production Code Administration (PCA), 131–34, 137, 139–41

professional associations, 5

professionalization of American literary culture, 21–22

proletarian literature, 72–73

propaganda, 25, 72, 167, 178

Provincial Letters, The (Pascal), 109

psychology, 56, 115–16, 165–66

pulp magazines, 30, 126, 128, 134–38, 142, 149, 208n34
Purcell, Edward, 167

Queen's Work Press, 14, 36
Quigley, Martin, 129–30, 133

radicalism, 37
radio, 125, 128, 149, 208n34
reading circles, 8
Readings for Catholic Action (Confrey), 16
realism, 21, 38–46, 48, 53, 163, 167–68
reconciliation, 153–72
Red Silence (Norris), 42–43
Reformation Protestantism, 3, 8, 86, 88, 91, 92–93, 97, 122
Religion and the Study of Literature (Brother Leo), 23, 27
religious liberty, 57, 144, 146–47
religious toleration, 65
Renaissance, 87
Renascence, 159
repetition. *See* innovation/repetition
Repplier, Agnes, 35
Rerum Novarum (Leon XIII), 11, 58
"Revelation" (O'Connor), 173
Rhythm of Sterility and Fertility in Women, The (Latz), 118–19
Richardson, Samuel, 108
Rich Mrs. Burgoyne, The (Norris), 12
Rimbaud, Arthur, 58
Rise of Silas Lapham, The (Howells), 38–39
Rite of Spring (Stravinsky), 75
Robey, David, 188–89
"Roman" Index of Forbidden Books, 94
Roman Index of Forbidden Books Briefly Explained, The (Betten), 105
romanticism, 3, 37, 74–75, 155
Roosevelt, Franklin Delano, 138
Rose of the World (Norris), 68
Rossellini, Roberto, 140
Ruskin, John, 8
Ryan, John A., 11, 58

St. Anthony Messenger, 14
St. Bede College (Peru, Ill.), 121
St. Joseph's University, 134
St. Mary's College (Moraga, Calif.), 12–13
Sand, George, 108
Sapphira and the Slave Girl (Cather), 69
Sartre, Jean-Paul, 193
Scharper, Philip J., 184
Schlesinger, Arthur, Jr., 85, 87

Schneider, H. Joseph, 103
Scholasticism, 28–29
science, 8, 16, 17, 49, 50, 53, 56, 71, 87, 97, 155, 156
Science and Civil Life (Eisenstein), 98
Scott, Nathan, 189
secularism, 3
segregation, 217n26
separation of church and state, 57, 61, 94, 146
sexuality, 30, 38, 56–57, 118, 134, 135–36, 145, 162, 164, 217n17
Shadows on the Rock (Cather), 68–69
Shahan, Thomas J., 16–17
Shakespeare, William, 185
Shaw, George Bernard, 40
Sheed and Ward publisher, 67
Sheen, Fulton, 150
Sheridan, John Desmond, 30–31
Ship of Fools (Porter), 173
Shurlock, Geoff, 141
Shuster, George, 64–65
Sign, The, 89
Sinatra, Frank, 150
Sloyan, Father Gerard, 194
Smith, Al, 47
Smith, Barbara Herrnstein, 68
Smith, Betty, 145, 162
socialism, 3, 8, 11–13, 40, 52, 58, 67
social justice, 3, 11, 57–58
Society of Catholic College Teachers of Sacred Doctrine, 194
sodalities, 14
Sollicita ac Provida (Benedict XIV), 97, 100
Song of Bernadette, The, 202n42
Sound and the Fury, The (Faulkner), 59–60
Soviet Union, 3, 11, 121–22, 137, 151, 166–67, 178, 180–82, 185, 186
Spain, 87, 99
Spalding, Martin John, 8
Spellman, Cardinal Francis, 140
Stalin, Joseph, 137
Stamboul Train (Greene), 160
Steinbeck, John, 30, 201–2n27
Steinhuber, Cardinal Andreas, 119
Stendhal, 108
Stowe, Harriet Beecher, 121
Straton, John Roach, 47
Stravinsky, Igor, 75
stream-of-consciousness, 53, 78
Sullivan, Ed, 150
Sullivan, Richard, 16, 29, 33, 41, 43–45, 154, 204n69
Summa Theologiae (Thomas Aquinas), 34, 36

Summer after Summer (Sullivan), 44
Supreme Court, U.S., 137, 138, 140, 151
Survey of Catholic Literature (McDermott and Brown), 16
Syllabus of Errors, 98
Sylvester, Harry, 43–44, 153–54, 183

Talbot, Francis X., 13, 23, 41, 42–43, 115
Talmud, 91
Tate, Allen, 24, 165
Taylor, Charles, 16
Teilhard de Chardin, Pierre, 191
television, 149, 186
"Tenets for Readers and Reviewers" (Gardiner), 162
Tentler, Leslie, 213n31
Testem benevolentiae, 50–51
theological education, 175, 176
theological modernism, 6, 25, 48–55, 71, 81, 83, 98, 156
Thompson, Francis, 15
Thoreau, Henry David, 22
Tierney, Rev. Richard H., 115
Time magazine, 217n17
Tolstoy, Leo, 39
Tompkins, Jane P., 6, 25, 206n3
Transcendentalists, 155
Transition: A Sentimental Story of One Mind and One Era (Durant), 111
Tree Grows in Brooklyn, A (Smith), 145, 162
Tremendous Trifles (Chesterton), 40
Trilling, Lionel, 68, 69
Trinity College, 168–69
truth, 25, 29, 31–34, 45, 51–52, 90, 91, 110–11, 114, 120–23, 168–69, 188, 190
Tully, John C., 44
Turgenev, Ivan, 39
Twain, Mark, 65–66

Ultramontanism, 55
Ulysses (Joyce), 2, 30, 39, 61, 64, 65, 67, 78
Uncle Tom's Cabin (Stowe), 121
Undset, Sigrid, 15, 41–42, 203n61
UNESCO, 64
University of Bologna, 97
University of Chicago, 105
University of Notre Dame, 29, 44, 138, 154, 158, 195
University of Padua, 96

Vatican Councils: First (1869–70), 55, 98, 100; Second (1962–65), 6, 51, 57, 82, 88, 144, 146, 154, 190, 192–93, 194

Vatican Library, 96
Venables, The (Norris), 43
Victorianism, 21, 22, 24–25, 29, 57, 72, 78, 167, 178, 185
Vitale, Philip, 29
Volkening, Henry, 166
Voltaire, François, 97, 108, 110, 119

Walker, Frank, 138–39
Walker, Herbert O'Halloran, 36
Walsh, Frank, 134
Walsh, Moira, 164, 190
Walsh, Thomas, 13, 27
Ward, Leo L., 204n69
Warren, Robert Penn, 177–78
Washington Post, 139
Waste Land, The (Eliot), 64, 67, 74, 80, 159, 179
Watkin, E. I., 67
Waugh, Evelyn, 77, 195–96
We Hold These Truths (Murray), 143, 144–45
Well of English, The (Kelly), 26
Wells, H. G., 24, 33, 39, 40, 58
West, Mae, 125
West, Morris, 150
Wharton, Edith, 80
What Is the Index? (Burke), 105
When the Sleeper Wakes (Wells), 24, 33
White, Victor, 165
White Christmas, 180
Whitman, Walt, 22
Whittier, John Greenleaf, 22
Wilde, Oscar, 31
Williams, Gluyas, 43
Williams, Michael, 119
woman's suffrage, 30
women's literature, 68
Woodstock College, 143
Woolf, Virginia, 2, 39–40
Wordsworth, William, 78
working class, 3, 11, 58, 72–73, 79
World of Idella May, The (Sullivan), 43
World Parliament of Religions, Columbian Exposition, 9
World War II, 148, 163, 167, 184
Wright, Richard, 33
Wright, Teresa, 167–68
Wycliffe, John, 91
Wynhoven, Peter, 15

Yorke, Anthony, 34

Zola, Émile, 38, 39, 108